THE CONSTITUTION OF NEW ZEALAND

This book examines New Zealand's constitution through the lens of constitutional realism. It looks at the practices, habits, conventions and norms of constitutional life. It focuses on the structures, processes and culture that govern the exercise of public power – a perspective that is necessary to explore and account for a lived, rather than textual, constitution.

New Zealand's constitution is unique. One of three remaining unwritten democratic constitutions in the world, it is characterised by a charming set of anachronistic contrasts. 'Unwritten', but much found in various written sources. Built on a network of Westminster constitutional conventions but generously tailored to local conditions. Proudly independent, yet perhaps a purer Westminster model than its British parent.

Flexible and vulnerable, while oddly enduring, it looks to the centralised authority that comes with a strong executive, strict parliamentary sovereignty, and a unitary state. However, its populace insists on egalitarian values and representative democracy, with elections fiercely conducted nowadays under a system of proportional representation. The interests of indigenous Māori are protected largely through democratic majority rule. A reputation for upholding the rule of law, yet few institutional safeguards to ensure compliance.

Pictorial Narrative

The Constitution of New Zealand: *Tides of Harmony and Dissonance*

A complex geometric interplay of rectangles and triangles encapsulates the essence of New Zealand's constitutional history, culture and geography.

The eye is drawn into the heart of the composition by a dominant rectangle in the central foreground, itself comprised of juxtaposed triangles. The vivid yellow 'crab claw' sail of a waka (canoe) and taiaha (spear) of legendary chief Kupe, notionally colliding with the forward staysails in orange and red from Captain Cook's *Endeavour*, brandishes the Cross Pattée and fleurs-de-lis from the British Crown. The sail is placed at the apex of a triangle containing at its base a reference to the distinctive interior of the Supreme Court building, with the dome-shaped beehive pattern of the modern Parliament stacked above it. To the left, the reference to the '1840 Waitangi' Treaty serves as a further reminder of the conflict between settlers and the indigenous population. Swirling below in the bottom left are the deconstructed red, white and blue elements from the British national flag that is still part of New Zealand's flag.

The kaleidoscope of triangles and rectangles to the right from bottom to top refer to culture, politics and nature. In shades of magenta and cobalt blue, the traditional elements of a Māori meeting house are depicted, above it the green fronds of the fern unfurling. This is flanked further to the right by the green, red, blue and yellow dots referring to the partisan seating plan of the House of Representatives. The skyward rectangle of mountains and sky in green, yellow and azure portrays the natural beauty of the Southern Alps, above the ocean waves. Capping the composition, the night sky displays the twinkling stars of the Southern Cross constellation, echoing New Zealand's national flag and coat of arms. It also features the predominant sporting icon with a dynamic spinning rugby ball.

Putachad
Artist

Constitutional Systems of the World
General Editors: Benjamin L Berger, Rosalind Dixon, Andrew Harding, Heinz Klug, and Peter Leyland

In the era of globalisation, issues of constitutional law and good governance are being seen increasingly as vital issues in all types of society. Since the end of the Cold War, there have been dramatic developments in democratic and legal reform, and post-conflict societies are also in the throes of reconstructing their governance systems. Even societies already firmly based on constitutional governance and the rule of law have undergone constitutional change and experimentation with new forms of governance; and their constitutional systems are increasingly subjected to comparative analysis and transplantation. Constitutional texts for practically every country in the world are now easily available on the internet. However, texts which enable one to understand the true context, purposes, interpretation and incidents of a constitutional system are much harder to locate, and are often extremely detailed and descriptive. This series seeks to provide scholars and students with accessible introductions to the constitutional systems of the world, supplying both a road map for the novice and, at the same time, a deeper understanding of the key historical, political and legal events which have shaped the constitutional landscape of each country. Each book in this series deals with a single country, or a group of countries with a common constitutional history, and each author is an expert in their field.

Published volumes

The Constitution of the United Kingdom; The Constitution of the United States; The Constitution of Vietnam; The Constitution of South Africa; The Constitution of Japan; The Constitution of Germany; The Constitution of Finland; The Constitution of Australia; The Constitution of the Republic of Austria; The Constitution of the Russian Federation; The Constitutional System of Thailand; The Constitution of Malaysia; The Constitution of China; The Constitution of Indonesia; The Constitution of France; The Constitution of Spain; The Constitution of Mexico; The Constitution of Israel; The Constitutional Systems of the Commonwealth Caribbean; The Constitution of Canada; The Constitution of Singapore; The Constitution of Belgium; The Constitution of Taiwan; The Constitution of Romania; The Constitutional Systems of the Independent Central Asian States; The Constitution of India; The Constitution of Pakistan; The Constitution of Ireland; The Constitution of Brazil; The Constitution of Myanmar; The Constitution of Czechia; The Constitution of New Zealand

Link to series website

www.bloomsburyprofessional.com/uk/series/
constitutional-systems-of-the-world

The Constitution of New Zealand

A Contextual Analysis

Matthew S R Palmer
and
Dean R Knight

•HART•
OXFORD • LONDON • NEW YORK • NEW DELHI • SYDNEY

HART PUBLISHING
Bloomsbury Publishing Plc
Kemp House, Chawley Park, Cumnor Hill, Oxford, OX2 9PH, UK
1385 Broadway, New York, NY 10018, USA
29 Earlsfort Terrace, Dublin 2, Ireland

HART PUBLISHING, the Hart/Stag logo, BLOOMSBURY and the Diana logo are trademarks of Bloomsbury Publishing Plc

First published in Great Britain 2022

First published in hardback, 2022

Paperback edition, 2023

A catalogue record for this book is available from the British Library.

Library of Congress Cataloging-in-Publication data

Names: Palmer, Matthew, 1964- author. | Knight, Dean R. (Dean Robert), author.

Title: The Constitution of New Zealand : a contextual analysis / Matthew S.R. Palmer, Dean R. Knight.

Description: Oxford, UK ; New York, NY : Hart Publishing, an imprint of Bloomsbury Publishing, 2022. | Series: Constitutional systems of the world | Includes bibliographical references and index.

Identifiers: LCCN 2021053511 (print) | LCCN 2021053512 (ebook) | ISBN 9781849469036 (hardback) | ISBN 9781509956456 (paperback) | ISBN 9781849469050 (pdf) | ISBN 9781849469043 (Epub)

Subjects: LCSH: Constitutions—New Zealand. | Constitutional law—New Zealand. | New Zealand—Politics and government.

Classification: LCC KUQ1750 .P37 2022 (print) | LCC KUQ1750 (ebook) | DDC 342.93—dc23/eng/20211109

LC record available at https://lccn.loc.gov/2021053511

LC ebook record available at https://lccn.loc.gov/2021053512

ISBN: PB: 978-1-50995-645-6
ePDF: 978-1-84946-905-0
ePub: 978-1-84946-904-3

Typeset by Compuscript Ltd, Shannon

To find out more about our authors and books visit www.hartpublishing.co.uk. Here you will find extracts, author information, details of forthcoming events and the option to sign up for our newsletters.

Preface and Acknowledgements

WE HAVE WRITTEN this book based on three convictions: our constitution matters; it can only be understood by understanding how it works in reality; and it is important for as many New Zealanders as possible to understand it. The book aims to explain rather than advocate. It is written for the interested and intelligent observer. We hope it might of use to judges, legislators, public servants, academics, lawyers, law and political science students, and others. It has been confined by space requirements but that has made it a better book.

Our families have borne the brunt of the writing process. We are grateful to them for their love and support and some for their comments on the text. Kia ora and thanks to Matthew's family: Ruth, Russell, Kathryn, Andrew, Jeremy, Helena and Kate; fa'afetai and thanks to Dean's partner: Alan. Creation of a book, on top of busy day jobs, unfairly intrudes into family life and we appreciate the space and tolerance they gifted to us to complete the project, over several years. We hope they and others find something of value in the result.

We also thank the many who have contributed thoughts and critiques during the (overly-lengthy) writing process (and who bear no responsibility for the result). Ben Berger and Ros Dixon have provided supportive guidance and helpful comments on the draft manuscript. We are also very grateful for comments from: Rachel Hayward, Deputy Secretary to the Cabinet and her team; David Wilson, Clerk of the House of Representatives; Peter Hughes, Public Services Commissioner and his team; Una Jagose, Solicitor-General, and her team; Andrew Butler; Claire Charters; Alberto Costi; Claudia Geiringer; Andrew Geddis; Geoff McLay; Janet McLean; Sir Geoffrey Palmer; Guy Fiti Sinclair; and unnamed judges. Thanks also to Dean's research assistants, who helped out with research and other assistance with the drafting process: Maisy Bentley; William Britton; Alex Ladyman; Anna Prestidge; and Pita Roycroft; and Matthew's clerks who helped with research and proofing have been of invaluable assistance: Yasmin Olsen; Jessica Storey; Antonio Bradley; Jessica Fenton; Jessica Sutton; and Leilani Taula.

This book covers law, practice and developments as at July 2021.

Contents

Preface and Acknowledgements......*vii*
Table of Cases......*xv*
Table of Legislation......*xxi*
Table of International Instruments......*xxvii*

1. New Zealand Constitutionalism......**1**
I. Introduction......1
II. Constitutional Essence......2
A. Constitutional Collision and Evolution......2
B. Constitutional Sketch......5
III. Constitutional Perspective......9
A. Constitutional Realism......9
B. Constitutional Elements......11
IV. Constitutional Culture......14
A. Egalitarianism......16
B. Faith in Authority......17
C. Fairness......18
D. Pragmatism......20
V. Constitutional Dialogue......21
VI. Conclusion......24
Further Reading......24

2. Aotearoa New Zealand......**26**
I. Introduction......26
II. Māori and Pākehā......27
III. He Whakaputanga o te Rangatiratanga o Nu Tireni: The Declaration of Independence of New Zealand......29
IV. Te Tiriti o Waitangi: The Treaty of Waitangi......31
V. Assertion of British Sovereignty......33
VI. Conclusion......35
Further Reading......35

3. Head of State and the Crown......**36**
I. Introduction......36
II. Sovereign as Head of State......37
III. Governor-General as De Facto Head of State......39

IV. Governor-General's Functions and Powers 41
A. Constitutional, Ceremonial and Community Functions 41
B. Prerogative and Statutory Powers 42
C. Reserve Powers....43
D. Parliamentary Powers....45
V. Executive Council 45
VI. The Crown in Law 46
VII. Conclusion....48
Further Reading....48

4. Democratic Government....49
I. Introduction....49
II. Representative Government: An Elected House 49
A. Evolution of the Electoral System....50
B. MMP Electoral System in Operation....53
C. Political Parties....56
D. Effect of MMP 58
E. Entrenched Provisions....60
III. Responsible Government: A Parliamentary Ministry 62
A. Government, Cabinet and Ministers....62
B. Formation of Government 63
C. Coalition, Confidence-and-supply and Support Agreements 66
D. Expiration or Dismissal of Government 69
E. Transition between Governments and Caretaker Convention....72
IV. Conclusion....74
Further Reading....75

5. Executive....76
I. Introduction....76
II. Cabinet Government 77
A. Cabinet 77
B. Cabinet Manual and Cabinet Office 78
C. Collective Responsibility....79
III. Prime Minister and Ministers....84
A. Ministers....84
B. Individual Ministerial Responsibility....87

IV. Public Service 91
A. Departments 93
B. Conventional Public Service Duties 94
V. Wider State Sector 100
VI. Public Finance and Managerialism 102
VII. Conclusion 105
Further Reading 105

6. Parliament 107
I. Introduction 107
II. Parliamentary Institutions 107
A. Parliament 107
B. House of Representatives 108
C. Speaker and Clerk 110
D. Committees 112
III. Parliamentary Functions 114
A. Law-making 115
B. Provider of Government 118
C. Control of Public Finances 119
D. Holding the Executive to Account 120
E. Forum for Party Political Contest 124
F. Symbol of Representative Government 124
IV. Parliamentary Dynamics under MMP 124
V. Legislative Supremacy and its Limits 126
A. Origins 127
B. Nature 129
C. Possible Limits 132
VI. Conclusion 135
Further Reading 136

7. Judiciary 137
I. Introduction 137
II. The Rule of Law and Forms of Law 137
A. The Rule of Law 138
B. Statutory Interpretation 140
C. Common Law 144
D. Tikanga 145
III. The Judiciary as an Institution 147
A. Court Structure and Processes 147
B. Judges and the Judiciary 151
C. The Daily Practice of Judges and the Judiciary 155

IV. Judicial Independence and Accountability 156
A. Protection of Judicial Independence 156
B. Judicial Direction and Executive Operation of the Court System 158
C. Judicial Removal and Accountability 160
V. Conclusion 163
Further Reading 164

8. Accountability and Transparency 165
I. Introduction 165
II. Accountability 166
A. Judicial Review 168
B. Statutory Appeals 174
C. Administrative Tribunals 175
D. Ombudsman 177
E. Controller and Auditor-General 179
F. Inquiries 180
III. Transparency 181
A. Official Information 182
B. Public Records 186
C. Reason-giving 186
IV. Conclusion 187
Further Reading 188

9. Human Rights 189
I. Introduction 189
II. New Zealand Bill of Rights Act 1990 190
A. Protected Rights 191
B. Operational Scheme 192
C. Impact on the Functions of Government 194
D. Sites of Contest 199
E. Efficacy 202
III. Fundamental Rights and the Common Law 203
IV. Other Statutory Rights Protections 206
V. Conclusion 207
Further Reading 207

10. Te Tiriti o Waitangi 208
I. Introduction 208
II. A Brief History of the Status of Te Tiriti 208
A. Creation 208
B. Te Tiriti o Waitangi Ignored 210

C. Te Tiriti Revisited 212
D. The Waitangi Tribunal 215
E. Legislative References and Judicial Enforcement 216
F. Reinterpretation through Dialogue 218
III. Te Tiriti in the Constitution Today 219
A. Contemporary Meaning 219
B. Legal Force and Effect 220
C. Reconciliation and Settlement 222
D. Constitutional Place 225
IV. Conclusion 228
Further Reading 229

11. Local and Global Governance 230
I. Introduction 230
II. Local Government 230
III. Māori Governance 234
IV. Non-State Bodies and the Private Sector 236
V. Global Institutions and International Relationships 237
VI. Conclusion 241
Further Reading 241

12. Constitutional Futures 242
I. Introduction 242
II. A Written Constitution? 242
III. A Māori-centred Nation State? 244
IV. A New Zealand Head of State? 246
V. Pragmatic Tinkering? 247
VI. Enhanced Protection of Rights? 251
VII. Localism versus Globalism? 252
VIII. Conclusion 254
Further Reading 254

Index 255

Table of Cases

AI (Somalia) v Immigration and Protection Tribunal [2016] NZHC 2227, [2016] NZAR 1471 171
Air Nelson Ltd v Minister of Transport [2007] NZAR 266 (HC) 171
AMM, Re [2010] NZFLR 629 (HC) 200
Anisminic v Foreign Compensation Commission [1969] 2 AC 147 (HL) 173
Arani v Public Trustee [1920] AC 198 (PC) 145
Ashby v Minister of Immigration [1981] 1 NZLR 222 (CA) 238
Associated Provincial Picture Houses Ltd v Wednesbury Corporation [1948] 1 KB 223, [1947] 2 All ER 680 (CA) 171
Attorney General for Canada v Attorney General for Ontario [1937] UKPC 6, [1937] AC 326 238
Attorney-General for New South Wales v Trethowan [1932] AC 526 (PC) 133
Attorney-General v Chapman [2009] NZCA 552, [2010] 2 NZLR 317 172
Attorney-General v Chapman [2011] NZSC 110, [2012] 1 NZLR 462 .... 47, 172
Attorney-General v New Zealand Maori Council [1991] 2 NZLR 129 (CA) 218
Attorney-General v Ngāti Apa [2003] 3 NZLR 643 (CA) 130, 145
Attorney-General v Taylor [2017] NZCA 215, [2017] 3 NZLR 24 .... 110, 170, 198, 201
Attorney-General v Taylor [2018] NZSC 104, [2019] 1 NZLR 213 51
Attorney-General v Udompun [2005] 3 NZLR 204 (CA) 198
Attorney-General v Van Essen [2015] NZCA 22 172
Austin, Nichols & Co Inc v Stichting Lodestar [2007] NZSC 103, [2008] 2 NZLR 141 174
Barton-Prescott v Director-General of Social Welfare [1997] 3 NZLR 179 (HC) 222
Borrowdale v Director-General of Health [2020] NZHC 2090, [2020] 2 NZLR 864 .... 192, 201
Boscawen v Attorney-General [2009] NZCA 12, [2009] 2 NZLR 229 201
Bribery Commissioner v Ranasinghe [1965] AC 172 (PC) 133

Brooker v Police [2007] NZSC 30, [2007] 3 NZLR 91 200
Bugdaycay v Secretary of State for the Home Department
[1987] AC 514, [1987] 2 WLR 606 (HL) 204
Bulk Gas Users Group v Attorney-General [1983]
NZLR 129 (CA) 173
Carter Holt Harvey Ltd v North Shore City Council [2006]
2 NZLR 787 (HC) 171
Child Poverty Action Group Inc v Attorney-General [2013]
NZCA 402, [2013] 3 NZLR 729 200
Combined Beneficiaries Union Inc v Auckland City COGS
Committee [2009] 2 NZLR 56 (CA) 196
Commerce Commission v Fonterra Co-operative Group Ltd
[2007] NZSC 36, [2007] 3 NZLR 767 142–143
Commissioner of Inland Revenue v Chesterfields Preschools Ltd
[2013] NZCA 53, [2013] 2 NZLR 679 172
Comptroller of Customs v Terminals (NZ) Ltd [2012] NZCA 598,
[2014] 2 NZLR 137 171
Continental Shelf (Libyan Arab Jamahiriya v Malta) [1985]
ICJ Rep 13 238
Cooper v Attorney-General [1996] 3 NZLR 480 (HC) 134
Cropp v Judicial Committee [2008] NZSC 46, [2008]
3 NZLR 774 203
Curtis v Minister of Defence [2002] 2 NZLR 744 (CA) 170
Drew v Attorney-General [2002] 1 NZLR 58 (CA) 196
Dunlea v Attorney General [2000] 3 NZLR 136 (CA) 198
Dunne v CanWest TVWorks Ltd [2005] NZAR 577 (HC) 169, 236
Electoral Commission v Cameron [1997] 2 NZLR 421 (CA) 236
Ellen Street Estates Ltd v Minister of Health [1934]
1 KB 590 (CA) 129, 131
Ellis v R [2020] NZSC 89 146
Entick v Carrington (1765) 19 Howell's State Trials 1029,
95 ER 807 206
Fitzgerald v Muldoon [1976] 2 NZLR 615 (SC) 129–30, 165
Governor of Pitcairn Islands v Sutton [1995] 1 NZLR 426 (CA) 238
Gwynn v Napier City Council [2018] NZHC 1943, [2018]
NZAR 1410 204
H v Refugee and Protection Officer [2019] NZSC 13, [2019]
1 NZLR 433 174
Hansen v R [2007] NZSC 7, [2007] 3 NZLR 1 199
Harris v Minister of the Interior 1952 (2) SA 428 (AD) 133

Hauraki Coromandel Climate Action Inc v Thames-Coromandel District Council [2020] NZHC 3228 204
Helu v Immigration and Protection Tribunal [2015] NZSC 2; [2016] 1 NZLR 298 240
Henderson Borough Council v Auckland Regional Authority [1984] 1 NZLR 16 (CA) 129
Hopkinson v Police [2004] 3 NZLR 704 (HC) 200
Hosking v Runting [2005] 1 NZLR 1 (CA) 197
Hu v Immigration and Protection Tribunal [2017] NZHC 41, [2017] NZAR 508 171
Huakina Development Trust v Waikato Valley Authority [1987] 2 NZLR 188 (HC) 145, 222
Institute of Chartered Accountants of New Zealand v Bevan [2003] 1 NZLR 154 (CA) 171
Invercargill City Council v Hamlin [1984] 3 NZLR 513 (CA) 145
Invercargill City Council v Hamlin [1996] 1 NZLR 513 (PC) 145
Jackson v Attorney-General [2006] 1 AC 262 (HL) 133
Kim v Minister of Justice [2016] NZHC 1490, [2016] 3 NZLR 425 204
Kim v Minister of Justice of New Zealand [2019] NZCA 209, [2019] 3 NZLR 173 .... 171, 204
Korokai v Solicitor-General (1912) 32 NZLR 321 (CA) 212
McGrath v Minister of Justice [2014] NZHC 3279, [2015] NZAR 122 204
McGuire v Secretary for Justice [2018] NZSC 116, [2019] 1 NZLR 335 174
McLiver v Macky (1856) 211
Mangawhai Ratepayers' and Residents' Association v Kaipara District Council [2014] NZHC 1147, [2014] 3 NZLR 85 234
Martin v District Court at Tauranga [1995] 2 NZLR 419 (CA) 199
Minister of Energy v Petrocorp Exploration Ltd [1989] 1 NZLR 348 (CA) 169
Minister of Justice v Kim [2021] NZSC 57 204
Ministry of Health v Atkinson [2012] NZCA 185, [2012] 3 NZLR 456 200
Ministry of Transport v Noort [1992] 3 NZLR 260 (CA) 199
Moonen v Film and Literature Board of Review [2000] 2 NZLR 9 (CA) 199–200
Morse v Police [2011] NZSC 45, [2012] 2 NZLR 1 200

New Health New Zealand Inc v South Taranaki District Council [2018] NZSC 59, [2018] 1 NZLR 948 201
New Zealand Airline Pilots' Association v Attorney-General [1997] 3 NZLR 269 (CA) 240
New Zealand Council of Licensed Firearms Owners Inc v Minister of Police [2020] NZHC 1456 134
New Zealand Drivers' Association v New Zealand Road Carriers [1982] 1 NZLR 374 (CA) 134
New Zealand Fishing Industry Association Inc v Minister of Agriculture and Fisheries [1988] 1 NZLR 544 (CA) 171
New Zealand Maori Council v Attorney-General (Lands Case) [1987] 1 NZLR 641 (CA) 165, 217, 222
New Zealand Maori Council v Attorney-General [1994] 1 NZLR 513 (PC) 218
New Zealand Maori Council v Attorney-General [2013] NZSC 6, [2013] 3 NZLR 31 218
Ngaronoa v Attorney-General [2017] NZCA 351, [2017] 3 NZLR 643 200
Ngaronoa v Attorney-General [2018] NZSC 123, [2019] 1 NZLR 289 .... 61–62, 132, 200, 204
Ngāti Hurungaterangi v Ngāti Wahiao [2017] NZCA 429, [2017] 3 NZLR 770 161
Ngāti Whātua Ōrākei Trust v Attorney-General [2018] NZSC 84, [2019] 1 NZLR 116 .... 170, 252
Nireaha Tamaki v Baker [1901] AC 561 145
Parata v Bishop of Wellington (1877) 3 NZJur (NS) 72 (SC) 145, 212
Phipps v Royal Australasian College of Surgeons [2000] 2 NZLR 513 (PC) 169
Police v Beggs [1999] 3 NZLR 615 (HC) 199
Proprietors of Wakatu v Attorney-General [2017] NZSC 17, [2017] 1 NZLR 423 222
Puli'uvea v Removal Review Authority [1996] 3 NZLR 538 (CA) 205
Quilter v Attorney-General [1998] 1 NZLR 523 (CA) 200
R (Brind) v Secretary of State for the Home Office [1991] UKHL 4, [1991] 1 AC 696 240
R (Datafin plc) v Panel on Takeovers and Mergers [1987] QB 815 (CA) 169
R (ex parte Guinness Plc) v Panel on Takeovers and Mergers [1990] 1 QB 146 (CA) 171
R (Miller) v Prime Minister [2019] UKSC 41, [2020] AC 373 170

R (Miller) v Secretary of State for Exiting the European Union [2017] UKSC 5, [2017] 2 WLR 583 238
R (Privacy International) v Investigatory Powers Tribunal [2019] UKSC 22, [2019] 2 WLR 1219 134
R (Simms) v Secretary of State for the Home Department [2000] 2 AC 115, [1999] 3 WLR 328 (HL) 203
R (Smith) v Ministry of Defence [1996] QB 517, [1996] 2 WLR 305 (CA) 204
R v Fineberg [1968] NZLR 119 (SC) 133
R v Hansen [2007] NZSC 7, [2007] 3 NZLR 1 .... 192–93, 199
R v Oakes [1986] 1 SCR 103 192
R v Pora [2001] 2 NZLR 37 (CA) 199, 205
R v Poumako [2000] 2 NZLR 695 (CA) 199, 203
R v Symonds (1847) NZPCC 387 (SC) 144, 211
Remuneration of Judges, Reference re [1997] 3 SCR 3 158
Resolution to Amend the Constitution, Re [1981] 1 SCR 753 12
Ririnui v Landcorp Farming Ltd [2016] NZSC 62; [2016] 1 NZLR 1056 171
Royal Australasian College of Surgeons v Phipps [1999] 3 NZLR 1 (CA) 236
Seales v Attorney-General [2015] NZHC 1239, [2015] 3 NZLR 556 201
Shaw v Commissioner of Inland Revenue [1999] 3 NZLR 154 (CA) 134
Simpson v Attorney-General (Baigent's Case) [1994] 3 NZLR 667 (CA) 197–99
Singh v Auckland Co-Operative Taxi Society Ltd [2019] NZHC 1759 170
Smith v Attorney-General [2017] NZHC 1647, [2017] NZAR 1094 169
Stafford v Accident Compensation Authority [2020] NZCA 164 47
Tainui Maori Trust Board v Attorney-General [1989] 2 NZLR 513 (CA) 218
Takamore v Clark [2011] NZCA 587, [2011] 1 NZLR 573 146
Takamore v Clark [2012] NZSC 116, [2013] 2 NZLR 733 146
Tannadyce Investments Ltd v Commissioner of Inland Revenue [2011] NZSC 158, [2012] 2 NZLR 153 173–74
Taunoa v Attorney-General [2007] NZSC 70, [2008] 1 NZLR 429 .... 172, 198–99
Tavita v Minister of Immigration [1994] 2 NZLR 257 (CA) 205, 240

Taylor v Attorney-General [2017] NZCA 215, [2017] 3 NZLR 24 142
Taylor v Attorney-General of Queensland (1917) 23 CLR 457 133
Taylor v New Zealand Poultry Board [1984] 1 NZLR 394 (CA) 6, 134
Te Heuheu Tukino v Aotea District Maori Land Board [1941] NZLR 590 (PC) 212, 221
Te Runanga o Muriwhenua v Attorney-General [1990] 2 NZLR 641 (CA) 218
Thoburn v Sunderland City Council [2003] QB 151, [2002] EWHC 195 (Admin) 206
Town Investments Ltd v Department of the Environment [1978] AC 359 (HL) 46
Trans-Tasman Resources Ltd v Taranaki-Whanganui Conservation Board [2020] NZCA 86, [2020] NZRMA 248 .... 146, 222
Waikato Regional Airport Ltd v Attorney-General [2002] 3 NZLR 433 (CA) 120
Wallis v Solicitor-General [1903] AC 173, (1903) NZPCC 23 212
Wellington City Council v Woolworths New Zealand Limited (No 2) [1996] 2 NZLR 537 (CA) 171
Westco Lagan Ltd v Attorney-General [2001] 1 NZLR 40 (HC) 62, 133–34
Whiteley v Chappell (1868) LR 4 QB 147 141
Wilson v Attorney-General [2011] 1 NZLR 399 (HC) 162
Wolf v Minister of Immigration [2004] NZAR 414 (HC) 171, 204
Ye v Minister of Immigration [2009] NZSC 76, [2010] 1 NZLR 104 .... 205, 240
Zaoui v Attorney General [2005] 1 NZLR 577 (CA) 205
Zhang v Minister of Immigration [2020] NZHC 568 171

Table of Legislation

Bill of Rights 1688 (UK) 1 Will and Mar c 2
art 1 130
art 9 110
Chatham Islands Council Act 1995 232
Child Poverty Act 2018 105
Colonial Law Validity Act 1865 (UK) 128
Companies Act 1993 101
Constitution Act 1986 .... 4, 21, 60, 103, 250
Pt 4 157
s 2(2) 38
s 3 39
s 5 37
s 6 84
s 6(2)(a) 70
s 6(2)(b) 70
s 10 50
s 14 .... 45, 50, 108
s 15(1) 115, 127, 129
s 16 .... 44, 118
s 17(1) 61, 69
s 19 65
s 22 .... 119, 179
s 23 157
Court of Appeal (Civil) Rules 2005 147
Court of Appeal (Criminal) Rules 2001 147
Crimes of Torture Act 1989, ss 16 and 27 177
Crown Proceedings Act 1950 198
Crown Entities Act 2004 100
Declaratory Judgments Act 1908 .... 133, 169
Defence Act 1990 41
District Court Act 2016
s 11 154
s 15 151
s 29 161
s 38 157

District Court Rules 2014 147
Economic Stabilisation Act 1948 86
Electoral (Disqualification of Sentenced Prisoners) Amendment Act 2010 51
Electoral (Integrity) Amendment Act 2019 58
Electoral (Registration of Sentenced Prisoners) Amendment Act 2020 198
Electoral Act 1956 .... 52, 61
Electoral Act 1993 .... 50, 53, 109
  Pts 4, 6, 6A and 6AA 57
  s 28 60
  ss 55AAB–55E 58
  s 71 57
  s 268 60
Electoral Referendum Act 1993 53
English Laws Act 1858 .... 144, 211
Environment Act 1986 216
Foreshore and Seabed Act 2004 130
Fiscal Responsibility Act 1994 .... 4, 103
High Court Rules 2016 147
Human Rights Act 1993 .... 151, 206–7
Immigration Act 2009
  s 127(3) 239
  Sch 1 239
Imperial Laws Application Act 1988 37
  s 5 144
Inquiries Act 2013 180
Interpretation Act 1924, s 5(j) 141
Interpretation Act 1999
  s 5(1) 142
  s 27 198
Interpretation Ordinance 1851 141
Judicature Amendment Act 1972 168
Judicature Amendment Act 1979, s 2 148
Judicial Conduct Commissioner and Judicial Conduct Panel Act 2004 .... 157, 162
Judicial Review Procedure Act 2016 .... 168, 170
  s 16 172
Kaipara District Council (Validation of Rates and Other Matters) Act 2013 234
Legislation Act 2012 116

Legislation Act 2019 142
Pt 5 86
Letters Patent 1839 31
Letters Patent Constituting the Office of Governor-General of New Zealand 1983 .... 39, 41, 46
cl 1 37–38
cl 2 38–39
cl 16 43
Letters Patent issued on 16 November 1840, known as The New Zealand Charter 127
Local Electoral Act 2001 231–32
Local Government (Auckland Council) Act 2009 232
s 8 233
Local Government (Rating) Act 2002 .... 231, 233
Local Government Act 2002 .... 228, 231, 233
s 10 233
s 21 232
s 41 233
s 94 180
Sch 2, pt 3, cl 3 232
Local Government Official Information and Meetings Act 1987 177
s 4 182
Maori Affairs Amendment Act 1967 212
Maori Community Development Act 1962 234
Maori Fisheries Act 2004 221
Māori Language Act 2016, *see* Te Ture mō Te Reo Māori 2016
Maori Representation Act 1867 51
Māori Television Service (Te Aratuku Whakaata Irirangi Māori) Act 2003 221
New South Wales Continuance Act 1840 (UK) 3 & 4 Vict c 62 127
New Zealand Bill of Rights Act 1990 .... 4, 14, 51, 131, 135, 170, 172, 189–203, 206, 216, 228, 236, 239, 252
s 3 192
s 4 .... 192, 194, 196
s 5 .... 191–93, 196, 207
s 6 .... 193, 196
s 7 .... 194–95, 202
s 14 191
s 19 207

s 27(1) 196
s 27(2) 196
New Zealand Constitution (Amendment) Act 1857 (Imp) 128
New Zealand Constitution (Amendment) Act 1947 (UK) 128
New Zealand Constitution Act 1852 (Imp) 3, 21, 44, 50, 127–28
s 18 128
s 32 108
New Zealand Constitution Amendment (Request and Consent) Act 1947 (NZ) 128
New Zealand Constitution Amendment Act 1973 (NZ) 129
New Zealand Superannuation Act 1974 130
Official Information Act 1982 .... 99–101, 177, 181, 186
s 2 182
s 4 182
s 6 183
s 9 183
s 9(1) 84
s 9(2)(f) 83
s 9(2)(g)(i) 98
s 18 183
s 22 184
s 23 187
s 24 184
Official Secrets Act 1951 182
Ombudsmen Act 1975
ss 3 and 6 177
s 13 177
s 22 178
Privacy Act 2020 .... 186, 206
s 22 184
Public Audit Act 2001 179
s 14 179
s 16 180
s 18 180
Public Finance Act 1989 .... 4, 91, 103
s 4(1) 119
s 5 .... 119, 179
ss 65U–65ZB 179
s 266 104

Public Records Act 2005 186
s 3(c) 186
Public Safety Conservation Act 1932 86
Public Service Act 1912 91
Public Service Act 2020 .... 92–94, 97, 99, 102
s 12 94
s 52 93
s 54 .... 88, 95
s 104 93
Resource Management Act 1991 228
Royal Succession Act 2013 37
Royal Titles Act 1974 37–38
Sale of Goods (United Nations Convention) Act 1994 239
Seal of New Zealand Act 1977 38
Senior Courts Act 2016 139
s 3(2) 127
s 74 148
s 74(3) 227
s 94 151
s 100 .... 43, 153
Standing Orders of the House of Representatives 2020 108
SO 35 57
SO 77 112
SO 144 57
SOs 185 and 189 112
SO 257 115
SO 270 133
SOs 326(1) and 327(2) 114
SOs 326–333 86
SO 396 121
SOs 405–408 240
SO 409 113
State Sector Act 1988 .... 4, 91–93, 102
State-Owned Enterprises Act 1986 .... 4, 91, 101, 216
s 9 217
Statute of Westminster 1931 .... 4, 52
Statute of Westminster Application Act 1947 128
Supreme Court Act 2003 149
Supreme Court Rules 2004 147
Te Ture mō Te Reo Māori 2016 221
Te Ture Whenua Maori Act 1993 221

Te Urewera Act 2014 225
Treaty of Waitangi (State Enterprises) Act 1988 217
Treaty of Waitangi Act 1975 215
preamble 215
ss 6(3), 8A, 8HB and 8HJ 223
Sch 1 209
Tribunals Powers and Procedures Legislation Act 2018 176
Tūhoe Claims Settlement Act 2014 225
s 10 225
Waikato Raupatu Claims Settlement Act 1995 38
Waterfront Strike Emergency Regulations 1951 86

Table of International Instruments

Convention Relating to the Status of Refugees 239
International Covenant on Civil and Political Rights 189, 239
Singapore Closer Economic Partnership Agreement 81
Statute of the International Court of Justice 237
te Tiriti o Waitangi/Treaty of Waitangi 2, 4, 9, 15, 20, 22, 26–27, 31–33, 35, 38, 47, 127, 148–49, 151, 176, 190, 203, 208–28, 235, 243, 248, 250, 252
  preamble 32
  first article 32, 209
  second article 32, 209, 213
  third article 32, 210, 213
United Nations Declaration on the Rights of Indigenous Peoples 228, 253
he Whakaputanga o te Rangatiratanga o Nu Tireni/Declaration of Independence of New Zealand 26, 29–30, 35

1

New Zealand Constitutionalism

Introduction – Constitutional Essence – Constitutional Perspective – Constitutional Culture – Constitutional Dialogue – Conclusion

I. INTRODUCTION

New Zealand's constitution is a charming set of anachronistic contrasts in the twenty-first century. Its practitioners and commentators think of it as 'unwritten' although its contents are found in various written sources. It can change dramatically overnight but has retained its essential character for over 150 years. It proudly asserts its independence but is now a purer Westminster model than that in Westminster. It still looks to the centralised authority that comes with a strong executive, strict legislative supremacy and a unitary state, while its populace insists on egalitarian values and representative democracy. It aims to protect the interests of indigenous Māori through democratic majority rule. It is proud of its reputation for upholding the rule of law but has few institutional safeguards to ensure that happens.

These contrasts make New Zealand's constitution a rich area for exploration. Its distinctive features hark back to an age of public trust in government institutions and the power of convention. They are flexible and vulnerable but oddly enduring. They also make exploration of a lived, rather than textual, constitution a necessity rather than a choice. New Zealand's constitution resides in the practices, habits, conventions and norms of constitutional life. That is not just how this book explores it: that is how New Zealand constitutional practitioners and commentators conceive of it. Constitutional lawyers in New Zealand do not study a text. They study the life and times of the constitution as performance art. As authors of this book, we are explicit about our approach: constitutional realism. In this introductory chapter we explain our approach and use it to explore constitutional concepts, New Zealand constitutional culture. But first, we provide an overview of the essence of New Zealand's constitution.

II. CONSTITUTIONAL ESSENCE

A. Constitutional Collision and Evolution

The cultural and legal collision in New Zealand in the first half of the nineteenth century was between British law and Māori law. British settlers brought their legal traditions to a land occupied by Māori and governed in accordance with their tikanga, as we explain further in Chapter 2.

From Cook's three visits in 1769–1779 until the 1830s, there was increasing contact and trade between Europeans and Māori iwi (tribes) and hapū (sub-tribes), especially once Sydney was established in 1788. There were engagements, tensions and conflict between the differing interests of British commercial, religious and government groups and the differing interests of iwi in the 1830s. They culminated in 1840 in the negotiation of te Tiriti o Waitangi / the Treaty of Waitangi and a British assertion of sovereignty. 1840 was the closest New Zealand got to a constitutional 'moment' of the kind identified in many foreign constitutional textbooks.[1] It marked the point at which the coercive force of the British Crown began to be brought to bear in New Zealand, through establishment of British government in New Zealand.

The relationships between the Crown, Māori and other New Zealanders have continued to be fundamental to New Zealand culture and society and to constitutional dynamics. They have, as could be expected, bubbled up through whatever legal system developed, as seen in other colonised nations. The relationships between Māori and the Crown have been a live wire, charged with tension and often generating sparks. There have been painful and dark passages in time that today provide embarrassment, regret and fodder for grievance. More recently there has been a growing willingness to recognise both world views.

In recent times, the primary constitutional avenue in which this constitutional collision has been manifested in New Zealand constitutional dialogue is te Tiriti o Waitangi. From the 1970s to the 1990s, the meaning and legal status of te Tiriti was reinterpreted through iterative constitutional dialogue between the Waitangi Tribunal, the executive, the courts and Parliament (as we detail in Chapter 10). The resulting relational meaning of te Tiriti has become a settled part of New Zealand's

[1] B Ackerman, *We the People: Foundations* (Cambridge, Harvard University Press, 1993).

constitutional landscape. Its legal force has been uncertain, accidental and politically charged, but has grown inexorably.

There are other legal manifestations of the constitutional collision between Māori and the Crown, as also outlined in Chapter 10. The common law of customary rights is the subject of constitutional dialogue that is ongoing. Fiduciary rights are also sometimes litigated, relying on traditional common law conceptions. Perhaps most important, as we speculate in Chapter 7, is the recognition and/or enforcement of Māori tikanga by the common law that has now begun. Whatever directions these developments take, there is no doubt that they relate to an enduringly significant dimension of the character of the New Zealand constitution.

Since 1840, there have not been many constitutional moments of the same intensity. Rather, New Zealand's constitution has evolved in fits and starts, with a couple of more intense periods of constitutional realignments, from the 1840s to 1860s and the 1980s to 1990s. We provide only a very potted outline here, but more details are provided where relevant in each chapter.

British forms of governance followed its assertion of sovereignty in 1840. The 1840s to the 1850s saw the British settlers largely wrest control of government from the Colonial Office through their demands for representative and responsible government. They achieved this through the Imperial Parliament's establishment of a New Zealand Parliament and the Colonial Office acceptance of a doctrine of ministerial responsibility in 1854–56. In 1858, around the time settlers began to outnumber Māori, the New Zealand Parliament gained the ability to amend parts of its constitutive statute, the New Zealand Constitution Act 1852 (Imp).

The increasing political power of settlers reflected and engendered increasing armed conflicts between the Crown and many Māori iwi, from the mid-1840s to the late 1860s.[2] The Crown, with the assistance of other iwi, eventually got the better of these conflicts. But it was probably not until the 1920s that the government effectively controlled all of New Zealand. There were significant difficulties of communication and transportation around the two main islands of New Zealand – which stretch from the equivalent of around Brittany, France to North Africa. Accordingly, early British governance was based on a series of provincial divisions, until these were eventually abolished in 1875. Since then, New Zealand has been a unitary state.

[2] V O'Malley, *The New Zealand Wars* (Wellington, Bridget Williams Books, 2019).

From then, there were only isolated significant constitutional changes for around 100 years. There was a period of political and social ferment in the 1870s to 1890s, with government establishment of national infrastructure and a significant welfare state. These were accompanied constitutionally by the establishment of the first political party (the Liberal Party) in 1891; women's suffrage in 1893; the decision not to join the Australian federation in 1901; and establishment of a politically neutral public service in 1912.

The reaction to the 1930s depression saw the consolidation of the welfare state and development of a two-party electoral system contested by the Labour and National parties. Even the acquisition of independence from Britain was a hesitant series of specific steps, including the acquisition of dominion status in 1907; the passage of the Statute of Westminster by the United Kingdom allowing effective independence in 1931; and New Zealand's eventual adoption of independence under the Statute of Westminster in 1947. The latter move was motivated at least partly by domestic political considerations, in particular the desire to abolish the appointed upper house (the Legislative Council), which was effected in 1950. From then until the 1990s, New Zealand's Cabinet government effectively exercised unbridled power.[3] A small number of ministers dominated the Cabinet, which dominated the governing party, which always had a majority in the small House of Representatives, which exercised legislative supremacy.

The Muldoon administration from 1975 to 1984 demonstrated the autocratic potential of unbridled power, causing an economic crisis. A constitutional backlash followed in the mid to late 1980s. Measures introduced by subsequent governments included restructuring of the public service by the State-Owned Enterprises Act 1986, State Sector Act 1988, Public Finance Act 1989 and Fiscal Responsibility Act 1994. The Constitution Act 1986 brought together the scattered constitutional provisions in the statute book in one ordinary statute. Changes to parliamentary procedures made the House of Representatives more effective. The New Zealand Bill of Rights Act 1990 protected civil and political rights and freedoms with the power of an ordinary statute. From 1986 to 1996, politics was fundamentally restructured as the electoral system was changed from first-past-the-post (FPP) to mixed-member-proportional (MMP). And over all this period of relatively intense constitutional activity, te Tiriti o Waitangi was given legal recognition by the establishment

[3] GWR Palmer, *Unbridled Power?* (Melbourne, Oxford University Press, 1979).

of the Waitangi Tribunal in 1975; the Tribunal's reinterpretation of the principles of te Tiriti from 1983 to 1986; passage of legislation recognising those principles in various Acts from 1986; and court confirmation and enforcement of the principles from 1987. Overall, executive power has been significantly bridled.[4]

Since the 1990s, the pace of constitutional development has slackened, as all these measures have been reviewed, confirmed, tweaked and bedded in. The removal of the Judicial Committee of the Privy Council as New Zealand's highest court in favour of a patriated Supreme Court, in 2003, has been the main additional development. Two current developments that may prove significant are the adoption of well-being as a public finance yardstick and the increasing recognition and enforcement of tikanga by the courts.

B. Constitutional Sketch

The bare essence of the resulting series of contemporary constitutional relationships can be sketched in seven points. These are relationships between the people, Parliament, the Sovereign, Cabinet, ministers, the public service and the judiciary. They are encapsulated in principle and convention and reinforced by legislation and interpretations. But these relationships are not bound up in, or overridden or constrained by, superior legal rules.

(a) *Representative democracy:* New Zealanders have a deep attachment to democracy, manifested through the election of members to the relatively small (120 member) House of Representatives, which is the only house of Parliament. Since 1990, the introduction to the Cabinet Manual, written by one of New Zealand's foremost constitutional scholars, Sir Kenneth Keith, has presented democracy as *the* 'underlying principle' of New Zealand's constitution.[5] The primacy of this principle is reinforced by the rare entrenchment of a handful of electoral laws. Changes to the franchise and electoral system have been central to New Zealand's constitutional story over time. Māori men got the vote in 1867 and Māori and Pākehā women in 1893.

[4] GWR Palmer and MSR Palmer, *Bridled Power*, 4th edn (Melbourne, Oxford University Press, 2004).

[5] K Keith, 'On the Constitution of New Zealand' in Cabinet Office, *Cabinet Manual 2017*, 3.

The change from a FPP electoral system to a MMP system is the most fundamental constitutional reform of recent times. We explain the nature and significance of representative democracy in Chapter 4 (Democratic Government).

(b) *Legislative supremacy (parliamentary sovereignty):* In New Zealand, Parliament may still 'make or unmake any law whatever'.[6] Parliament may also make and unmake governments. The legislative power of Parliament is not subject to formal constraint and, despite occasional extra-judicial musings,[7] the judiciary is not supposed to be able to strike down legislation for any reason. This legislative supremacy flows on from the strong commitment to representative democracy. Historical struggles – initially for representative and responsible government and later to shake off the law-making limits of a colonial legislature – have also reinforced the centrality of legislative supremacy vested in Parliament. We explain the principle of legislative supremacy and its realisation in New Zealand in Chapter 6 (Parliament).

(c) *Sovereign's obligation to act on ministerial advice:* This convention is fundamental to the democratic nature of New Zealand's constitution. Legislation confers on the Governor-General, as local representative of the Sovereign, many legal powers which, if exercised without check, would revive the monarchical nature of government. But convention requires that almost all of the Sovereign's powers may only be exercised on the advice of ministers. In so doing, this convention plays a key role in converting the monarchy into a constitutional monarchy. The convention also comes with an important qualifying condition. The Governor-General acts on the advice of ministers *only* if ministers have the confidence of the House of Representatives. This safety valve reinforces the foundational importance of democratic legitimacy of executive government, tying it back to the notion of representative democracy. We explain the role of the Governor-General, as local representative of the Sovereign, in Chapter 3 (Head of State and the Crown) and the role confidence plays in enabling executive government to advise the Head of State in Chapter 5 (Executive).

[6] AV Dicey, *Lectures Introductory to the Study of the Law of the Constitution* (London, MacMillan & Co, 1885) 36.

[7] See eg O Woodhouse, 'Government Under Law' (Wellington, Price Milburn for New Zealand Council for Civil Liberties, 1979); R Cooke, 'Fundamentals' (1988) *New Zealand Law Journal* 158; *Taylor v New Zealand Poultry Board* [1984] 1 NZLR 394 (CA), 398.

(d) *Collective Cabinet responsibility:* Parliament expresses its confidence in the government as a whole, not individual ministers. This democratic mandate is gifted to the collective of ministers, led by the Prime Minister and operating through Cabinet's deliberative processes. Key parliamentary votes confirm whether a Prime Minister and their Cabinet commands the confidence of the House of Representatives. But it falls to the Governor-General to assess the position on confidence, based on publicly known statements and information, during transitions between governments. The collective character of Cabinet also generates conventions of confidentiality and solidarity. Cabinet and ministers must speak as one and should not reveal difference and dissent. These conventions promote unity, functionally and ostensibly: Cabinet aggregates the power of individual ministers to itself as a collective entity to create 'Cabinet Government'. This collective entity is able to override and to exercise the powers of any individual minister, because ministers are obliged to support the decisions of the Cabinet. In New Zealand, the demands of multi-party government ushered in with proportional representation have tested the virtue of unity. Several innovations allow coalition and support parties to maintain their distinctive positions on some matters even if at variance from the government. We explain how governments gain and lose the confidence of Parliament in Chapter 4 (Democratic Government) and the conventions about how Cabinet and ministers operate in Chapter 5 (Executive).

(e) *Individual ministerial responsibility:* The convention of individual ministerial responsibility remains a bedrock foundation for executive government, even if somewhat overshadowed by collective responsibility.[8] The power of this convention lies in the simple allocation of responsibility: this convention makes clear the identity of the political actor to whom responsibility for a matter of government policy or operations is assigned. The minister so designated by the Prime Minister is responsible to the House of Representatives for all matters within their portfolio. Under the convention, responsibility principally means the obligation to explain, especially to the House – and, as necessary, fix things within their portfolio – more than the

[8] Palmer and Palmer (n 4) 89–94; GWR Palmer, 'The Cabinet, the Prime Minister and the Constitution' (2006) 4 *New Zealand Journal of Public and International Law* 1.

misconceived popularised obligation to resign for governmental mistakes. The explanatory and remedial aspects of the convention drive much of the rhythm of life within Parliament and politics; questions of culpability are more secondary and more circumstantial. We explain these aspects of the convention in Chapter 5 (Executive) and identify the key mechanisms the House uses to hold ministers to account in Chapter 6 (Parliament).

(f) *Public service neutrality and loyalty:* Convention requires public servants to be loyal to the government of the day, to be politically neutral, and to provide ministers with free and frank advice. These conventions complete the series of conventions that link the people to Parliament, Parliament to the Cabinet and to ministers, the Cabinet to ministers, and public servants to ministers. The public service is composed of officials in government departments. Government departments, directed by ministers, are the core of the legal entity known as the Crown. The duty of loyalty requires public servants to do what ministers say. In a real sense, it is this that enables ministers to exercise power. But, importantly, it is subject to the requirements that public servants must maintain their political neutrality between different political parties and that they must provide free and frank advice to ministers. We explain the shape of the public service, along with the conventions and law that regulate the relationship between Cabinet, ministers, departments and officials in Chapter 5 (Executive).

(g) *Rule of law and judicial independence:* At its most basic, the rule of law expresses the ideal that it is the law itself that should rule rather than those individuals who make, administer or interpret the law. Judges are charged with ensuring that the demands of the rule of law are met, through adjudicating on disputes, interpreting legislation and developing the common law and, now, recognising tikanga. Judicial independence provides a necessary condition for them to do so. Most of the other principles and conventions above preserve the monopoly of coercive power of the state intact and specify the relationships between the legislative and executive institutions that exercise it. But, together with representative democracy, the rule of law is a key constraint on the exercise of that power – a constraint which fortifies the overall system as a *constitutional* monarchy. We explain the rule of law and the related principle of judicial independence in Chapter 7 (Judiciary), and other sources of power besides central government in Chapter 11 (Local and Global Governance). We explore some of the key means of constraining government in

Chapters 8 (Accountability and Transparency), Chapter 9 (Human Rights) and Chapter 10 (Te Tiriti o Waitangi).

Together these seven principles and conventions sketch the fundamentals of how public power is exercised in New Zealand. They also illustrate how important it is to understand the underlying reality of the constitution, rather than just its formal clothes. The approach of constitutional realism enriches but complicates the basic task of identifying and explaining the constitution and its elements, as we explain further below. A written constitution is easily explained by showcasing the main constitutional instrument: some master text cloaked in special sanctity. But a formal account misses operational and cultural aspects to which constitutional realists are attentive. The frequent mismatch between legal form and practical reality – or constitutional masquerade – is one of the most striking aspects of New Zealand's constitutional character.

III. CONSTITUTIONAL PERSPECTIVE

A. Constitutional Realism

Our approach is one of 'constitutional realism'. It involves delving beneath the formal legal robes of the constitution to detect the functional substance of how things work in reality.[9]

As an analytical approach, we articulate constitutional realism explicitly in the terms used to describe the approach to law of the American legal realists of the 1920s and 1930s. While describing that 'jurisprudential tendency' as 'ambiguous, unsettled and undefined', Neil Duxbury admits that 'realism describes accurately what was possibly the single unifying ambition of so-called realists: namely, the commitment to candour, to telling it – whatever "it" happened to be – as it is'.[10] The early American realists did not focus much of their attention on constitutional matters. Felix Frankfurter examined realism in constitutional law through the impact of facts influencing the outcome of constitutional

[9] One of us has labelled and used this approach in previous writing; see eg MSR Palmer, 'What is New Zealand's Constitution and Who Interprets It?' (2006) 17 *Public Law Review* 133.

[10] N Duxbury, *Patterns of American Jurisprudence* (Oxford, Clarendon Press, 1995) 65 and 71.

cases.[11] Karl Llewellyn was more comprehensive in one article: 'For the working Constitution consists not merely in powers of the specialists, nor merely in their existing ways of action; it includes no less their attitudes toward the Document and its language.'[12] The American realists' commitment to candour about the reality of law is as applicable to the Constitution as it was to any other law as more recent American constitutional scholars have demonstrated.[13]

Understanding a constitution as a living set of practices was also an approach adopted as an implicit matter of faith and assumption by nineteenth century English constitutionalists. In 1885 law professor Albert Venn Dicey said, in a statement this book could adopt in New Zealand today: 'Constitutional law, as the term is used in England, appears to include all rules which directly or indirectly affect the distribution or the exercise of the sovereign power of the state.'[14] Sir Ivor Jennings made the implications of this clear:[15]

> A constitution, in anything more than a formal sense, is only an organisation of men and women. Its character depends upon the character of the people engaged in governing and being governed. In this respect it is a transient thing, changing like the colours of the kaleidoscope; and an examination of its working involves an examination of the social and political forces which make for changes in the ideas and desires and habits of the population and its various social strata. A public lawyer will not understand [their] constitution unless [they] understand these aspects of it.

Similarly, one of New Zealand's most distinguished jurists, Sir John Salmond, wrote a few years later of the distinction between constitutional fact and constitutional law from a jurisprudential perspective. He noted that:[16]

> [T]he constitution is both a matter of fact and a matter of law. The constitution as it exists *de facto* underlies of necessity the constitution as it exists *de jure*. Constitutional law involves concurrent constitutional practice.

[11] F Frankfurter, 'Hours of Labor and Realism in Constitutional Law' (1916) 29 *Harvard Law Review* 353.

[12] KN Llewellyn, 'The Constitution as an Institution' (1934) 34 *Columbia Law Review* 1, reprinted with notes in *Jurisprudence* (Chicago, University of Chicago Press, 1962) 239–40.

[13] LH Tribe, *The Invisible Constitution* (Oxford, Oxford University Press, 2008); AR Amar, *America's Unwritten Constitution* (New York, Basic Books, 2012).

[14] Dicey (n 6) 24.

[15] WI Jennings, *The Law and the Constitution*, 3rd edn (London, University of London Press, 1943) xv.

[16] JW Salmond, *Jurisprudence or the Theory of the Law* (London, Stevens and Haynes, 1902) 202.

In this tradition, the approach of constitutional realism deployed in this book emphasises substance over form and reality over theory. It looks to behaviour and actions as a more reliable guide to the reality of the constitution than words and doctrines. It stresses the importance of context and the dependence of institutions and procedures on the path by which they have evolved over time. The 'constitution' which affects the behaviour of the actors who exercise public power resides in the influences on those behaviours in reality – their incentives, constraints and powers that extend beyond formal processes and rules to encompass attitudes, beliefs, norms and cultures. That holistic approach to the nature of a constitution underlies this book's identification of the factors which influence the exercise of public power in New Zealand.

Our brief sketch above illustrates that New Zealand's constitution formally vests powers in certain institutions but, in reality, they are actually exercised by others. The Governor-General exercises the powers of the Sovereign. Cabinet and ministers effectively control those decisions. Cabinet can override most decisions that apparently belong to individual ministers. Cabinet and the executive stage-manage much of Parliament's work. Political parties negotiate over the formation of executive government and the exercise of Parliament's powers. Many of these principles and conventions are inconsistent with the formal substance of constitutional laws. This is a salient feature of many Westminster constitutions. But most Westminster constitutions have, superimposed on top of these features, a written constitution, bill of rights or superior document that stamps malleable convention with more rigid legal rules. New Zealand does not. A proper understanding of our constitutional system – and the ways the different component parts militate against misuse of power – needs a realist's eye.

B. Constitutional Elements

A core task of explaining a constitutional system is identifying the key elements that shape the constitution. In the case of unwritten constitutions, this usually involves itemising the various sources which supply constitutional rules in the absence of a complete and superior instrument. But that task often devolves into a long – almost infinite – shopping list of legal elements that might generate some constitutional-looking norms. And, of course, drawing up this shopping list is inherently subjective, especially in the absence of any widely-accepted rule of recognition for constitutional rules. There is notable variation in the list of sources identified in other accounts of the New Zealand constitution, both between the different accounts and across time.[17]

We think this descriptive exercise should be guided by a definition that reflects constitutional realism: a rule, norm or practice (an element) should be regarded as constitutional 'if it plays a significant role in influencing the generic exercise of public power – whether through structures, processes, principles, rules, conventions or even culture'.[18] Consistent with the conceptual purpose of constitutions, the key focus is on public power and the rules which shape that power – whether enabling or limiting power. It sifts rules regulating power to avoid the constitution being equated with a vast mass of rules affecting government down to the smallest minutiae. Significance and genericism qualify the group of rules that should be treated as constitutional. The definition also enlarges the corpus of constitutional rules beyond the formal, ensuring more subtle human aspects that empower or constrain government are not lost. We attend to the continuum of the most formal instruments of black-letter legislation and judge-made common law and interpretation as well as systemic tensions, patterns of political dynamics, constitutional character and even constitutional culture.

For convenience, the constitutional elements associated with each branch of government can be further conceptualised in four categories: conventions, common law, instruments, and interpretations of those instruments. Inevitably there is some overlap, but this systemic approach presents a fuller and more meaningful account of constitutional rules than an ad hoc shopping list approach.

(a) *Constitutional conventions:* Conventions are social norms that constrain behaviour within government: a practice, norm or understanding which has gradually crystallised so that it is recognised by constitutional actors and commentators to exist and, normatively, to govern the exercise of public power.[19] Conventions are binding constitutional practices that arise independently from, or overlap, the strict legal scope of legislative or other powers. There must also be a reason for a convention; it must fulfil a function consistent

[17] See eg PA Joseph, *Joseph on Constitutional and Administrative Law*, 5th edn (Wellington, Thomson Reuters, 2021); Keith (n 5); B Harris, *New Zealand Constitution: An Analysis in Terms of Principles* (Wellington, Thomson Reuters, 2018).

[18] Palmer (n 9) 152.

[19] See Dicey (n 6); Jennings (n 15), 129–31; *Re Resolution to Amend the Constitution* [1981] 1 SCR 753. See also G Marshall, *Constitutional Conventions*, rev edn (Oxford, Clarendon Press, 1986).

with the wider constitutional system. As conventions are not legal rules, they can be breached without formal legal consequences – conventions are not directly enforceable in court (although courts sometimes acknowledge them). Instead, sociological dynamics and reactions – civic virtue, moral-suasion, disapprobation, political cost, public reaction – help condition actors to do the right thing. A convention may change through a consistent change in behaviour over time.

Throughout this book, we explain many conventions, from the cardinal constitutional convention that the Governor-General must act on the advice of their ministers, to the public service obligation to tender free and frank advice. The informality of conventions means there is often debate about the existence and nature of a particular convention, especially how practices over time should be interpreted, whether those practices serve important constitutional purposes, and whether deviation from practice amounts to a breach or reformulation of a convention. Increasingly we are seeing conventional rules being signalled through expressed expectations about the proper way power should be exercised, for example, in Cabinet circulars, the Cabinet Manual and speeches from important office-holders. Whether these top-down statements of expectations are successful in influencing the conscience and practice of those exercising public power depends on their normative force and the context in which the expectations are expressed.[20] In principle, conventions can be created in this way but it is difficult to measure that success until put to the test in practice.

(b) *Common law:* The common law is more formal than constitutional conventions because the norms are expressed through adjudication in court judgments and are enforceable through coercive means. Judge-made law, through adjudication in individual disputes, is the emblematic form of common law. However, we can speak of norms generated by other branches of government in this way too, such as a common law of Parliament, where some of its rules and customs are subject to formal adjudication and enforcement.

(c) *Instruments of each branch of government*: The most formal rules are those recorded in instruments of each branch of government, whether in legislation, standing orders, rules of court, prerogative

[20] A Perry and A Tucker, 'Top-Down Constitutional Conventions' (2018) 81 *Modern Law Review* 765.

instruments, the Cabinet Manual and so forth. Importantly, those charged with interpreting and adjudicating compliance with these instrumental rules often differ from those creating them.

(d) *Interpretations of instruments:* The meanings given to instrumental rules can also be elements of the constitution. The judiciary has a primary role in interpreting legislation but some legislation will naturally fall for interpretation by other officeholders. For example, the Controller and Auditor-General may have a more dominant role in giving meaning to the public finance provisions set out in legislation. Standing Orders of the House of Representatives are interpreted by the Speaker and committees of the House. The Cabinet Manual provisions are given life by the Prime Minister and Secretary of the Cabinet. And, as we identify throughout this book, instances of overlapping responsibility for interpretation of some constitutional rules means different branches of government and different officeholders effectively engage in dialogue about the meaning and significance of the rules.

Throughout this book, we are guided by these key definitions of what a constitution is and what the elements of New Zealand's constitution are. But our broad lens of constitutional realism stresses not only formal legal instruments. It also extends to attitudes that affect the generic exercise of public power.

IV. CONSTITUTIONAL CULTURE

In considering constitutional matters, lawyers tend to focus primarily on institutions, procedures and particular cases, consistent with their training. Constitutional law in most common law jurisdictions is largely the study of a text and cases. New Zealand and the United Kingdom have adhered less to this kind of constitutional law than other jurisdictions, because of the absence of a foundational constitutional text. Even so, and particularly since the enactment of the New Zealand Bill of Rights Act 1990, most constitutional law analysed by lawyers and judges is doctrinal in nature and more interested in the detail of individual cases than the contextual sweep of political interactions. But in reality, the ebb and flow of underlying public opinion about how public power is and should be exercised influences the evolution of unwritten constitutional events more directly than do particular cases. In other words, it is useful to reflect on constitutional culture as well its legal infrastructure and doctrinal form.

We use a concept of 'culture' that refers to a general understanding of a group of people – their collective mindset or way of thinking about the world: 'the collective programming of the mind which distinguishes the members of one group or category of people from another' or 'interpretive community'.[21] Naturally, there is a close relationship between the culture and the identity of a community. In this sense culture is 'constitutive' of a community, in determining how that community is distinct from others. We consider any adequate conception of a 'constitution' must deal with the cultural elements that underpin it. We identify key norms of New Zealand constitutional culture that appear to endure over time. These norms are shaped by, and shape, the constitution. We take a long-term view of patterns of constitutional culture.[22]

We note some caveats though. First, distilling cultural norms is inherently impressionistic and reflects our own observations and experiences of the operation of New Zealand's constitution in reality. Secondly, in the current context, there are limits on how far we can identify national constitutional norms, across the communities which constitute Aotearoa New Zealand. Culture exists within any group, and groups and cultures overlap with each other at all levels of society. We do not deny the importance of examining the large number and varieties of cultures that overlap and nestle within New Zealand. In particular, the aspects of Māori culture that intersect with the New Zealand constitution have a separate and important existence that is not drawn out in our account but deserves its own treatment – as Māmari Stephens has recently demonstrated so ably and Carwyn Jones further develops.[23] We applaud these and any other efforts to understand the various cultures that exist and evolve within New Zealand. By necessity, the constitutional culture we posit here is the amorphous but recognisable 'culture' across Aotearoa New Zealand. It eddies in and out of overlapping and component cultures but retains its own discernible current of how those involved in the exercise of public power perceive the general nature of 'public' opinion.

[21] G Hofstede, GJ Hofstede and M Minkov, *Cultures and Organisations*, 3rd edn (New York, McGraw Hill Professional, 2010); S Fish, *Doing What Comes Naturally* (Durham and London, Duke University Press, 1989) (especially in his response to Owen Fiss, ch 6).

[22] MSR Palmer, 'New Zealand Constitutional Culture' (2007) 22 *New Zealand Universities Law Review* 565; MSR Palmer, *The Treaty of Waitangi in New Zealand's Constitution and Law* (Wellington, Victoria University Press, 2008) 278–82.

[23] M Stephens, 'A Loving Excavation' (2013) 25 *New Zealand Universities Law Review* 820; C Jones, 'Whakaeke i ngā ngaru – riding the waves' in L Ford and T Rowse (eds), *Between Indigenous and Settler Governance* (Abingdon, Routledge, 2013) 174.

We suggest there are four key cultural attitudes to the exercise of public power in New Zealand which are at the heart of its constitutional culture and which support four constitutional norms: egalitarianism, faith in authority, fairness and pragmatism. Overall, these constitutional norms pull in contradictory directions and manifest in different aspects of our constitutional arrangements. But identifying them enables us to understand the overall 'grain' of New Zealand's constitutional culture. In the end, it is these sorts of cultural attitudes that 'constitute' New Zealand, in a more enduring though evolving manner than particular institutions, procedures or cases.

A. Egalitarianism

New Zealand sees itself as a fundamentally egalitarian society. Ideas of equality and a belief in the collective have existed from an early stage of New Zealand's settler society. Team spirit matters. In Māoridom the interests of the collective tribal unit – the iwi or hapū or whānau – dominate. In early settler society the cohesiveness of the crew was crucial. An aspect still seen today, particularly by New Zealanders returning from overseas, is New Zealand's 'tall poppy syndrome', where those over-inflating their own importance are cut down to size.

Perhaps this aspect of New Zealand culture is changing. There is empirical evidence that the distribution of wealth in New Zealand society has become markedly more unequal than it used to be, and that expectations that the government should redress that inequality have fallen.[24] In popular culture there seems to be more individualism in New Zealand society now than in the past, associated with celebration of celebrity-oriented international culture. Even the attention paid to individual rugby players now rivals that paid to the All Blacks collectively. Celebrity culture focuses on individual politicians in a more presidential way than it used to. But during the struggle against coronavirus in 2020, Prime Minister Jacinda Ardern constantly evoked, and commentators picked up, the image of the 'team of five million' – in other words, New Zealanders acting collectively.[25] We consider that the underlying egalitarian ethos and rhetoric from

[24] M Rashbrooke (ed), *Inequality: A New Zealand Crisis* (Wellington, Bridget Williams Books, 2013).

[25] DR Knight, 'Stamping out Covid-19 in New Zealand: Legal Pragmatism and Democratic Legitimacy' [2021] Public Law 241.

the foundational elements of New Zealand culture still subsist in New Zealanders' attitudes to the exercise of public power.

Egalitarianism still underlies and reinforces what we regard as the strongest constitutional norm in New Zealand: *representative democracy*, explored in Chapter 4. Māori tikanga expects rangatira (chiefs) to express the consensus of the iwi or hapū.[26] The demand for representative government was the natural expectation for a settler society conceived in the era of the Great Reform movement of 1830s Britain. That demand was pushed, hard, in the 1850s by those who successfully demanded representative and responsible government. Māori men voting in 1867; all European men voting in 1879; women voting in 1893; the abolition of plural voting in 1889 – all of these indicate that the ballot box was seen as the means of giving groups a stake in settler society. The biggest constitutional change in twentieth century New Zealand was the introduction of MMP in 1993.

As Neil Atkinson states 'it is clear that the act of voting is still deeply rooted in the collective [New Zealand] psyche'.[27] The central position of representative democracy in New Zealand's constitution today is also cemented by other aspects of the constitution. The confidence of the elected House of Representatives is the lifeblood of government. The Governor-General may only ignore their ministerial advisors if those ministers have lost the confidence of the people's representatives. The only provisions in New Zealand law entrenched against amendment by a simple majority of the House are certain provisions relating to electoral law. Democracy is *the* 'underlying principle' of New Zealand's constitution, as Sir Kenneth Keith records in his preface to the Cabinet Manual, which is probably the most authoritative account of the constitution.

B. Faith in Authority

New Zealanders generally trust their governors. We put our faith in government to look after us and our wellbeing.[28] Collective action, by the state on behalf of the community, is not seen as the enemy of the people.

[26] J Williams, 'He Aha Te Tikanga Māori' (unpublished draft paper for the Law Commission, 1998) 12, quoted in Law Commission, 'Māori Custom and Values in New Zealand' (NZLC SP9, 2001) 34.

[27] N Atkinson, *Adventures in Democracy* (Dunedin, Otago University Press, 2003) 10.

[28] In the previous work of one of us that underlies these concepts, parliamentary sovereignty was previously supported by a norm of 'authoritarianism' (Palmer, 'Constitutional Culture' (n 22)). We think faith in authority better captures our meaning.

Māori revere strong rangatira. New Zealanders generally admire strong Prime Ministers: Norman Kirk, Rob Muldoon, Helen Clark, John Key and Jacinda Ardern in recent years. Settler society in New Zealand always looked to the state rather than away from it – as long as it was directed by those chosen in New Zealand rather than London. Whether it was advancing settler interests against Māori, building national infrastructure in the 1870s; creating the welfare state in the 1890s or 1930s; mantling or dismantling economic protectionism in the 1940s or 1980s; leading New Zealanders to war in the 1900s, 1910s and 1940s; or fighting coronavirus, Pākehā New Zealanders have generally expected and trusted government to solve their problems and look after their interests. This is where the contrast with American constitutional culture is at its highest. The separation and equilibration of powers by the United States constitution directly reflect the distrust of the state into which that nation was born. (Pākehā) New Zealanders never had or wanted a revolution; they wanted efficient government that could do things for them, as it has done.

The cultural demand for, and trust in, authority found ideal expression in the principle of *legislative supremacy* explored in Chapter 6. Irrespective of questions over its historical existence, legislative supremacy has never been seriously questioned in New Zealand since (Pākehā) New Zealanders seized the reins of parliamentary sovereignty in 1858. New Zealand appears to be the last outpost where citizens appear content to dice with Dicey. In New Zealand, Parliament can, and still does, make or unmake any law whatsoever, unconstrained by a 'higher' law, a written constitution or European law.[29]

We do not want to overstate this degree of trust though. Māori and Pasifika attitudes are much more ambivalent, especially towards Pākehā-dominated majoritarian government. And faith is not blind; trust must be earned. The introduction of MMP sought to bridle executive power by restructuring the political sector after both Labour and National governments were seen to have broken promises. But, so far, a turn to judicial authority to counterbalance politicians' sovereignty has not found favour with most New Zealanders.

C. Fairness

Fairness is a core animating ideal of New Zealand culture. Historian David Hackett Fischer rightly identifies our 'highly developed vernacular

[29] Dicey (n 6), 36.

ideas of fairness', in contrast to the American embrace of freedom, as our societal organising principle.[30] Fairness has both procedural and substantive dimensions, both of which are familiar to lawyers but not usually conceived by lawyers as pertaining to popular attitudes. A substantive meaning captures ideas like 'not taking undue advantage of others' or 'doing unto others as we would have them do unto us'.[31] Procedural meanings are more about 'playing by the rules', and related ideas of honesty, impartiality and decency.[32] These ideas of fairness, we think, bear on New Zealanders' attitudes to how public power should be exercised.

We might expect fairness to translate into, and support, the rule of law as a strong constitutional norm (and, perhaps, by association, judicial independence too).[33] Justice and the rule of law can be seen as formal corollaries of the notion of fairness, reflecting both its procedural and substantive dimensions. But, while we detect a strong cultural commitment to the broad notion of fairness, we are not convinced that New Zealanders see the courts as the primary guardians of fairness. As one of us said in 2007 (and we both still agree), '[v]aluing the notion of giving people a fair go does not necessarily require that you value the judiciary giving it to them'.[34] Our impression is that the rule of law is a vulnerable constitutional norm in New Zealand. As a former High Court judge said in 2009, 'the constitutional importance of the judicial arm of government and its independence are imperfectly understood and not deeply entrenched in New Zealand's culture'.[35] While we endorse the normative value of the rule of law (supported by judicial independence), we are not convinced New Zealanders understand the rule of law or, in a crunch, would necessarily stand by it in the face of a collective objective seen as important.[36]

Indeed, various law reform exercises in New Zealand over the years have exhibited a consistent suspicion about entrusting decision-making to court processes, whether because of perceptions of their slowness, expense or formality. Examples include the institution of the Ombudsmen as a check on executive government from 1962; the replacement of the right to sue for personal injury by the accident

[30] DH Fischer, *Fairness and Freedom* (New York, Oxford University Press, 2012) 479–80.
[31] Ibid 486.
[32] Ibid 486.
[33] Palmer, 'Constitutional Culture' (n 22) 588.
[34] Ibid 588.
[35] J Priestley, 'Chipping Away at the Judicial Arm?' (2009) 17 *Waikato Law Review* 1, 23.
[36] Palmer, 'Constitutional Culture' (n 22).

compensation scheme in 1972; the creation of the Waitangi Tribunal in 1975, rather than reference to the courts, to investigate allegations of the breaches of te Tiriti o Waitangi; and establishment of a myriad of complaints or oversight agencies about aspects of executive government (Independent Police Conduct Authority, Human Rights Commission, Privacy Commissioner, Children's Commissioner, Health and Disability Commissioner, Inspector-General of Intelligence and Security). And when distrust in politics engendered a demand for constitutional change in the early 1990s, it was the electoral system, not a judicial check, that was reached for.

Yet public opinion polls seem to indicate that, on balance, the courts do not fare too badly in terms of popular confidence. Or at least – which is not quite the same thing – they tend to fare better than politicians.[37] Periodic public reviews have become gradually less antagonistic to the notion that the power of the judiciary might desirably increase.[38] To us, this reflects gradually decreasing negativity regarding the role of the judiciary in New Zealand. But it does not, yet, necessarily indicate comfort about entrusting more positive public power to judges.

D. Pragmatism

We identify the fourth aspect of New Zealand culture relevant to the exercise of power to be pragmatism. Grand theorising is suspicious unless it relates to something concrete. Problems should be fixed as they appear, preferably with 'number 8 fencing wire' after tinkering in the constitutional shed. Just get on with it – and 'it' is preferably something practical rather than theoretical. In that regard, New Zealanders do value innovation in our pragmatic tinkering – and are not averse to, and rather proud of, doing something no one else has ever done (regardless of whether there were good reasons for that). But they would apparently rather make up constitutional innovations on the spot than think too much about it in advance.

[37] UMR polls in 2013 placed Parliament last on a list of 18 institutions, with the courts 10th, but are no longer available online. See UMR, 'Mood of the Nation Archive' (www.umr.co.nz).

[38] See also a later review of the issue by the promoter of the Bill of Rights Act in GWR Palmer, 'The Bill of Rights after Twenty-One Years' (2013) 11 *New Zealand Journal of Public and International Law* 257.

This pragmatic element of New Zealand culture appears to lie behind our determined assertion that New Zealand has, and should have, an unwritten constitution. It is not clear why New Zealanders have asserted this, and have done so since the 1860s.[39] New Zealand has always had a constitution of some sort, whether a Charter, the unrequited 1846 Imperial Act, the long-lasting 1852 Imperial Act or the patriated Constitution Act 1986. Those Acts are not significantly different in nature to those of Canada, Australia or other former British colonies. Yet New Zealand constitutional discourse has insisted that we had an unwritten constitution.[40]

Perhaps this reflected the early appeal to constitutional convention regarding responsible government in the 1850s. Perhaps it is related to the early abolition of the provinces in 1877, and the associated power of the judiciary to strike down legislation on federalism grounds. If Parliament is sovereign to the extent that it can unmake any (constitutional) law whatever without restraint by the judiciary, how could anyone reasonably talk about anything but an unwritten constitution? But the enduring nature of this assertion also seems to us to be connected with New Zealanders' cultural aversion to tying their hands in the future; a preference for presentism rather than originalism. This is also consistent with the incrementalism that has characterised any constitutional change, as we outlined above.

Periodic suggestions that we should write down our key constitutional rules are still greeted with suspicion. And this does seem to be consistent with Māori constitutional values, as our unwritten constitution, like tikanga Māori to some degree, privileges flexibility and pragmatic evolution. Our suspicion is greater if a proposal for a written constitution appears to transgress constitutional norms of representative democracy and/or legislative supremacy by installing the judiciary as enforcers. That too may change, incrementally, in the future.

V. CONSTITUTIONAL DIALOGUE

Finally, in this book we use the structure of the traditional division of government into three branches: the executive, the legislature and the

[39] Palmer, 'Constitutional Culture' (n 22) 95 and 590–91.

[40] J McLean, 'The Unwritten Political Constitution and Its Enemies' (2016) 14 *International Journal of Constitutional Law* 119.

judiciary. But we attempt to weave into these chapters on the executive, legislature and judiciary a sense of their contribution to constitutional dynamics. We characterise each branch as having its own voice and speaking its own language. This is a development of the metaphor of constitutional dialogue, where each branch of government issues its judgments, passes its legislation or executes its policies in reaction to each other's decisions, over time. We do not see the metaphor as a means of achieving normative constitutional prescriptions.[41] Rather, it is one way of capturing an understanding of an important part of how New Zealand constitutional dynamics actually function in practice.[42]

One value of the metaphor is that it moves academic debate away from the arid old question of which branch of government is, or should be, 'supreme'. That question is inadequate. It fails to capture what happens over time, when different branches of government express and then change their position on a question of law or policy in reaction to the views of other branches. Time and again, we have seen important features of New Zealand's constitution develop through an iterative series of interactions between the different branches of government, and also other institutions with a voice in the exercise of public power, such as the Waitangi Tribunal and the Law Commission. Our use of the dialogue metaphor also captures less rosy instances of inter-institutional discourse. Sometimes one branch may speak on a matter when other branches are not attentive or fail to listen closely. Or branches may speak past each other, as if they are speaking different languages. Nor will these dialogical developments always generate linear, neat or progressive outcomes. Rather, dialogue is a way of capturing inter-branch dynamics and interactions – both harmonious and discordant.

We cover a number of examples of constitutional dialogue in detail, particularly in relation to Māori rights and human rights more widely. These include the meaning and legal force of te Tiriti o Waitangi; Māori claims to customary rights to particular areas of foreshore and seabed; and the development of remedies (damages and declarations of legislative inconsistency) for breaches of fundamental rights and freedoms. We also identify instances of dialogue between the branches of government about the limits of the powers of different institutions of government: the scope of Parliamentary privilege; immunity of public servants for

[41] A Kavanagh, 'The Lure and Limits of Dialogue' (2016) 66 *University of Toronto Law Journal* 83, 85.

[42] See MSR Palmer, 'Constitutional Dialogue and the Rule of Law' (2017) 47 *Hong Kong Law Journal* 505.

negligent acts committed in good faith; and the judiciary's approach to the interpretation of legislation.

On all these and other constitutional issues, the dynamics of iterative dialogue involve each branch having different perspectives – effectively speaking in different languages and at different volumes:

- Politicians in Parliament speak the language of politics.
- The judiciary speaks the language of the common law.
- The public service speaks the languages of policy and management.
- Ministers speak, and translate between, the languages of politics and policy.

The most fundamental distinctions between these languages, however, are when the pragmatism of politics or the generic nature of policy meets the specificity and principle of law. That happens particularly over issues of fundamental human rights, including the rights of individuals and the rights of Māori. The judiciary and its language of the common law seems likely to feel more confident on specific cases of injustice focusing on 'rights' than it does on, for example, issues of generic social or economic policy. Rights are at the cutting edge of the relationship between the state and citizens, and the effects of the state's coercive powers. These are the issues on which the judiciary has been prepared to 'raise its voice' in constitutional dialogue with the political branches of government. They are the issues on which constitutional dialogue in New Zealand has been particularly noticeable.

The examples of constitutional dialogue over the nature and extent of the powers of different government institutions reveal another, unsurprising, pattern. The views of the judiciary have prevailed over those of other branches regarding the nature of the judiciary's own approach to statutory interpretation. The views of the political branches, the executive and Parliament, have been more influential in relation to the nature and extent of their own powers – the extent of Parliamentary privilege, the immunities of the public service or the surveillance powers of the police.

It makes sense to us that constitutional dialogue in New Zealand concerns the relationship between citizens and the state, and the nature and extent of the powers of the institutions of government. Those are, after all, the questions which matter in reality about a constitution. It also makes sense to us that the constitutional settings reached in New Zealand, for whatever period of time, reflect different perspectives of different institutions which evolve over time. We consider it is constitutionally healthy that generic policies and principles, mediated through political negotiation and competition should be checked in terms of their specific impacts on the rights of individuals and groups in particular contexts. There is value to different kinds of thinking, including thinking fast and slow, as they have become popularised.[43] An individual benefits from different parts of the brain impelling urgent demands for action as well as more considered reflection on the value of that action. Our considered view is that the same is true for a constitutional polity.

VI. CONCLUSION

New Zealand is a country of five million people in the South Pacific. It has a single House of Parliament, a unitary state, no supreme law and a Cabinet used to getting its own way. The legal form of its constitution is that of a monarchy and its monarch lives in Britain. By convention, however, the monarch's representative acts only on advice from Ministers. who have the confidence of the House of Representatives. Cabinet acts collectively and is advised by a loyal and politically neutral public service who usually provide free and frank advice. New Zealanders fiercely uphold their right to vote out the government in general elections every three years.

Against that backdrop and with a strong realist's eye, we set out to explore New Zealand's constitution. First, in Chapters 2 to 7, we look at the institutions which constitute the state and wield public power. Then we examine the norms and processes that constrain that power.

FURTHER READING

Cabinet Office, *Cabinet Manual 2017*.

Constitutional Advisory Panel, 'New Zealand's Constitution: A Report on a Conversation' (Wellington, New Zealand Government, 2013).

Harris, B, *New Zealand Constitution: An Analysis in Terms of Principles* (Wellington, Thomson Reuters, 2018).

Joseph, PA, *Joseph on Constitutional and Administrative Law*, 5th edn (Wellington, Thomson Reuters, 2021).

Palmer, GWR, and Palmer, MSR, *Bridled Power: New Zealand's Constitution and Government*, 4th edn (Melbourne, Oxford University Press, 2004).

[43] D Kahneman, *Thinking, Fast and Slow* (London, Allen Lane, 2011).

Palmer, MSR, 'What is New Zealand's Constitution and Who Interprets It?' (2006) 17 *Public Law Review* 133.
Palmer, MSR, 'New Zealand Constitutional Culture' (2007) 22 *New Zealand Universities Law Review* 565.

2

Aotearoa New Zealand

Introduction – Māori and Pākehā – He Whakaputanga o Te Rangatiratanga o Nu Tireni: The Declaration of Independence of New Zealand – Te Tiriti o Waitangi: The Treaty of Waitangi – Assertion of British Sovereignty – Conclusion

I. INTRODUCTION

A COLLISION BETWEEN two legal systems sparked the emergence of what is now recognised as the nation state of New Zealand. As Sir Joe Williams, now a Supreme Court judge, explains metaphorically: the first and second laws of New Zealand are those brought to New Zealand by two great explorers, Kupe and Cook.[1] Kupe's law for te Ao Māori (the Māori world) was carried by Māori when they first settled the land later known as Aotearoa. At its core is 'tikanga Māori', which represents Māori concepts of correctness, rightness or justice. Tikanga expresses the customs and expected behaviours within and between Māori communities and reflects a holistic perspective of kinship with the physical and metaphysical world. Cook's law was English law and custom, statute and common law, generally reflecting materialist, individualistic and Christian perspectives. It implicitly accompanied British visitors to Aotearoa and was then more explicitly invoked by British settlers in New Zealand.

Te Tiriti o Waitangi / the Treaty of Waitangi was 'the mechanism through which these two systems of law would be formally brought together in some sort of single accommodation' in 1840.[2] Te Tiriti has been described by New Zealand's most distinguished jurist, Lord Cooke of Thorndon, as 'simply the most important document in New Zealand's

[1] J Williams, 'Lex Aotearoa' (2013) 21 *Waikato Law Review* 1, 4.
[2] Ibid 7.

history'.[3] Its signing was a 'constitutional moment' in the history of New Zealand.[4] But it did not 'found' Aotearoa. Māori did that. They formed iwi (tribes), which were shifting coalitions of hapū (sub-tribes) composed of various whānau (extended families). In te Tiriti, Māori rangatira (chiefs) agreed that the Crown could exercise some form of public power in Aotearoa, particularly over Europeans. In short order Britain asserted, and later exercised, its own concept of sovereignty over all those in New Zealand.

The legal and constitutional significance of te Tiriti and its context deserves book-length treatment.[5] This chapter outlines the story of legal creation sparked by the signings of te Tiriti o Waitangi.

II. MĀORI AND PĀKEHĀ

Māori hapū and iwi exercised public power over their various rohe (geographical areas) from the time of their (multiple) arrivals from elsewhere in the Pacific over at least 800 years ago. Hapū were the core social, economic, political and constitutional units of governance. Numbering at least in the hundreds, hapū formed, dissolved and reformed as larger iwi in a constantly shifting series of alliances – preparing for and reacting to the presence or absence of external threats and internal divisions.[6] Rangatira provided political leadership of collective units, where the exercise of decision-making power within a hapū was regulated by complex norms and belief systems including mana (status), tapu (sacredness), noa (ordinary, free from tapu), utu (reciprocity), tikanga (procedure), whakapapa (genealogy), whanaungatanga (kinship), manaakitanga (nurturing

[3] R Cooke, 'Introduction' (1990) 14 *New Zealand Universities Law Review* 1. We refer to it as te Tiriti o Waitangi because, as explained in this chapter, rangatira overwhelmingly signed the Māori language version, and in 1841 the United Kingdom House of Commons published the certified copies of the two language versions with the Māori language version first, under the title 'TREATY.', followed by the English language version, under the title '(Translation.)'.

[4] This chapter draws on MSR Palmer, 'Indigenous Rights: New Zealand' in DS Law (ed), *Constitutionalism in Context* (Cambridge, Cambridge University Press, forthcoming 2022).

[5] For example, C Orange, *The Treaty of Waitangi* (Wellington, Bridget Williams Books Ltd, 1987); MSR Palmer, *The Treaty of Waitangi in New Zealand's Law and Constitution* (Wellington, Victoria University Press, 2008); Waitangi Tribunal, 'He Whakaputanga me te Tiriti' (Wai 1040, 2014).

[6] A Ballara, *Iwi* (Wellington, Victoria University Press, 1998).

others) and kaitiakitanga (guardianship).[7] The islands, later collectively known as Aotearoa, were governed by a dynamic pattern of distributed power amongst Māori iwi and hapū. We do not explore the intricacies of the history of this governance here, partly because we are not well enough informed to do so and partly because in this chapter we focus on the clash between Māori and British governance.

In 1642 Abel Tasman sighted, but did not land on, Aotearoa. Dutch mapmakers named the islands 'Nieuw Zeeland', which was picked up by later European visitors starting with Captain James Cook in 1769 and later transliterated by Māori as 'Nu Tireni'. Further European and Māori contact was boosted by Britain's establishment of a penal colony in 1788 in 'nearby' Port Jackson, New South Wales, which became Sydney. Trade and migration led to the gradual arrival of British and other visitors, who sometimes stayed. Māori called the Europeans 'Pākehā' and this label is still in common use in New Zealand. British, French and American visitors, as well as other Europeans, came to Aotearoa from 1800 for whaling and sealing. Timber and flax and other resources were traded. A number of Māori visited Sydney and Europe. By the 1820s there was a thriving trans-Tasman trade between, particularly, the north of Aotearoa, Sydney and Europe. 1825 also saw the formation of the first New Zealand Company, headed by Lord Durham, advocating organised private British settlement in New Zealand.

Christian missionaries arrived and established missions in New Zealand from 1814. A number of Māori became interested in Christian theology, marrying it with aspects of Māori beliefs and eventually converting to Christianity in not insignificant numbers. Inter-hapū Māori power dynamics were also changed by contact with European technology. Hongi Hika of Ngāpuhi visited England in 1820, gaining an audience with King George IV. On his way back, he acquired a large quantity of muskets in Sydney, which enabled Ngāpuhi to gain an upper hand over other iwi in the 'musket wars' which lasted into the 1830s. In that decade diseases brought by foreign contact also killed thousands of Māori.

During all this time Māori well outnumbered Pākehā in Aotearoa. Māori exercised public power throughout the land. Transgressions of tikanga Māori, including by Pākehā, were punished by iwi and hapū. For example, in 1809 Māori killed most of the crew of the *Boyd* in response to the flogging of a rangatira. This, in turn, led to reprisals

[7] HM Mead, *Tikanga Māori*, 2nd edn (Wellington, Huia Publishers, 2016); Waitangi Tribunal (n 5) ch 2; C Jones, *New Treaty, New Tradition* (Vancouver, UBC Press, 2016) ch 2.

against other Māori and to inter-tribal conflict. The British government, and successive governors of the British colony of New South Wales, became increasingly agitated about the conduct of British subjects in New Zealand.[8] The Governor of New South Wales issued five proclamations from 1804 to 1814 attempting to regulate the transport of, and conduct toward, Māori. Under the last of these, three Māori rangatira and a British clergyman were appointed as justices of the peace in New Zealand. The United Kingdom Parliament passed statutes in 1817, 1823 and 1828 extending criminal law and procedure to crimes committed by British subjects in the foreign territory of New Zealand.

By the 1830s there was increasing pressure on the British government from the missionaries and intending settlers to influence or participate in the exercise of public power in New Zealand. Unscrupulous land-dealings also reflected cross-cultural misunderstandings. A series of incidents of grisly cross-cultural misunderstanding and malice by both Māori and British, well publicised in Britain, engendered British outrage. A prime example in 1830 was when the captain of the British brig *Elizabeth* allowed Te Rauparaha, rangatira of Ngāti Toa, and 100 of his warriors to use the ship. In an exercise of utu (or rebalancing) after the earlier killing of Ngāti Toa rangatira, they captured and killed a Ngāi Tahu rangatira and his wife and daughter, killed a number of Ngāi Tahu, and destroyed their settlement. Captain Stewart was put on trial in Sydney in 1831 as an accessory to murder but it failed to proceed.

III. HE WHAKAPUTANGA O TE RANGATIRATANGA O NU TIRENI: THE DECLARATION OF INDEPENDENCE OF NEW ZEALAND

In 1831, a number of rangatira, encouraged by missionaries, petitioned King William IV for recognition of British friendship and guardianship. The Crown's letter in response in 1833 appointed James Busby as 'British Resident', its official emissary to investigate complaints against British citizens and attempt to protect Nu Tireni from outrage by British subjects. The aim was to extend to Aotearoa all the benefits it could gain from 'alliance' with Britain. Busby would do this primarily by exercising soft power. He facilitated rangatira of northern iwi and hapū choosing a national flag in 1834. A number of British Navy ships helped resolve disputes within New Zealand by both diplomatic and destructive means.

[8] Palmer (n 5) ch 2.

In 1835, northern rangatira, again facilitated by Busby, signed he Whakaputanga o te Rangatiratanga o Nu Tireni (the Declaration of Independence of New Zealand). The immediate catalyst was a perceived French threat from claims by Anglo-French adventurer Charles de Thierry to have acquired sovereignty in northern Aotearoa. Busby may also have been motivated by rivalry over law-making procedures with another newly appointed British Resident.

British legal practice was (and is) to emphasise the importance of the text of such documents. It seems likely that Busby did the initial draft which was translated into te reo Māori (the Māori language) by missionary Henry Williams and debated and amended by the rangatira. On 28 October 1835, 34 rangatira of northern iwi and hapū debated and agreed he Whakaputanga – a declaration of their independence. There were four articles:

- The chiefs of northern Nu Tireni declared their 'rangatiratanga', which was translated as 'independence' in the English version.
- They declared that all sovereign power and authority of the land, or 'ko te kingitanga ko te mana i te wenua', resided with the rangatira who would not allow any wakarite ture or legislative authority, or any function of kāwanatanga (a transliteration of governorship translated as government in the English version) other than themselves in their collective capacity in Congress assembled.
- They agreed to meet in Congress in autumn each year.
- They agreed to send a copy of he Whakaputanga to the King of England to thank him for his acknowledgement of their flag and, in return for the friendship and protection they would show to his subjects, asked for his protection against attempts on their independence.

Busby communicated the English language version of he Whakaputanga to the Crown in Sydney and London, as well as to de Thierry. He also continued to collect further signatures of rangatira, eventually totalling 52, until as late as 1839. But the text of he Whakaputanga was not as important in Māori tikanga as the relationships understood to have been formed at the time. As the Waitangi Tribunal has found, he Whakaputanga was a written assertion of the mana, rangatiratanga and independence of those who signed.[9] Ultimate public authority in Aotearoa remained, and was declared to remain, with hapū.

[9] Waitangi Tribunal (n 5) 203.

The 1830s saw an increase in Pākehā settlement in Aotearoa although there were still vastly more Māori, who were clearly in control. Missionaries agitated for assertions of British authority while other Pākehā increased trade and land purchases and made proposals for organised private settlements in New Zealand. Britain in the 1830s had extended its electoral franchise and outlawed slavery in the Empire. Lord Melbourne's Whig administration, from 1835 to 1841, had close connections to missionary lobbyists. A number of British parliamentary inquiries in the 1830s expressed concern at the effect of colonisation on native inhabitants around the Empire and outside it and specifically in New Zealand.[10]

From 1837, there were negotiations between the New Zealand Association and the Colonial Office over the terms of colonisation of New Zealand. Both envisaged negotiation of a treaty with Māori, as recommended by British Resident Busby and Captain Hobson of the Royal Navy. Negotiations in London foundered. A bill in Parliament to approve New Zealand colonisation, promoted by leading members of the New Zealand Association, failed.

More direct action by the settlers impelled British government action. On 12 May 1839 a shipload of British settlers from the New Zealand Company left for New Zealand on the *Tory*. In June 1839 the Colonial Secretary, Lord Normanby, requested a law officers' opinion on how any territory acquired in New Zealand could be lawfully annexed to New South Wales. Letters Patent were issued in June 1839 including any such territory acquired. And on 14 August 1839 Normanby authorised Captain Hobson to treat with the 'natives' of New Zealand for recognition of British sovereignty over the whole or any part of New Zealand which 'they may be willing to place under Her Majesty's dominion'.

IV. TE TIRITI O WAITANGI: THE TREATY OF WAITANGI

Hobson arrived at Waitangi in northern New Zealand on 29 January 1840. He issued proclamations to the British subjects about land sales needing to be confirmed by the Crown before their validity would be acknowledged. Then, at a meeting with rangatira at Waitangi on 5 and 6 February, he proposed a treaty. There was much debate amongst the rangatira. As with he Whakaputanga o te Rangatiratanga, there were

[10] Palmer (n 5) 44.

two written versions of te Tiriti o Waitangi – in Māori and in English. Again its text was short, with a preamble and only three articles.[11]

The preamble recited Queen Victoria's interest in preserving Māori rangatiratanga and land (in the Māori version) or protecting Māori rights and property (in the English version) and her appointment of Captain Hobson to treat with Māori for establishment of her kāwanatanga (in Māori) or recognition of her Sovereign authority (in English).

In the *first article* the rangatira gave completely to the Queen kāwanatanga of their land (in Māori) or all the rights and powers of sovereignty (in English).

In the *second article* the Queen agreed to protect (in Māori) rangatira, hapū (chiefs and sub-tribes) and all the people of New Zealand in their tino rangatiratanga (unqualified exercise of chieftainship) over their whenua, kāinga and taonga (lands, villages and all their treasures) or (in English) the full, exclusive and undisturbed possession of their lands, estates, forests, fisheries and other properties. The rangatira also gave to the Queen the exclusive right (in Māori) of sale of such lands as they were willing to sell or (in English) of pre-emption.

In the *third article* the Queen agreed to protect Māori and imparted to them the tikanga (in Māori) or the rights and privileges (in English) of British subjects.

Almost all Māori who signed te Tiriti o Waitangi signed te reo Māori version. After 6 February 1840, Hobson sent out emissaries around Aotearoa to gather more signatures from other rangatira. By 3 September 1840 around 530 rangatira, including a few women, had signed nine copies of te Tiriti o Waitangi. Only one of those, with 39 signatures, was the English version. Some iwi and hapū did not sign. And although some notable rangatira did not sign, it is understandable that so many did. The British navy was more powerful than any individual iwi when it was present in Aotearoa. Inter-hapū rivalry, exacerbated by the musket wars, as well as the prospect that Britain might be able to control their own subjects, could be expected to have impelled signatures.

The textual differences in meaning between the two language versions are significant, which has been troubling for British and New Zealand lawyers ever since. But in Māori tikanga, as with he Whakaputanga, the text was less important than the conception of the relationship engendered by the discussions at the signing events. Principles of tikanga such as whanaungatanga, manaakitanga, mana and good faith, and their

[11] The full text of the articles are set out in ch 10.

understandings of dynamic relationships between iwi and hapū, would have been seen by Māori as controlling the ongoing relationship reflected in, but not defined by, the text. Even for the British, there is evidence of an understanding of a '*fourth article*', formulated at the instigation of Catholic missionary Pompallier, when the Governor agreed in discussion that the faiths of England, of the Weslayans, of Rome and also Māori custom (te ritenga Māori) would be protected.[12]

V. ASSERTION OF BRITISH SOVEREIGNTY

In the midst of the process of gathering signatures for te Tiriti, Hobson learned that New Zealand Company settlers in Wellington had obtained signatures of rangatira there to a provisional constitution in early March 1840. Around the same time, Governor Gipps of New South Wales was concerned about French designs on New Zealand and urged Hobson to take prompt measures to secure sovereignty over the South Island, if necessary by discovery.[13] Hobson despatched militia to Wellington to assert the Crown's authority in practice. On 21 May 1840, he made two proclamations which asserted the British Crown's sovereignty over New Zealand. The proclamation of sovereignty over the North Island of New Zealand relied on rangatira having ceded sovereignty through te Tiriti, though signatures were still being collected. The proclamation of sovereignty over the South Island, made in ignorance of signatures being collected there too, was simply asserted and said to be based upon discovery.

On hearing from Hobson, the New South Wales legislature passed an Act in June 1840 declaring the laws of New South Wales to extend to Her Majesty's dominions in New Zealand. On 2 October 1840 the Colonial Office published Hobson's proclamations of sovereignty in the London Gazette. The two certified language versions of te Tiriti were published by the House of Commons in 1841 with te reo Māori version entitled 'Treaty.' and the English language version entitled '(Translation.)'.

The differences between the two language versions could be expected to create problems. Rangatira had declared their rangatiratanga, or independence, in he Whakaputanga o te Rangatiratanga, signed from 1835 to 1839. In te reo Māori version of te Tiriti, Britain agreed to protect

[12] Orange (n 5) 53.
[13] M Wright, *Waitangi* (Auckland, Bateman Books, 2019) 107.

te tino rangatiratanga while rangatira allowed Queen Victoria to set up some sort of governance (kāwanatanga), probably over Pākehā. In the English version Britain acquired sovereignty over New Zealand. The meaning in te reo Māori may not have been too far from the initial intention of Captain Hobson and the Colonial Office.[14] But the terms of the English translation were clear about the cession of sovereignty. That is what the Colonial Office and successive settler governments in New Zealand emphasised, after the British declaration of sovereignty. Under British law te Tiriti, as an international treaty, had no domestic legal force without being incorporated into law by statute. Its purpose, illustrated by Normanby's instructions, was a moral or political one to gain Māori consent for a British assertion of sovereignty. As far as British law was concerned, it was the proclamations of sovereignty by Hobson, their endorsement in London, acceptance by other nations, and eventual enforcement in fact that constituted Britain's acquisition of sovereignty.

In 1842, the New Zealand Attorney-General issued an opinion that 'the title of Great Britain to the sovereignty of New Zealand rests partly upon discovery, partly upon cession, partly upon assertion, and partly upon occupation'.[15] This line of thinking was quickly closed down by the Colonial Secretary, Lord Stanley, in London. At law, and for colonial officials, it was sufficient that the Queen had pursued the course she did and asserted her power.[16]

At British law, te Tiriti was a political condition to the assertion of sovereignty. But assertion of sovereignty was not the same as the actual exercise of sovereignty. Even backed by the Royal Navy, Governor Hobson was not able to enforce British will throughout New Zealand. How and when Britain eventually came to exercise sovereignty in practice throughout New Zealand remains opaque. The wars between the Crown (supported by some iwi) and other iwi in the 1860s were key. An agreement between the Crown and Tūhoe, legislated in 1896 and subsequently

[14] See N Fletcher, 'A Praiseworthy Device for Amusing and Pacifying Savages?' (PhD thesis, University of Auckland, 2014). But see also M Hickford, 'Interpreting the Treaty' in B Patterson, RS Hill and K Patterson (eds), *After the Treaty* (Wellington, Steel Roberts, 2016) 92, 123.

[15] Minutes of Executive Council of 29 December 1842, enclosed in Despatch from Acting Governor Shortland of 31 December 1842 in Appendix 19 of 'Report from the Select Committee on New Zealand; with the Minutes of Proceedings' (1844) (556) Vol XIII *British Parliamentary Papers* 457.

[16] Despatch from Lord Stanley to the Officer Administering the Government, 21 June 1843, in Appendix 19 (n 15).

dishonoured by the Crown, enabled the Crown to assert power over what was probably the last significant area of independent Māori control.[17]

In 2014, after lengthy hearings about the circumstances of the events leading to the signings of he Wakaputanga and te Tiriti, the Waitangi Tribunal concluded that rangatira did not cede their sovereignty but agreed to share power and authority with the Governor.[18] How that was to occur was left to be worked out over time. This is also the conclusion previously reached by a variety of scholars, including one of us.

VI. CONCLUSION

Te Tiriti o Waitangi guaranteed rangatiratanga but permitted the Crown to establish kāwanatanga. In 1840, the expectations of how te Tiriti would work in practice reflected the dominant political power of Māori in New Zealand. After the wars of the 1860s, it was the Crown that dominated the exercise of political power in New Zealand. As an international treaty, te Tiriti could not generally be enforced by Māori in British courts. Over its first century or so te Tiriti generally failed to assume real legal status. But events from the 1970s saw greater recognition of te Tiriti in law and deeper infiltration of te Tiriti o Waitangi into the consciousness of New Zealand's constitution. We explain this in Chapter 10.

Before that, we explain the main institutions of New Zealand's constitution – including the Crown, Executive, Parliament and judiciary – how they work in practice and the key constraints on them.

FURTHER READING

Orange, C, *The Treaty of Waitangi* (Wellington, Bridget Williams Books Ltd, 1987).

Palmer, MSR, *The Treaty of Waitangi in New Zealand's Law and Constitution* (Wellington, Victoria University Press, 2008).

Waitangi Tribunal, 'He Whakaputanga me te Tiriti: The Declaration and the Treaty' (Wai 1040, 2014).

[17] R Boast, 'Treaties Nobody Counted On' (2011) 42 *Victoria University of Wellington Law Review* 663.

[18] Waitangi Tribunal (n 5) 526–27.

3

Head of State and the Crown

Introduction – Sovereign as Head of State – Governor-General as de facto Head of State – Governor-General's Functions and Powers – Executive Council – The Crown in Law – Conclusion

I. INTRODUCTION

> The Queen reigns but the government rules so long as it has the support of the House of Representatives.[1]

SO SAYS SIR Kenneth Keith in his introduction to the Cabinet Manual. This triumvirate – Sovereign, ministers and the House of Representatives – forms the backbone of New Zealand's constitutional system of government. The relationships between them are animated by, and give effect to, the principle of democracy. Formally, as a constitutional monarch, the Sovereign of New Zealand – Queen Elizabeth II, represented locally by the Governor-General – sits at the apex. But the Sovereign wields little real power and is largely consigned to a symbolic, figurehead role. In reality, the Crown's executive power is exercised by ministers of the Crown, drawn from and responsible to the House of Representatives. Those democratic representatives are, in turn, accountable at the ballot box to the people. In this way, New Zealand's constitutional system is founded on the notion of responsible and representative government, which is explained in the next chapter.

This chapter explains the role of the Sovereign as Head of State and the role of the Governor-General as the Sovereign's local representative or New Zealand's de facto Head of State. We also explain the nature of the Crown and its legal significance.

[1] K Keith, 'On the Constitution of New Zealand' in Cabinet Office, *Cabinet Manual 2017*, 3. The first part of the mantra – she reigns but does not rule – has been attributed to W Bagehot: C Munro, *Studies in Constitutional Law*, 2nd edn (London, Butterworths, 1997).

II. SOVEREIGN AS HEAD OF STATE

The Sovereign occupies the most senior formal office within New Zealand's constitutional framework. Putting aside the pomp, ceremony and mystique of the monarchy, the Sovereign serves as Head of State of New Zealand, as recognised in section 2 of the Constitution Act 1986. Queen Elizabeth II is the Queen of New Zealand, as well as the Queen of the other Commonwealth realms, such as the United Kingdom, Canada and Australia. The Realm of New Zealand over which she reigns includes several nations and territories: New Zealand, the Cook Islands, Niue, Tokelau and the Ross Dependency in Antarctica.[2] Nowadays, the Sovereign is styled and titled under the Royal Titles Act 1974 in a more New Zealand-oriented form – 'Elizabeth the Second, by the Grace of God Queen of New Zealand and Her Other Realms and Territories, Head of the Commonwealth, Defender of the Faith' – replacing the former unified British styles and titles. But the person reigning as the Sovereign in right of New Zealand is, in reality, the same person who reigns as Sovereign in right of the United Kingdom and other Commonwealth realms.[3]

The laws of succession for the Sovereign in right of New Zealand are now formally part of New Zealand law, rather than British law.[4] That contrasts with some other Commonwealth realms which rely directly on the identity of the Sovereign of the United Kingdom for the Sovereign in their realm. The imperial statutes comprising the laws of succession were declared to form part of New Zealand law under the Imperial Laws Application Act 1988 and subsequent amendment of those imperial statutes in the United Kingdom were disbarred from applying in New Zealand. In reality, though, succession laws are coordinated to ensure they are common across the realms. For example, in 2013, the New Zealand Parliament voluntarily passed amendments to the New Zealand version of the laws of succession to ensure that they remain harmonious with the laws of succession in the United Kingdom and other Commonwealth realms.[5]

[2] Letters Patent Constituting the Office of Governor-General of New Zealand 1983, cl 1.

[3] The other 15 Commonwealth realms are Antigua and Barbuda, Australia, the Bahamas, Barbados, Belize, Canada, Grenada, Jamaica, Papua New Guinea, Saint Kitts and Nevis, Saint Lucia, Saint Vincent and the Grenadines, Solomon Islands, Tuvalu and the United Kingdom. The Commonwealth itself comprises 54 nations, including the 16 realms, 5 other monarchies with different sovereigns and 33 republics.

[4] Constitution Act 1986, s 5.

[5] Royal Succession Act 2013.

So, the Queen formally holds the powers of Head of State and is invested with the authority of the Crown. But practice dictates that the Queen exercises little, if any, of this power and authority in reality. First, distance and practicalities mean the Queen cannot generally exercise the Head of State powers personally. Living in the United Kingdom, she is removed from New Zealand and its civic goings-on. Queen Elizabeth II was the first Sovereign to visit New Zealand (in 1953) and she has only done so 10 times in the years since (although members of her family are often now tasked with visiting New Zealand and her other realms). It is impractical for her to be briefed in a timely fashion, to fully appreciate the local conditions, to effectively discharge the Head of State functions on a day-to-day basis, or to meaningfully represent New Zealand on the international stage. She is understandably occupied by matters within the realm where she resides, as well as her other realms. Therefore, she relies on her local representative, the Governor-General, to fulfil her functions in New Zealand on her behalf.[6]

While the Sovereign retains the authority to exercise the powers delegated to the Governor-General, or to exercise any powers directly conferred on the Governor-General, by convention, she does not generally do so. By necessity, she must be involved in the appointment of the Governor-General.[7] Other rare occasions where she has personally exercised her functions include assenting to legislation of significance to the office of head of state,[8] and legislation authorising the first settlement of a historical grievance between the Crown and iwi/hapū under te Tiriti o Waitangi.[9] She also routinely approves grants of royal honours. The Clerk of the Executive Council and the Queen's private secretary facilitate the tendering of advice from the Prime Minister to the Sovereign, on the few occasions where it is necessary. By and large, the personal role of the Sovereign in New Zealand is limited and generally symbolic.

Secondly, in any event, democratic legitimacy dictates that the Sovereign's authority be exercised, by the Sovereign or the Governor-General, in accordance with the advice of responsible advisors: ministers responsible to the House of Representatives and ultimately the people. The cardinal constitutional convention requires, as Sir Kenneth Keith explained, that the Queen *reigns* but the government *rules*.

[6] Constitution Act 1986, s 2(2); Letters Patent Constituting the Office of Governor-General of New Zealand 1983, cl 1.

[7] Letters Patent Constituting the Office of Governor-General of New Zealand, cl 2.

[8] For example, the Royal Titles Act 1974 and Seal of New Zealand Act 1977.

[9] Waikato Raupatu Claims Settlement Act 1995.

III. GOVERNOR-GENERAL AS DE FACTO HEAD OF STATE

The Governor-General is the Sovereign's local representative in New Zealand and, in reality, discharges almost all functions of head of state. The Governor-General is authorised to exercise the Sovereign's functions (Constitution Act 1986, section 3) and legislation often directly confers authority on the Governor-General. The office was known as Governor until 1917, when it was reconstituted as Governor-General during the term of Lord Liverpool. The Letters Patent Constituting the Office of Governor-General of New Zealand 1983 – a key instrument prepared on behalf of New Zealand ministers specifically for local arrangements – constitutes the office and delegates head of state functions and powers to the Governor-General. The Governor-General is, among other things, authorised to exercise the Sovereign's 'executive authority' in New Zealand, 'either directly or through officers' (Letters Patent, clause 3).

Formally, the Governor-General is appointed by the Sovereign (Letters Patent, clause 2). By convention, the appointment is made on the recommendation of the Prime Minister. During the colonial era, appointments were made on recommendation of the British Prime Minister but the recommendation power has been patriated since the 1930s.[10] Before recommending a candidate for appointment, convention dictates the Prime Minister should seek informal approval of the candidate from the Sovereign in order that the Sovereign not be presented with a fait accompli.[11] In addition, convention suggests some limited degree of dialogue with other parliamentary leaders about the candidate. The precise nature of the obligation is somewhat opaque. At its highest, it has involved the Prime Minister consulting the Leader of the Opposition (and, in the age of multi-party politics, perhaps other parliamentary leaders) about a short-list of potential candidates. At other times, it has involved mere notification of the proposed candidate. The latter more diluted approach appears to prevail today, though such an approach sits uncomfortably with the desirability of a candidate commanding widespread support inside and outside Parliament.

[10] KJ Scott, *The New Zealand Constitution* (Oxford, Oxford University Press, 1962) 73.

[11] A Quentin-Baxter and J McLean, *This Realm of New Zealand* (Auckland, Auckland University Press, 2017) 119.

No formal credentials are prescribed for the office. However, the types of people appointed to the office of Governor-General reflect evolving expectations of the role. Historically, Governors and Governors-General were members of the British military or nobility. Today, it is unthinkable that the candidate would not be a New Zealander. Governor-General Freyberg (1946–1952) was the first Governor-General raised in New Zealand; Governor-General Porritt (1967–1972) was the first New Zealand-born Governor-General. Efforts have been made in recent decades to ensure a diversity of appointments, so that the office of Governor-General better reflects the community it serves. Of the seven Governors-General since 1985, three have been women, two have been Māori and one Fijian-Indian. The eighth, due to assume office in late 2021, is a Māori woman. Appointees in the last half century have been drawn from the judiciary, military, diplomatic and political office, as well as from business, medical and religious service. Appointments in the first decade or so of the mixed-member-proportional (MMP) electoral system (in 1996, 2001 and 2006) were drawn from the judiciary, reflecting concerns the Governor-General might be called on to exercise constitutional powers in relation to the formation of government. As the conventions around government formation have become more settled in the light of practice, the need for a legal background has diminished. Controversy has understandably accompanied appointment of those from national or local political office. That was so with the appointment of Sir Keith Holyoake in 1977, a former Prime Minister and then-serving Cabinet minister, and, to a lesser degree, Dame Catherine Tizard in 1989 as a then-serving mayor. The more active role for the Governor-General under MMP and the heightened need for the office-holder to be – and to be perceived to be – politically neutral, mean it is unlikely we will see appointees drawn from political office in the future.

The Governor-General is generally appointed for a term of five years but serves at the pleasure of the Sovereign. Thus, a Governor-General may be recalled by the Sovereign, although this has not occurred since the colonial era. As the power to recall is exercisable on advice of the Prime Minister, there is an awkward tension that may arise in times of crisis. While it has not been experienced in New Zealand, there is a tangible prospect of a Prime Minister, anticipating dismissal by the Governor-General, advising the Sovereign to dismiss the Governor-General. In 1975 in Australia, Governor-General Kerr dismissed Prime Minister Whitlam before the reverse occurred. This lack of security of tenure sits uncomfortably with any role the Governor-General might have as a constitutional watchdog in times of crisis.

The Governor-General is also styled as 'Commander-in-Chief' of New Zealand. The Letters Patent and the Defence Act 1990 recognise the Governor-General's role under the royal prerogative to raise and maintain armed forces in the name of the Sovereign. Although separately identified, the role as Commander-in-Chief is ceremonial and does not confer separate or additional substantive powers not already possessed by the Governor-General.

When the Governor-General is absent from New Zealand, or otherwise unable to perform their duties, the Chief Justice or next most senior judge performs the Governor-General's functions, as Administrator of the Government. So far no potential issues of conflict in this arrangement have arisen in New Zealand.

IV. GOVERNOR-GENERAL'S FUNCTIONS AND POWERS

A. Constitutional, Ceremonial and Community Functions

The Governor-General's functions (and, in theory, the Sovereign's functions) are usually explained as having three dimensions: *constitutional*, *ceremonial* and *community*. While these important functions are perennial, each Governor-General brings different emphasis to the role. Indeed, recent office-holders have issued strategic documents expressing their vision and mission. For example, during his term, Sir Jerry Mateparae recorded the ceremonial, community and constitutional functions as 'core functions' within the Governor-General's 'high level agenda' while identifying 'international' and 'heritage' as subsidiary areas of importance.[12] Dame Patsy Reddy described her 'mission' in terms of '[building] nationhood and a strong successful and vibrant Aotearoa New Zealand through the constitutional, ceremonial, international and community activities of the Governor-General', and outlined a vision for New Zealand, values of the office of Governor-General, and strategic priorities.[13]

The *constitutional* dimension captures a suite of legal and constitutional powers exercised by the Governor-General on behalf of the Sovereign, as we explore in more detail below. The term 'constitutional'

[12] 'Governor-General's Strategy 2011–2016' www.gg.govt.nz. See also A Satyanand, 'The Governor-General's Role' (Christchurch, University of Canterbury, August 2010).

[13] 'Governor-General's Strategy 2016–2021' (www.gg.govt.nz).

is used in contrast to ceremonial and community, rather than carrying a specifically constitutional meaning. Some of the powers may have a special constitutional character. Other powers, while having legal effect, may lack any higher-order or special status. And some constitutional functions may be exercised in ceremonial circumstances.

The *ceremonial* dimension captures the numerous instances where the Head of State personifies the Crown and state at formal occasions, rituals and memorials. This includes activities such as:

- officiating at the state opening of Parliament (a function which also has constitutional significance), including delivering the speech from the throne setting out the government's forthcoming plans;
- conducting investitures for those receiving honours;
- receiving the credentials of accredited diplomats; and
- attending memorial and remembrance ceremonies.

The Governor-General also entertains visiting heads of state and heads of government, which could be considered a ceremonial function. State visits abroad by the Governor-General – international but apolitical diplomacy on behalf of New Zealand – have increased markedly over recent decades.

The *community* dimension overlaps with the ceremonial but has a different emphasis. While the ceremonial role generally involves the Governor-General personifying and representing the Sovereign, the community function charges the Governor-General with reflecting and representing the people of New Zealand. This dimension also involves activities, functions, speeches and so forth, with the aim of expressing the values of the nation and its peoples. As one Governor-General put it, 'the value of the office of Governor-General [is] measured by the extent to which it is seen by New Zealanders to reflect their national values and identity, and to work as a unifying mechanism to that end'.[14]

B. Prerogative and Statutory Powers

In a strict legal sense, the powers held by the Governor-General include royal prerogative and statutory powers. Prerogative power is the remnants of royal authority previously held and exercised by the monarch. It is

[14] S Cartwright, 'The Role of the Governor-General' (Occasional Paper No 6, New Zealand Centre for Public Law, Wellington, 2001).

from the royal prerogative that executive government has the right to govern, sourced in the Sovereign's and Governor-General's right to exercise executive authority. The Governor-General's powers are also augmented by statute, either supplementing or superseding prerogative power. For example, section 100 of the Senior Courts Act 2016 provides that all High Court judges are to be appointed by the Governor-General 'in the name and on behalf of Her Majesty'. In practice, as explained in Chapter 7, the Governor-General follows the advice of the responsible minister, usually the Attorney-General, in relation to appointment of judges.

These prerogative and statutory powers are held and exercised by the Governor-General (on behalf of the Sovereign). But constitutional convention dictates that they be exercised in accordance with the advice of the Governor-General's responsible ministers who enjoy the confidence of the House of Representatives. This ensures the exercise of these powers has democratic pedigree, including ensuring they are subject to the demands of political and other accountability. And while the Governor-General acts on the advice of ministers, ministers are expected to keep the Governor-General 'fully informed concerning the general conduct of the Government' (Letters Patent, clause 16).

This is why New Zealand is a *constitutional*, not an *absolute*, monarchy. This key convention means the Sovereign and Governor-General wield little real power, even though much state power is formally and legally vested in them. As these powers are, in practice, mostly powers of executive government, we explore their nature and operation in more detail in our discussion of democratic and executive government in Chapters 4 and 5.

C. Reserve Powers

The Sovereign – or, in reality, the Governor-General – retains the right to exercise certain powers independently in rare cases, without or even potentially contrary to government advice. These powers are usually described as reserve powers, because they are held in reserve for exceptional circumstances. However, the 'reserve powers' label has, rightly, been described as a misnomer.[15] In reality, there is nothing unique about

[15] PA Joseph, *Joseph on Constitutional and Administrative Law*, 5th edn (Wellington, Thomson Reuters, 2021), [19.7.2].

these powers. They are legal powers vested in the Governor-General like all others and, legally, are exercised in the same way as other powers. The difference lies in the absence or rejection of government advice about when and how they should be exercised. A key characteristic of the reserve powers is that the Governor-General uses their own independent judgement about their exercise. Any exceptionality comes from the circumstances in which the powers are exercised, not the powers themselves.

There are a number of so-called reserve powers or powers that, it is commonly accepted, may be exercised independently by the Governor-General:

- appointment of a Prime Minister;
- dismissal of a Prime Minister;
- refusal of a request to dissolve Parliament for an election;
- forcing the dissolution of Parliament for an election; and
- theoretically, refusal of royal assent to a Bill passed by the House of Representatives.

The first four reserve powers arise from the limit on the constitutional convention to act on advice; ministers' advice must only be heeded while the ministers have the support of the House of Representatives. These reserve powers arise when governments are born or expire as canvassed in Chapter 4. By necessity, the Governor-General is called on to exercise independent judgement to appoint the leader of a new government, based on their understanding of who commands confidence. Once appointed, the Governor-General will act on the advice of their ministers, as long as that confidence is maintained. In other circumstances, if confidence is lost, the Governor-General may be called on to exercise independent judgement to ascertain where confidence lies and mandate any new government that emerges from the alternative political settlement.

The last reserve power is more controversial and is unlikely to be called on to be exercised. As a matter of law, under section 16 of the Constitution Act 1986, royal assent to legislation is necessary for a Bill passed by the House of Representatives to become law. But refusing to assent to legislation would involve the Governor-General overruling the wishes of a democratically elected House of Representatives. Ordinarily, that would strike at the heart of the democratic equilibrium on which our system is based. In colonial times, it was not unknown for assent to bills to be withheld or refused. The New Zealand Constitution Act 1852 (Imp) provided for refusal, reservation and disallowance by the

Governor and Sovereign.[16] However, that was when the legislature was a subordinate colonial legislature subject to law-making conditions and supervision by British ministers. Today, the House of Representatives is a fully omnipotent legislature and it would be unthinkable, short of the most exceptional circumstances, for a Governor-General to refuse to assent to a bill. The theoretical scenarios usually suggested, where it might be democratically defensible, include legislation seeking to fundamentally repudiate the constitutional foundations of our system, such as removing free and fair elections, abolishing courts and so forth. These circumstances are unlikely to arise and, if they did, the nation would already be in a constitutional imbroglio. Even then, there are other courses of action available to a Governor-General less dramatic than vetoing legislation, including delay, threatening resignation or assenting to a Bill to enable the constitutional validity of the legislation to be tested in the courts. In such circumstances, the Governor-General could seek advice from the Attorney-General and other constitutional advisors. This is how New Zealand's constitution evolves.

D. Parliamentary Powers

Parliament is formally defined as comprising the Sovereign and the House of Representatives (Constitution Act 1986, section 14). Together, as explained in Chapter 6, Parliament and the House undertake important functions of state, including making laws, mandating executive government, holding the executive to account, and providing actual and symbolic linkage between the government and the community.

The Governor-General discharges a number of specific powers in relation to the operation of Parliament on behalf of the Sovereign. These include formally summonsing and dissolving Parliament and, historically (but not now), proroguing Parliament too. Following an election, the Governor-General delivers the speech from the throne: a speech written by ministers setting out the new government's policy programme, within the parliamentary precinct in the old Legislative Council chamber.

V. EXECUTIVE COUNCIL

The primary way executive government advises the Governor-General to exercise their powers is through the Executive Council. Under

[16] See further ch 6, section V.A.

law, the Executive Council is the highest formal body of executive government. The Executive Council is created by the Letters Patent. Legally, the Letters Patent could be seen as the basis of New Zealand's executive government.[17] Formally, the Executive Council is composed of ministers of the Crown and is presided over by the Governor-General.

In practice, the Executive Council usually meets every Monday, after Cabinet, with a handful of ministers. The Executive Council carries out formal acts of executive government which require force of law.[18] For example, it has statutory power to make many regulations, under the legal formulation of 'the Governor-General in Council'. But the Council is a largely a formality; decisions to make regulations are taken, in reality, by Cabinet beforehand. The meeting does, however, provide an opportunity for the Governor-General, when in attendance, to exercise their soft powers by being briefed and asking questions of ministers.

VI. THE CROWN IN LAW

The other dimension of the Sovereign – or, more particularly, the Crown – is its role as a juristic entity. When we talk of the Sovereign, we usually mean the individual actions and functions of the person holding office as Head of State. When we talk of the Crown, we usually use it as a short-hand for the collective institutions of government or state, however defined.[19]

The Crown is, literally, 'a piece of jewelled headgear under guard at the Tower of London'.[20] But this is rarely what is meant when the Crown is used in constitutional conversations. Rather, the Crown is a 'metonym': a substitute term used to capture a number of different persona, in law and in practice.[21] The term 'the Crown' is sometimes employed to describe the Sovereign herself, as a 'natural body' or in her role as Head of State.[22] For example, a number of statutory instruments describe the Crown as 'Her Majesty the Queen in right of New Zealand' or as including, non-exhaustively, 'the Sovereign in right of New Zealand'.

[17] Quentin-Baxter and McLean (n 11) 3.

[18] Cabinet Office, *Cabinet Manual 2017*, [1.23].

[19] Ibid [1.4].

[20] *Town Investments Ltd v Department of the Environment* [1978] AC 359 (HL), 397.

[21] M Sunkin, 'Crown' in P Cane and J Conaghan (eds), *The New Oxford Companion to Law* (Oxford, Oxford University Press, 2008) 286.

[22] *Case of the Duchy of Lancaster* (1561) 1 Plow 212, 213; *Town Investments Ltd v Department of the Environment* (n 20) 397.

So, the term 'the Crown' is commonly used to express ideas of the state as a legal entity, in its various legal forms. Our constitutional system, and its British constitutional ancestor, does not recognise a singular concept of 'the state' as a legal or juristic entity. The concept of the Crown goes some way to fill this institutional gap. For example, the Crown is often taken to mean executive government, that is, the ministers, departments and officials that make up central government or, more abstractly, the concept of executive authority within the state. But the particular meaning of the Crown depends on context.[23] 'The common law itself contains distinct and competing versions of the Crown', Professor McLean says, concluding that there 'is no single or simple answer to "who is the Crown generally"'.[24] And the efforts to personify the state through the Crown is not without complications in law.[25] For example, the common law treated the Crown as having numerous privileges and immunities in litigation.[26] Legislative reform has been required to put state actors on the same footing as others in litigation and to ensure that their actions in the name of the Sovereign are not unduly removed from legal and other scrutiny.

The term 'the Crown' has special currency in relation to te Tiriti o Waitangi, where it is used to describe the state as a party to the treaty. In this sense, it is used primarily to connote New Zealand's executive government, rather than Queen Victoria as the original named party or her natural successors. However, this is not without some ambiguity.[27] And, as explained in Chapter 10, some Māori place special significance on the symbolism of the Sovereign being the party with whom they signed te Tiriti in 1840. The Crown also has legislative and judicial dimensions, with the Queen in Parliament and the Queen's judges. There is also a symbolic dimension, perhaps underpinning the other conceptions, where the Crown extends to include the people too, when exercising or expressing collective will.[28]

[23] *Attorney-General v Chapman* [2011] NZSC 110, [2012] 1 NZLR 462, [78]; *Stafford v Accident Compensation Authority* [2020] NZCA 164, [118]–[133].

[24] J McLean, 'Crown Him with Many Crowns' (2008) 6 *New Zealand Journal of Public and International Law* 35, 58.

[25] J McLean, *Searching for the State in British Legal Thought* (Cambridge, Cambridge University Press, 2012).

[26] Law Commission, 'The Crown in Court' (NZLC R135, 2015).

[27] McLean (n 24).

[28] McLean (n 24) 36. And see C Shore, DV Williams and S Raudon, 'Conclusion' in C Shore and DV Williams (eds), *The Shapeshifting Crown* (Cambridge, Cambridge University Press, 2019) 245.

VII. CONCLUSION

It is fundamental to New Zealand's constitution that the Sovereign is Head of State, which is why we have dealt with it as the first constitutional office. But the difference between the formality and reality of New Zealand's constitution is well illustrated by this fundamental element. The powers of the Sovereign residing in London, as Head of State, are exercised by her representative in New Zealand, the Governor-General. The vast majority of the legal powers of the Governor-General are exercised on the advice of responsible ministers, as long as they have the confidence of the House of Representatives. That provides the democratic basis for New Zealand government. The few constitutional powers which might be exercised independently of ministerial advice relate to the formation and termination of executive government administrations, which we address in the next chapter. The formal concept of the Crown also masks, rather than reflects, the reality of underlying constitutional arrangements. This 'shape-shifting', monarchal symbol is used to embody a number of different agents and institutions.

FURTHER READING

McLean, G, *New Zealand's Governors and Governors-General* (Dunedin, Otago University Press, 2007).

Quentin-Baxter, A, and McLean, J, *This Realm of New Zealand* (Auckland, Auckland University Press, 2017).

Shore, C, and Williams, DV (eds), *The Shapeshifting Crown* (Cambridge, Cambridge University Press, 2019).

Website of the Governor-General of New Zealand (www.gg.govt.nz).

4

Democratic Government

Introduction – Representative Government – Responsible Government – Conclusion

I. INTRODUCTION

THE CONCEPT OF representative and responsible government gives New Zealand's constitutional framework its democratic legitimacy. As explained in the previous chapter, the backbone of New Zealand's constitutional system of government is the maxim that the Queen reigns but the government rules so long as it has the support of the House of Representatives. We have already examined the institution that formally heads that triumvirate: the Sovereign. In this chapter, we look at the institutions that give the system its democratic lifeblood: an elected House and a parliamentary ministry.

Our focus in this chapter is on the way the House of Representatives and the executive government are constituted and their key relationships within the system. First, we look at the electoral system that determines the composition of the House of Representatives. We focus particularly on the significance of the mixed-member-proportional (MMP) system in renovating the constitutional dynamics in New Zealand since 1996. The adoption of MMP to replace the previous first-past-the-post (FPP) system was one of the most fundamental constitutional changes in the modern history of New Zealand's constitution. Secondly, we look at executive government and the way the Prime Minister and ministers are drawn from the democratically elected House. We explain, in some detail, the way a parliamentary ministry is formed.

II. REPRESENTATIVE GOVERNMENT: AN ELECTED HOUSE

Parliament stands at the centre of New Zealand's constitutional system and radiates the nation's strong commitment to representative democracy.

New Zealand has a unicameral legislature, unlike its Westminster counterpart: Parliament, is made up of one house, the House of Representatives, together with the Sovereign in right of New Zealand.[1] The House of Representatives is, in reality, the heart of Parliament.[2] The House and Parliament undertake various functions, the most high profile of which is law-making (discussed in detail in Chapter 6). The House also provides and sustains executive government, as the Prime Minister and other ministers are drawn from its members. The House itself is made up of 120 members of Parliament, sometimes more, elected every three years. The mechanics of the MMP electoral system are set out in the Electoral Act 1993. This electoral system is one of the most distinctive features of New Zealand's contemporary system of democratic government. In a formal sense, MMP is simply a means of selecting the membership of the House of Representatives, from which the political leaders of executive government are drawn. But, in reality, the adoption of MMP dramatically changed the dynamics of New Zealand's system of government and politics.

A. Evolution of the Electoral System

Representative democracy has been an ongoing project of reform. New Zealand is well-known for being the first nation where women achieved the vote, as well as for the reservation of a number of seats for Māori representatives. And the adoption of MMP has changed the face of politics in New Zealand. Here we sketch some of the key historic turns that have led to the current electoral settings.

Governors initially assumed executive responsibility following the assertion of British sovereignty in 1840, operating together with the Colonial Secretary and Treasurer as the Legislative Council from 1841. The first election was not held until 1853, following the passing of the New Zealand Constitution Act 1852 (Imp), with parliamentary institutions modelled on the British system. The Parliament, then known as the General Assembly, was made up of two houses. Members of the House of Representatives were elected and members of the Legislative Council – the upper House – were appointed. The original franchise for the House was tightly defined: a person needed to be male, a British subject, at least

[1] Constitution Act 1986, s 14.
[2] Constitution Act 1986, s 10.

21 years old, and had to individually own, lease or rent property of a certain value. Those criteria excluded women, virtually all Māori (who owned land collectively), non-British subjects and those with convictions for certain serious offences. Despite these restrictions, the proportion of the population allowed to vote was many times more than in the United Kingdom at the same time. Members of the House were initially elected for five-year terms.

Since that first election, a number of notable changes have been made. First, the franchise was enlarged. The property requirement was expanded in 1860 to also include those holding mining permits, and it was entirely removed in 1879. Māori electorates were adopted with the passing of the Maori Representation Act 1867. This enabled Māori men, and later women, to vote without meeting the property requirement – but only in four separate Māori seats. These separate seats, originally expected to be transitional, left Māori poorly represented based on their proportion of the population. Yet, this separate and undervalued form of representation continued for over a century until, in 1975, Māori were permitted to choose between enrolment in a general or a Māori electorate. It was not until 1996 that the number of Māori electorates was permitted to vary with the number of those on the Māori roll, to ensure parity between Māori and general electorates in numbers of electors. In 2021, there were seven Māori seats.

Following a powerful suffragette campaign and a number of failed attempts at reform, women achieved universal suffrage in 1893 and were enfranchised. However, it was only from 1919 that women were allowed to stand for office and it was not until 1933 that a woman (Elizabeth McCombs) was elected. The voting age was lowered to 20 in 1969, and to 18 in 1974. Permanent residents were allowed to vote alongside citizens from 1975. The ability of prisoners to vote has ebbed and flowed over time. In 2020, following the Supreme Court's declaration that a blanket ban on prisoner voting was inconsistent with the Bill of Rights Act, Parliament responded by allowing those sentenced to imprisonment for less than three years to vote.[3]

Secondly, the mechanics of elections have varied occasionally. In 1881, the parliamentary term was reduced from five to three years. For a brief period (1908–1911), the second ballot system replaced FPP: if no

[3] Electoral (Registration of Sentenced Prisoners) Amendment Act 2020, reversing the Electoral (Disqualification of Sentenced Prisoners) Amendment Act 2010, following the declaration issued by the Supreme Court in *Attorney-General v Taylor* [2018] NZSC 104, [2019] 1 NZLR 213.

candidate received an absolute majority of votes cast, there was a run-off vote between the two leading candidates. The passing of the Electoral Act 1956 led to the entrenchment of a number of key electoral provisions, including the secret ballot (first employed in 1871 for European electors and 1938 in Māori electorates).

Thirdly, the Legislative Council, Parliament's upper house, was abolished from 1951. Members of the Legislative Council were appointed, initially for life and then, from the 1890s, for seven-year terms. By the 1940s the Council was no longer seen as effective, relevant or useful. In August 1947, the National Party proposed that it should be abolished. In November 1947, the New Zealand Parliament acquired the power to amend the governing constitutional laws, through the adoption of the Statute of Westminster that had been passed by the United Kingdom Parliament in 1931. After National won the 1949 election, 29 new members of the Legislative Council were appointed, known as the 'suicide squad', bringing membership to 53. The Council assisted the abolition by voting itself out of existence.

Finally, the most notable change in living memory was the adoption of MMP as a result of a referendum in 1993. Dissatisfaction with the FPP system was the impetus for the move to MMP.[4] Key criticisms included: the dominance of two major parties; difficulties faced by minor parties in securing seats; disproportionate seat allocation as a party often received a far greater share of the seats in the House than its share of the vote; and instances where the governing party received fewer votes than the opposition party (such as in 1978 and 1981). Concerns were also expressed about the lack of diversity amongst MPs as well as the adversarial culture that tended to dominate parliamentary politics. In 1985, the fourth Labour Government established a Royal Commission and gave it very broad terms of reference to review the electoral system. The Commission's 1986 report, *Towards a Better Democracy*, recommended, among other things, that MMP replace FPP, subject to a public referendum.[5] During the 1987 election campaign, David Lange, the then Labour Prime Minister, inadvertently promised a referendum on proportional representation, but failed to deliver one while in office. Despite having reservations about

[4] A Geddis and C Morris, '"All is changed, changed utterly"?' (2004) 32 *Federal Law Review* 451.

[5] Royal Commission on the Electoral System, *Report of the Royal Commission on the Electoral System* (Wellington, Government Printer, 1986).

proportional representation, the 1990 National Government obtained cross-party support for referenda on electoral reform.[6]

The first referendum was held in 1992. Voters were asked if they wanted to change the existing electoral system and to indicate a preference for a replacement system from four options. With a turnout of 55 per cent, nearly 85 per cent voted for change and just over 70 per cent voted for MMP as the preferred alternative. The Electoral Referendum Act 1993 was then passed to provide for a second binding referendum – a straight run-off between FPP and MMP, in conjunction with the 1993 general election. With a strong turnout of 85 per cent, nearly 54 per cent voted to adopt MMP. The referendum result automatically triggered the commencement of the Electoral Act 1993, providing for the next general election in 1996 to be held under the MMP system.

B. MMP Electoral System in Operation

New Zealand's MMP electoral system is based on the system used for federal parliamentary elections in Germany. In general terms, electors have two votes:

- the *electorate vote* determines which candidate is elected as a member of Parliament to represent each electorate; and
- the nationwide *party vote* determines the total number of members of Parliament to which each party is entitled (whether electorate MPs or list MPs).

MMP is a proportional system because the overall number of MPs each party has in the House of Representatives broadly reflects the proportion of party votes each party receives.

The House is made up of at least 120 MPs, elected either as electorate MPs or list MPs. The electoral system currently provides for 72 electorate MPs and at least 48 list MPs, although the balance between electorate MPs and list MPs varies with population changes. Eligible voters (citizens and permanent residents over the age of 18) are divided into two electoral rolls: general and Māori rolls. Every five years, Māori electors exercise their option to be registered on either the general or

[6] S Levine and N Roberts, 'The New Zealand General Election and Electoral Referendum of 1993' (1994) 46 *Political Science* 40.

Māori roll. A Representation Commission, comprised mainly of neutral public servants with relevant expertise, divides each roll into equal electorates based on population. The South Island must be divided into 16 general electorates, thus determining the approximate size of the electoral population for all electorates. This size is then used to determine the corresponding number of general electorates in the North Island and Māori electorates across the country, subject to mandated tolerances. The Representation Commission determines the boundaries of the electorates, taking into account the required size, previous boundaries, communities of interest, communication facilities, topographical features and expected population growth. Following the representation review in 2020, the average size of each electorate is around 65,000 electors. There are 65 general electorates (49 in the North Island and 16 in the South) and seven Māori electorates.[7]

The electoral process commences with the Governor-General issuing a writ for a general election, usually on the advice of the Prime Minister near the end of a three-year term, following the dissolution of Parliament. Qualified electors may be nominated as electorate candidates, whether as independent candidates or as a candidate accredited to a political party. Political parties must register and provide a list of (ranked) list candidates. Party lists are closed lists; ranking is solely determined by the party and is not able to be influenced by electors, although parties are required to select their candidates using democratic procedures involving financial members of their party. Dual candidacy as a candidate for an electorate and on a party list is permitted.

Elections are run by the Electoral Commission, which is an independent Crown entity. On election day (always a Saturday), or some two weeks beforehand for advance voting, electors cast secret ballots. Voters get two votes, one for their preferred political party and one for their preferred electoral candidate. The ballot paper lists all registered political parties on the left-hand side and electoral candidates for the particular electorate on the right-hand side. Electors vote by ticking the circles next to their preferred political party and electoral candidate. Voting is not compulsory but the turn-out is usually high: generally 75–85 per cent in elections since MMP was introduced. Turn-out was 82.2 per cent in 2020. It is concerning that the turn-out has been drifting

[7] Representation Commission, 'NZ Electorate Boundary Review' (2020).

downwards over the last couple of decades, although it has strengthened slightly in the three most recent elections.

On election night, the Electoral Commission undertakes a preliminary count of advance votes and election day votes. This gives an indication of the result of the election. But special votes, including votes cast overseas, do not all come in until up to 10 days after the election. The final official count is declared when all those votes have also been counted.

The contest in each local electorate is determined on an FPP basis. The electoral candidate with the most votes is declared elected as the member of Parliament for the electorate. Additional list MPs are then declared elected from the party lists in order to achieve proportionality. For example, in general terms, if a party receives 40 per cent of the party vote, then it is entitled to 48 (which is 40 per cent) of the 120 MPs in the House; if 35 of its electoral candidates have been elected as electorate MPs, then 13 of its list candidates will be declared elected as list MPs. A party is, however, only entitled to list MPs if it achieves at least 5 per cent of the nationwide party vote or one of its candidates is elected as an electoral candidate. More precisely, the Sainte-Laguë method is used to calculate the total number of MPs to which each party is entitled, based on the nationwide party vote. List candidates elected as electorate MPs are omitted and list candidates are declared elected starting from the top of the list until the party achieves the total number of MPs in the House it is entitled to. If a party wins more electorate seats than it is entitled to, based on the party vote (commonly called an over-hang), then the total number of MPs in the House is increased to more than 120. This has happened when minor parties have performed more strongly in electorate contests than the nationwide party vote.

The results of electorate contests and allocation of seats from party lists are formally declared by the Electoral Commission. The names of those elected are communicated to Parliament through the return of the writ to the Clerk of the House of Representatives, signifying the end of the electoral process. Once MPs take their seats in the House, electorate and list MPs generally have the same status for parliamentary business and activities.

The results for the 2020 General Election are shown in Table 4.1 (unusually, one party secured a majority of party votes).[8]

[8] For historical election results, see the website of the Electoral Commission (www.electionresults.org.nz).

Table 4.1 2020 General Election Results

	Party Votes	Percentage of Votes	Electorate Seats	List Seats	Total Seats
Labour Party	1,443,545	50.0	46	19	65
National Party	738,275	25.6	23	10	33
Green Party	226,757	7.9	1	9	10
ACT New Zealand	219,031	7.6	1	9	10
Māori Party	33,630	1.2	1	1	2
New Zealand First Party	75,020	2.6	–	–	–
The Opportunities Party (TOP)	43,449	1.5	–	–	–
New Conservative	42,613	1.5	–	–	–
Advance NZ	28,429	1.0	–	–	–
Aotearoa Legalise Cannabis Party	13,329	0.5	–	–	–
ONE Party	8,121	0.3	–	–	–
Vision New Zealand	4,237	0.1	–	–	–
NZ Outdoors Party	3,256	0.1	–	–	–
TEA Party	2,414	0.1	–	–	–
Sustainable New Zealand Party	1,880	0.1	–	–	–
Social Credit	1,520	0.1	–	–	–
HeartlandNZ	914	0.0	–	–	–
Total	**2,886,420**		**72**	**48**	**120**

Source: Electoral Commission, '2020 General Election and Referendums – Official Result' (www.electionresults.govt.nz/electionresults_2020).

C. Political Parties

The political party is an important institution in New Zealand's democratic system of government. Candidates and MPs organise themselves into political parties in order to enhance their electoral and political prospects. Parties provide, amongst other things, ideological solidarity, collective infrastructure and policy distinctiveness for their members. Political parties first came onto the scene at the end of the nineteenth century with the formation of the Liberal party.

MMP has brought political parties out of the shadows, even if parties have, in reality, always played a significant role within the political arena.[9] MMP directly recognises the role of the political party by treating it as a formal electoral institution: the public now cast votes directly for their preferred political party and the number of a party's MPs elected to the House largely reflects the proportion of party votes cast for that political party. The transformation of the political party into an electoral institution also came with necessary layers of regulation. These include registration of parties; administrative, financial and transparency obligations; campaigning and advertising controls; and restrictions on donations.[10] The means of selecting candidates is also addressed but with a relatively light touch: parties must follow 'democratic procedures' when selecting candidates and current financial members must be allowed to participate directly or indirectly in the choice of candidates.[11]

This recognition has also flowed into the parliamentary domain, where House rules and customs now reflect the reality that MPs generally act collectively through political parties. Standing orders of the House explicitly recognise any political party with MPs as a parliamentary institution.[12] Matters such as membership of committees, speaking rights and the number of oral questions aim to reflect the plurality of parties and each party's share of MPs within the House. And almost all contested votes in the House are undertaken by a party vote, where the party whips announce how many votes are cast for or against the motion by MPs from their party.[13]

Political parties also play a significant role on the edges of the parliamentary domain. All MPs in a political party – known as caucus – meet regularly as a group, providing a mechanism for collective planning, deliberation and discipline. And behind caucus stands the non-parliamentary wing of political parties, wielding different degrees of influence on policy, strategy and governance. For example, the National Party elects its party leader through a vote by MPs in caucus. However, since 2012, the Labour Party has moved to a party-wide election process,

[9] A Geddis, 'The Legal Status of Political Parties under MMP' (2009) 7 *New Zealand Journal of Public and International Law* 21.

[10] Electoral Act 1993, especially pts 4, 6, 6AA and 6A.

[11] Electoral Act 1993, s 71.

[12] Standing Orders of the House of Representatives 2020, SO 35.

[13] Standing Orders of the House of Representatives 2020, SO 144.

where the leader is elected on a weighted system of votes (caucus 40 per cent; party membership 40 per cent; affiliated unions 20 per cent). The exception is within three months prior to a general election, when the leader is elected by caucus majority vote. Interestingly, after nine years of relatively unpopular Labour leaders chosen by the usual method, Jacinda Ardern became leader about six weeks before the 2017 election under this exception. After coalition formation negotiations, she became Prime Minister.

The significance of the political party as the dominant electoral and parliamentary institution has also been reinforced, at times, by party-hopping prohibitions. Under this regime, in force from 2001 to 2005 and since 2018, MPs who resign or are dismissed as a member of the political party they were originally affiliated with upon election can be ousted from office as MPs.[14] This regime has been, and continues to be, controversial. Some are concerned that party-hopping disrupts the essential proportionality in Parliament. Others worry that the regime vests too much power in political parties and unduly tempers the freedom of individual MPs in Parliament.

D. Effect of MMP

The MMP electoral system has significantly changed the nature of government and associated constitutional dynamics, both directly and indirectly.

First, MMP has changed the face of Parliament with greater diversity in its membership. Over the last two decades, the number of women, Māori, and other minority groups has increased dramatically, as was predicted by the Royal Commission.[15] The proportion of women MPs elected in the 2020 election under MMP, compared with those elected in the last Parliament under FPP in 1993, increased from 21 per cent to 48 per cent. The proportion of Māori MPs increased from 6 per cent to 21 per cent. For Pasifika MPs, this proportion increased from 1 per cent to 8 per cent, and for Asian MPs it increased from zero to nearly

[14] Electoral Act 1993, ss 55AAB–55E, inserted by the Electoral (Integrity) Amendment Act 2019. See A Geddis, 'Proportional Representation, "Party Hopping" and the Limits of Electoral Regulation' [2006] *Common Law World Review* 24.

[15] Parliamentary Library, 'Size of the House of Representatives: 120 or 99 MPs?' (5 October 1999) (www.parliament.nz); J Hayward, L Greaves and C Timperley, *Government and Politics in Aotearoa and New Zealand*, 7th edn (Oxford, Oxford University Press, 2021) 220–23.

7 per cent. LGBT+ identifying MPs increased from 1 per cent to 11 per cent of the total. Much of this increased diversity is attributable to party lists – more so than electorates.[16] Some list MPs also informally align themselves to different, often minority, communities of interest throughout the country. This provides an additional layer of electoral representation over and above the locality-based electoral approach.

Secondly, multi-party politics and government have become the norm. FPP's strong propensity towards two-party politics was a key driver for the adoption of MMP. The resulting change delivered on this promise. It is very rare for a single party to be able to govern alone. Governments have been made up of multiple political parties, operating under a variety of coalition agreements or other support arrangements. This has sparked evolution in a number of conventions regulating the executive, as noted in Chapter 5. The exception is the most recent election in 2020, where the Labour party secured a majority of the vote and of MPs. Even then, it entered into a cooperation agreement with the Green party.

Thirdly, the executive no longer enjoys the dominance over Parliament it did under FPP. Instead, under MMP, the executive has 'qualified control' over Parliament due to the usual expectation of multi-party government.[17] Successful implementation of a government's programme depends on inter-party agreement, both generally and in relation to specific matters. The effect of needing inter-party agreement is usually more moderate government programmes, with greater policy compromise, fewer initiatives, and fewer radical reforms. While the executive's power has been curtailed compared with FPP, the executive is still usually able to get its way including through constitutional innovations such as coalition, confidence-and-supply or support agreements. During negotiations, larger parties can offer roles to minor party MPs or allow speaking time in exchange for their support on supply bills and budgets. So, if the larger party is competent in its negotiations and is bargaining from a position of electoral strength, it may still enjoy substantive control over the executive in exchange for minor concessions.

Fourthly, the relationship between parliamentary select committees and the executive has changed because the government is no longer guaranteed a majority on every select committee. For example, from 2017 to 2020, the opposition had a majority on two-thirds of select committees. That is not to say select committees are beyond the scope of government

[16] Electoral Commission, 'Review of the MMP Voting System' (29 October 2012), [2.23].

[17] R Malone, *Rebalancing the Constitution* (Wellington, Institute of Policy Studies, 2008).

influence. Rather, under MMP, ministers must work harder and be more flexible in regard to the content of their bills in order to secure the same level of influence they enjoyed in relation to select committees under FPP.

Fifthly, with the adoption of MMP, the number of MPs increased from 99 to 120. The increased number of MPs in itself has somewhat weakened the executive's previous dominance of the House through strength of numbers. It also allows the work of select committees to be carried out more effectively, and offers a larger talent pool from which to draw ministers. However, despite increased numbers, we have not seen the emergence of an independent backbench like that in Westminster.

New Zealanders appear to remain committed to MMP, although there continues to be some frustration with its quirks. A further referendum was undertaken on the electoral system in 2011. MMP was endorsed by over 56 per cent of voters. Major reviews have been undertaken, by a select committee in 2001 and the Electoral Commission in 2012.[18] There have been recommendations to lower the percentage of the party vote required for list seats below 5 per cent and to remove the single electoral seat as an alternative threshold for list seats. So far, they have failed to garner sufficient support to be implemented. But following the 2020 election, the Labour-led government signalled an intention to pick up these recommendations in discussions to be held with other political parties on electoral settings.

E. Entrenched Provisions

The other notable aspect of the electoral framework is the protection of some key provisions regulating elections, first introduced in 1956. The method of protection is legally ambiguous yet curiously effective. It is a testament to the importance of representative democracy in New Zealand that the only provisions so protected relate to elections. Section 268 of the Electoral Act 1993 entrenches six 'reserved' provisions of that Act and one of the Constitution Act 1986 regulating the electoral process:

- the independent Representation Commission which sets electorate boundaries (Electoral Act 1993, section 28);
- the division of New Zealand into electoral districts (section 35);

[18] MMP Review Committee, 'Inquiry into the Review of MMP' [1999–2002] *Appendix to the Journals of the House of Representatives* I.23A; Electoral Commission (n 16).

- the mandated tolerance in the size of electorates (section 36);
- the minimum voting age of 18 (section 74);
- the method of voting (section 168); and
- the three-year parliamentary term (Constitution Act 1986, section 17(1)).

Not all important electoral provisions are reserved. For example, qualifications for voting other than age, such as ethnicity, are not specifically reserved.[19]

A simple majority in the House is insufficient to amend or repeal the reserved provisions. Instead, a 75 per cent majority of the House or a simple majority of a national referendum is required. Significantly, though, section 268 is not itself protected against amendment or repeal by simple majority. This single, rather than double, entrenchment means that there would be no legal impediment to the House amending the reserved provisions if it first repeals or amends section 268. Despite this, there have been no deliberate attempts to nefariously circumvent the single entrenchment; only amendments with the elevated support in the House have been made.

When the provisions were first entrenched, in the predecessor Electoral Act 1956, the then-dominant thinking about parliamentary sovereignty was that entrenchment was legally ineffective.[20] Parliament was not considered legally able to bind its successors, even on the manner of amendment or repeal of certain provisions. Parliament at the time was anxious to 'place the structure of [electoral] law above and beyond the influence of Government and party', but there were serious doubts about whether that was legally possible.[21] Entrenchment was intended to send a signal about the sacredness of the reserved provisions – to engender a constitutional convention that they not be amended other than through the enhanced procedures. That intention has been successful as, in practice, the entrenched provisions have generally assumed conventional force. In addition to protection by convention, Parliament's own internal processes also might prevent passage of a Bill that does not satisfy the entrenchment requirements.[22]

[19] *Ngaronoa v Attorney-General* [2018] NZSC 123, [2019] 1 NZLR 289, [70], [76], [125] and [135].

[20] E McLeay, *In Search of Consensus* (Wellington, Victoria University Press, 2018).

[21] Royal Commission on the Electoral System (n 5), [9.175] and [9.182].

[22] A Quentin-Baxter and J McLean, *This Realm of New Zealand* (Auckland, Auckland University Press, 2017) 243; T Shiels and A Geddis, 'Tracking the Pendulum Swing on Legislative Entrenchment in New Zealand' (2020) 41 *Statute Law Review* 207, 216–18.

Constitutional theory has evolved to match. Current thinking is that 'manner and form' entrenchment (enhanced procedural protections) is legally valid and enforceable by the courts.[23] Indeed, in a recent (unsuccessful) legal challenge to electoral amendments disenfranchising prisoners from voting, the Attorney-General conceded that failure to comply with entrenched manner and form requirements would naturally lead to the courts invalidating such legislation, although the Supreme Court did not need to express a view on the point.[24]

III. RESPONSIBLE GOVERNMENT: A PARLIAMENTARY MINISTRY

The engine room of executive government in New Zealand is Cabinet, led by the Prime Minister and made up of ministers from political parties comprising the government, as explained in the next chapter. Ministers must be members of Parliament. A parliamentary ministry is one of the distinctive features of Westminster-style government: the government is drawn from Parliament and responsible to Parliament – and, through Parliament, ultimately responsible to the electorate. The parliamentary ministry facilitates interlocking chains of accountability that ensure the actions of the government have a democratic mandate. In this section, we look at how governments are constituted, how they expire and the transitions between them.

A. Government, Cabinet and Ministers

The divide between form and reality is vividly seen in the institutions that head executive government. That continues within the government itself. Indeed, the term 'government' is not a constitutional term of art or a formal institution in itself. The term is often used rather loosely, to describe the ministry that leads the executive – although there is variation in its usage and who qualifies for inclusion is contested.

At the core of executive government lies Cabinet – the most important institution of New Zealand government. Real political power is exercised by ministers individually within their portfolios, by the Prime Minister

[23] See eg *Westco Lagan Ltd v Attorney-General* [2001] 1 NZLR 40 (HC), [93]; GWR Palmer, 'A Bill of Rights for New Zealand: A White Paper' [1984–1985] I *Appendix to the Journals of the House of Representatives,* A6 [7.7]–[7.24]. See further the detailed discussion of entrenchment in ch 6.

[24] *Ngaronoa* (n 19), [70] and [159].

as leader of executive government, and by Cabinet collectively. The Prime Minister's appointment comes first when a new government is mandated: the Prime Minister is the first minister of the Crown. Although Parliament expresses its confidence in a government or ministry collectively, it is the Prime Minister who is charged with that confidence and responsible for ensuring that ministers deliver on it. The process for determining which party leader should be appointed Prime Minister, usually following an election, is the story of the formation of government. Other ministers are appointed and dismissed by the Governor-General acting on advice of the Prime Minister, as we explain in more detail in Chapter 5.

B. Formation of Government

Prime ministers and governments are not directly elected, even though their mandate to lead executive government reflects electoral support. It is for the House of Representatives to express confidence in the Prime Minister and the government – effectively choosing which group of their members should be appointed as the government of the day. In the tradition of Westminster government, the government is only indirectly elected.

The advent of MMP led to greater attention to the constitutional conventions governing the formation of government. Previously, after the emergence of party government, FPP usually delivered a clear electoral winner, and the leader of the party with the majority of seats in the House was appointed Prime Minister without fuss. However, similar decisive outcomes are rare under MMP. Multi-party government is the norm. Parties must enter into different governance arrangements with other parties in order to ensure they have sufficient support to govern, as we explain in more detail in Chapter 5.

Understandings about the Governor-General's role in appointing the Prime Minister have come into sharp focus and have needed to evolve. A series of carefully worded constitutional speeches and papers by successive Governors-General, subsequently reflected in the Cabinet Manual, has clarified the relevant principles and processes around government formation.[25] This has avoided the debate and uncertainty that has plagued government formation in some other countries. The principles and processes are now well-settled and apply to any appointment of a

[25] M Hardie Boys, 'The Role of the Governor-General under MMP' (1996) 21(4) *New Zealand International Law Review* 2; M Hardie Boys, 'Continuity and Change' (1997) 5 *Waikato Law Review* 1; M Hardie Boys, 'Governing under MMP' (IPS Policy Paper No 1,

new government, whether immediately following an election or after a mid-term loss of confidence. Although government formation may take a bit of time, uncertainty and crisis is usually avoided.

The basic rule, which is part of the constitutional convention of collective responsibility, is a simple one: *the Prime Minister and government must command the confidence of the House.*[26] That is, a party or group of parties in government must have the confidence of the House and must be able to survive votes of confidence. Confidence votes include: express votes of confidence; votes declared by the Prime Minister to go to the House's confidence in the government; automatic votes of confidence on the matter of supply, such as the budget or annual taxation rates; and other votes which impliedly raise the issue of a government's survival in office.[27] These votes are won (or lost) by a simple majority of votes. The ability to govern is conditional on surviving this small sub-set of votes in the House. Governments may lose other votes (and have done so in the MMP era) without affecting their constitutional legitimacy. As one Governor-General put it, commanding the confidence of the House is the 'quantity' dimension of forming a new government.[28]

Beyond the basic principle of commanding confidence, there are no other constitutional requirements dictating the shape of government. For example, there is no constitutional presumption that the party with the most seats should govern or have first option on forming a government. Nor does the incumbent government hold any special privilege in the formation process. The governing bloc may be made up in various ways, as long as it commands the confidence of the House: a majority coalition government; a minority single party or coalition government supported by other parties on confidence and supply; or other cooperation arrangements providing the necessary support (or abstentions) on confidence and supply. For most of the time since the advent of MMP, the party securing the most seats in the House formed and led government. But that need not be so. In 2017, for example, Labour and New Zealand First

Wellington, Institute of Policy Studies, 1999); S Cartwright, 'The Role of the Governor-General' (Occasional Paper No 6, Wellington, New Zealand Centre for Public Law, 2001); A Satyanand, 'The Governor-General's Role' (Christchurch, University of Canterbury, August 2010); J Mateparae, 'Address to Press Gallery Dinner' (Wellington, November 2013); P Reddy, 'Address to Returning Officers and Registrars of Electors' (Wellington, March 2020).

[26] Cabinet Office, *Cabinet Manual 2017*, [6.58].

[27] M Harris and D Wilson (eds), *McGee: Parliamentary Practice in New Zealand*, 4th edn (Auckland, Oratia Books, 2017) 128–31.

[28] Mateparae (n 25).

formed a coalition government, supported by the Greens, even though National was the largest single party.

The second dimension of government formation is 'clarity'. Governors-General in New Zealand have wisely treated the process of government formation as a political one, to be undertaken by politicians. Reflecting the neutrality of their office, the Governor-General does not take any active role in negotiations – their sole role is to ascertain where the confidence of the House lies. Thus, convention dictates that party leaders provide clear, public statements on their intentions on matters of confidence following the completion of negotiations. This is so that the Governor-General and the public are left in no doubt about each party's allegiances and which party leader would have the confidence of the House such that they should be appointed Prime Minister. Parties usually do this by publicly disclosing their coalition, confidence-and-supply or other support agreements. Governors-General have emphasised the need for certainty and transparency in order that they may fulfil their role of assessing which party or group of parties commands confidence, at arm's length from the political fray. If there is no clear outcome following negotiations, the Governor-General may find it necessary to talk to party leaders but this has not yet been necessary; political parties have, so far, reached clear arrangements within a few weeks of the election. The Clerk of the Executive Council is responsible for liaising with party leaders during this process on behalf of the Governor-General and provides official, impartial support and constitutional advice to the Governor-General.

No formal timeframe is set for the process of government formation, either following an election or a mid-term loss of confidence. The caretaker convention (discussed below) means much of the business of government continues, albeit subject to additional restrictions. The political process of garnering the necessary support can take as much or as little time as is needed. Key milestones help to nudge that process along. The formal declaration of election results, usually now made within three weeks of election day, provides certainty about the final make-up of the House, which may be especially significant in close contests. Parliament must also meet no later than six weeks after the day fixed for the return of the writ, as required by section 19 of the Constitution Act 1986. While government need not be formed before Parliament reconvenes, this date provides an incentive for parties to conclude their negotiations – in effect, giving a window of convenience of six weeks or so for negotiations. The length of time required has varied. The first government of the MMP era in 1996 was not settled for eight-and-a-half weeks after election night, until the eve of Parliament reconvening. Since then, government blocs have been negotiated and formalised much more quickly, partly as parties have become more familiar with the demands of government formation (and aware of public impatience at too long a delay).

The House of Representatives does not take any formal role in government formation. The Governor-General is constitutionally responsible for appointing the Prime Minister, as well as being the sentinel of confidence within the House. The Governor-General anticipates the outcome of confidence votes when appointing a Prime Minister. Confidence votes within the House serve to test and confirm, or contradict, their assessment. The first test is often a confidence vote moved in the Address-in-Reply to the Speech from the Throne – typically moved by the opposition as an amendment expressing no confidence in the newly appointed government. If a new government has not been formed before Parliament meets, an early vote on confidence may help resolve any uncertain stalemate.

The birth of a new government is signified by a formal appointment ceremony, where the Prime Minister is sworn into office by the Governor-General. Once the Prime Minister is sworn into office, the democratic legitimacy and full authority of government is restored. The Prime Minister can then advise the Governor-General to appoint ministers within the administration and proceed with the usual business of government. Since the advent of MMP, the practice has been to hold a formal appointment ceremony even in cases where the incumbent Prime Minister is to remain in office.

C. Coalition, Confidence-and-supply and Support Agreements

How a party (or parties) garners the necessary support on matters of confidence and structures their ministry is a matter of politics. The MMP era has generated a number of experiments in multi-party governance, with a variety of different support arrangements being adopted.[29] These arrangements are recorded in coalition, confidence-and-supply, cooperation or support agreements which are routinely made public at the end of negotiations about the formation of government.

[29] J Boston and others, *Left Turn* (Wellington, Victoria University Press, 2000); J Boston and D Bullock, 'Experiments in Executive Government under MMP in New Zealand' (2009) 7 *New Zealand Journal of Public and International Law* 39.

The pattern of negotiations will depend on the political numbers in the new House. If one of the two larger parties, National or Labour, can form a government with its natural allies, it will do so. Some smaller parties, such as the NZ First, United and Māori parties, position themselves in the centre between the two larger parties. If they hold the balance of power or might fortify a governing bloc, they may negotiate concurrently with the two larger parties. Smaller parties have to choose their role carefully: in government, supporting government or in opposition. Tight relations with the lead party typically bring short-term power but often at the cost of longer-term party identity and distinctiveness. As explained further below and in Chapter 5, a mid-way option has also developed where a smaller party acquires a few ministerial positions outside Cabinet, leaving space to distance itself from government on other matters if it wishes.

Coalition agreements in the early days of MMP tended to emphasise unity within the governing bloc. For example, the first coalition under MMP from 1996 to 1998, between National and NZ First, took the form of a traditional coalition. Ministers from both parties sat in Cabinet, along with a number of appointments outside Cabinet. An extensive series of policy commitments were recorded in the coalition agreement, along with coalition management procedures. Strong collective responsibility within the coalition was expected. Similarly, the Labour-Alliance and Labour-Progressive coalitions that followed in 1999 and 2002 also saw ministers inside Cabinet from both parties, albeit with lighter agreements on policy commitments and greater emphasis on processes for policy formation. Labour was supported on matters of confidence by other parties outside government: United Future supported on matters of confidence and supply, while the Greens supported on matters of confidence and supply in 1999 and agreed to abstain in 2002.

From 2005, most governance agreements have taken the form of confidence-and-supply agreements. Such agreements guarantee support from the junior party on matters of confidence and supply in return for a few ministerial (or other executive) positions outside Cabinet being guaranteed to the junior party. A handful of policy commitments are recorded in the agreement, along with the processes for management, consultation and policy development. Significantly, the agreements also provide for the expression of dissent on the part of junior parties. In many respects, the key to mastering the tricky 'unity-distinctiveness' conundrum has been through innovative approaches to Cabinet collective responsibility, as discussed in Chapter 5.[30]

[30] Boston and Bullock (n 29) 39.

Recent elections have seen slightly different arrangements, reflecting the dynamics of electoral results. In 2017, Labour entered into a full coalition agreement with New Zealand First, as well as a confidence-and-supply arrangement with the Greens, when New Zealand First held the balance of power and it was plausible that it could enter into governing arrangements with either main political party. In 2020, after Labour secured a majority of MPs itself and did not need to enter any deal to secure confidence, it entered into a relatively loose and modest cooperation agreement with the Greens.

Since MMP was adopted, the shape of governments has been as shown in Table 4.2.

Table 4.2 Forms of Government under MMP

		TOTAL MPs	**GOVT MPs**	ACT	Alliance	Green	Labour	Mana	Māori	National	NZ First	Progressive Coalition / Progressive	United / United Future
1996	National-led government	**120**	**61**	8	13	–	37	–	–	***44**	**#17**	–	1
1999	Labour-led	**120**	**66**	9	**#10**	^7	***49**	–	–	39	5	–	1
2002	Labour-led	**120**	**62**	9	–	9	***52**	–	–	27	13	**#2**	^8
2005	Labour-led	**121**	**61**	2	–	ϕ6	***50**	–	4	48	^7	**#1**	^3
2008	National-led	**122**	**69**	^5	–	9	43	–	^5	***58**	–	1	^1
2011	National-led	**121**	**65**	^1	–	14	34	1	^4	***59**	8	–	^1
2014	National-led	**121**	**64**	^1	–	14	32	–	^2	***60**	11	–	^1
2017	Labour-led	**120**	**63**	1	–	^8	***46**	–	–	56	**#9**	–	–
2020	Labour-led	**120**	**75**	10	–	**ϕ10**	***65**	–	2	33	–	–	–

* Lead government party

\# Coalition party

^ Confidence and supply party

ϕ Cooperation party

Note: Based on government numbers following election and not including mid-term changes.

D. Expiration or Dismissal of Government

Governments change or expire. But, strictly speaking, there is always a government because the Sovereign and Governor-General cannot be left without responsible advisors. There are two key ways a government expires and the ministry changes. First, a government may lose its mandate to govern following an election, where the mood of the electorate changes and the existing government can no longer command the confidence of the House of Representatives. Once a new government is formed and assumes office, the previous incumbent government vacates office; only one grouping of parties is ever able to command confidence. Secondly, and more rarely, a government may expire mid-term, if it loses the confidence of the House and fails to form a successor government from any political resettlement. A new government may emerge but, if not, Parliament dissolves or expires for an election.

i. Expiration Following an Election

In the ordinary course of events, a government's mandate expires through a cascading series of events tied, in part, to the electoral process.

The Governor-General issues a proclamation dissolving Parliament for an election, usually on advice of the Prime Minister who maintains the confidence of the House. A Prime Minister who has lost confidence cannot unilaterally request dissolution of Parliament for an election (a request in those circumstances is subject to the caretaker convention, as explained below). As a formal back-stop, if a request to dissolve is not made earlier, Parliament's term expires three years after the day fixed for the return of the writ for the previous election.[31] A government's full authority is not affected by dissolution, unless confidence has already been lost. Unlike some other Westminster systems, there is no pre-election caretaker (or 'purdah') convention obligating a government to restrict activity after an election is called or the House is dissolved. However, successive governments have, as a matter of voluntary restraint, chosen to avoid certain actions in the three months before an election, such as significant appointments or some government advertising.[32] The longer this practice continues the more it looks like a constitutional convention. Arguably, it is now.

[31] Constitution Act 1986, s 17(1).

[32] Cabinet Office, *Cabinet Manual 2017*, [6.5]–[6.15].

Election day changes the electoral and representative settings on which a government's mandate to govern is predicated. Usually this means the existing government no longer has the confidence of the House. Unlike the FPP days where there was usually a definitive election day result for one party, a new government needs to be constituted or reconstituted. The caretaker convention kicks in and restricts the power of the incumbent caretaker government until there is clarity about the next government and any new Prime Minister is sworn in. Election day also sees all MPs formally vacate their office, until new MPs assume office after the writ is returned or a declaration of list members is notified to Parliament. However, an election does not upset existing ministers' legal entitlement to office. An exception to the usual rule that ministers must be MPs allows an incumbent minister who has lost their seat in an election to continue to be a minister for 28 days after the election.[33] Conversely, electoral candidates may be appointed as ministers after election day (for up to 40 days), in anticipation of their formal return as MPs.[34]

Once a new government emerges, the incumbent Prime Minister and government must vacate office in favour of the new administration, unless the Prime Minister has been able to renew their democratic mandate to govern. In practice, the incumbent government's formal resignation from office is staged to coincide with the formal appointment of the incoming government: outgoing ministers tender their resignation, with those resignations taking effect when the incoming Prime Minister is sworn in. If the incumbent Prime Minister and government are returned with a fresh mandate then, strictly speaking, resignation and formal appointment is not needed because the legal authority to govern continues. However, recent practice has seen the Prime Minister and government ceremonially reappointed, in order to signal the end of the caretaker convention and fresh minting of the administration.

ii. Expiration Mid-term Following Loss of Confidence

The situation where a government loses the confidence of the House mid-way through a term is unusual in New Zealand's modern constitutional history. As with formation of government, the Governor-General is the sentinel of confidence. Ultimately, the Governor-General is the sole judge of whether a government retains or has lost the confidence of the

[33] Constitution Act 1986, s 6(2)(b).
[34] Constitution Act 1986, s 6(2)(a).

House, exercising their independent judgement. Formal evidence of loss of confidence includes losing an express vote of confidence. This is rare. Not since 1928 has a New Zealand government lost a vote of confidence. Losing a critical vote on the budget or supply Bill, or failing to pass a budget, also implicitly signals a loss of confidence, although a degree of judgement may be needed on the part of the Governor-General in order to assess whether the loss or failure undermines the government's ability to govern.

We also take the view that loss of confidence may be manifested through other means, absent a formal loss of a vote of confidence in the House. For example, actions or statements which indicate that one of the parties of government has repudiated the coalition, confidence-and-supply or support agreements on which the government grouping was predicated may indicate a loss of confidence. Clear public evidence of the existence of an alternative group of parties capable of and wishing to govern, in accordance with the quantity and clarity requirements of the government formation protocols, might raise similar uncertainty about whether the government still commands confidence. We consider clear cases of changes to an underlying political settlement could trigger the consequences of loss of confidence. In such circumstances it would be prudent for the Governor-General to invite public clarification of confidence if the position is uncertain. As one former Governor-General, Sir Michael Hardie Boys, explained, where support becomes unclear, 'politicians have a duty to clarify within a fairly short timeframe – allowing a reasonable period for negotiation and reorganisation – where the confidence of the House lies'.[35]

If a government loses confidence, it formally continues in office, subject to the caretaker convention, until there is an opportunity for a new government to emerge following a new political settlement. Notably, if a government has lost the confidence of the House, then a request by the Prime Minister to dissolve Parliament is subject to the caretaker convention and constitutional principle suggests it should only be made and agreed to if the request has majority support in the House.[36] Thus, unlike the position in some other Westminster democracies, an early election does not inevitably follow from a loss of confidence. Indeed, a Prime Minister who has lost confidence cannot unilaterally request

[35] Hardie Boys, 'Governing under MMP' (n 25).

[36] Cabinet Office, *Cabinet Manual 2017*, [6.63]–[6.64]. Some other constitutional commentators disagree with this; see Quentin-Baxter and McLean (n 22) 195–96.

dissolution for an early election. This understanding of the caretaker convention obviates the potential uncertainty about whether a Governor-General should accede to or refuse a request for early dissolution if there is a possibility of an alternative government being formed. Such judgement is unnecessary because reliance on the caretaker convention focuses the Governor-General solely on whether the request for dissolution has majority support in the House, as it should in terms of constitutional principle.

The only example of a mid-term breakdown under MMP was in 1998 when the National-New Zealand First coalition fell apart. But the Prime Minister was able to quickly regain support for a reconfigured ministry without the need for an election.[37] Following a dispute about Cabinet decision-making protocols, Prime Minister Jenny Shipley advised the Governor-General to dismiss Winston Peters, the leader of her coalition partner, New Zealand First, from his ministerial positions. A few days later, the parties advised the Governor-General that their coalition agreement would terminate in a week's time. Within days of that termination, the Prime Minister convinced enough former members of New Zealand First to support her leading a new administration, as well as garnering support from other parties and MPs. These new support arrangements confirmed the Prime Minister continued to command the confidence of the House, allowing the new ministry to be sworn in. Uncertainty was avoided during this process because the Prime Minister gave assurances, both publicly and to the Governor-General, that she continued to maintain majority support. And, just over a week after the new ministry was sworn in, a vote of confidence in the government was moved and won, reinforcing its legitimacy. Then Governor-General Sir Michael Hardie Boys described this formal testing of confidence following a mid-term political resettlement as 'an important precedent that will provide sound constitutional guidance to political leaders confronted by the same situation in the future'.[38]

E. Transition between Governments and Caretaker Convention

The transition between administrations is carefully regulated by constitutional convention, especially under MMP. Under FPP, the next government

[37] P Aimer and R Miller, 'New Zealand Politics in the 1990s' in J Vowles, S Banducci and J Karp (eds), *Proportional Representation on Trial* (Auckland, Auckland University Press, 2002) 1; Hardie Boys, 'Governing under MMP' (n 25).

[38] Hardie Boys, 'Governing under MMP' (n 25).

was normally known on election night. However, under MMP, parties generally have to negotiate to form the next government. As mentioned earlier, there is no formal limit to how long these negotiations can last. For example, in 1996, a caretaker government functioned for eight-and-a-half weeks before New Zealand First formed a government with National. After the 2017 election, Labour, New Zealand First and the Greens took 26 days to form a government.

The caretaker convention applies when an incumbent government loses its democratic mandate to govern: either following an election or a mid-term loss of confidence. The incumbent government retains, as a matter of law, full executive authority, with all the powers and responsibilities that go with that. The Governor-General can never be left without advisors and the business of government must go on during the transition period. However, by convention, the incumbent government's use of that authority is conditioned and restricted to reflect the absence of a democratic mandate, with the convention varying depending on whether it is clear who the incumbent's successor will be. These expectations are authoritatively set out in the Cabinet Manual.[39]

Where it is *clear* which party or group of parties will form the next government, but the incoming government has not been sworn in, the incumbent government is essentially required to give effect to the wishes of the incoming government. That is because, in reality, the incoming government has the democratic mandate to govern. This means the incumbent government should not undertake any new policy initiatives during the caretaker period. If any matter of significance cannot be delayed until the incoming government takes office, the outgoing government must act on the advice of the incoming government until the new government takes office, even if the outgoing government disagrees with the proposed response. This aspect of the convention was clarified by the outgoing Deputy Prime Minister and Attorney-General, Jim McLay, after the 1984 election.[40] The outgoing National Prime Minister, Sir Robert Muldoon, initially refused to accede to advice from the incoming Labour government to devalue the New Zealand dollar in response to an economic crisis. In the end, Muldoon took McLay's advice that it was constitutionally proper for an outgoing Prime Minister to agree to such a request from the incoming government. But, if Muldoon had failed to do

[39] Cabinet Office, *Cabinet Manual 2017*, [6.21]–[6.37].

[40] J McLay, '1984 and All That' (2012) 10 *New Zealand Journal of Public and International Law* 267, 273–77; GWR Palmer, *Unbridled Power*, 2nd edn (Oxford, Oxford University Press, 1987) 34–36; Quentin-Baxter and McLean (n 22) 174–75 and 221–22.

so, there was a very real prospect he would have been toppled as leader of the National Party or the Governor-General would have dismissed him as Prime Minister.

Where it is *unclear* which party or group of parties will form the next government, the convention reflects this uncertainty in the location of the democratic mandate. The focus turns to whether a particular action has majority support in the House and thus whether such action has democratic legitimacy.[41] The normal business of government and general day-to-day administration continues, along with policy initiatives implemented before the caretaker period. However, significant policy initiatives and appointments should be deferred, or temporary measures which do not commit the government in the longer term should be adopted. If neither deferral nor temporary solutions are available, the incumbent government should consult other parties in order to establish whether the proposed action has the support of a majority of the House.

Post-election government formation typically involves a period where the outcome is unclear (following the election, while parties are engaged in negotiations), then a short period where the outcome is clear (following the announcement of the new government until that new government is sworn in). The key principle that colours the caretaker convention is the need for a democratic mandate. Whatever action the government takes needs to have the mandate of majority support in the House – either implicitly, because government as an institution has that general mandate, or otherwise on an ad hoc basis, because any particular initiative has such a mandate.

IV. CONCLUSION

Democratic government is delivered in New Zealand by the executive, being drawn from, and being responsible to, an elected House of Representatives. At the apex of executive government, Cabinet, led by the Prime Minister, holds real power. It is entitled to advise the Governor-General and direct civil servants to carry out the ministry's wishes. As a parliamentary ministry, Cabinet's mandate to govern comes from the confidence expressed in it by the collective of MPs in the House. Ministers must explain and justify their priorities and actions on an ongoing basis in order for that mandate to continue. Regular elections,

[41] Cabinet Office, *Cabinet Manual 2017*, [6.25].

conducted under the MMP electoral system, ensure that the House's actions generally have majority support amongst the public. And electoral proportionality delivers multi-party politics in the House, weakening the executive's command over the legislature. Executive government cannot take for granted support for everything it does, thereby enhancing parliamentary accountability.

FURTHER READING

Cabinet Office, *Cabinet Manual 2017* (www.dpmc.govt.nz).

Electoral Commission, *Review of the MMP Voting System* (Electoral Commission, 29 October 2012).

Geddis, A, *Electoral Law in New Zealand: Practice and Policy*, 2nd edn (Wellington, LexisNexis, 2013).

Hayward, J, Greaves, L, and Timperley, C, *Government and Politics in Aotearoa and New Zealand*, 7th edn (Oxford, Oxford University Press, 2021).

Malone, R, *Rebalancing the Constitution: The Challenge of Government Law-making under MMP* (Wellington, Institute of Policy Studies, 2008).

Quentin-Baxter, A, and McLean, J, *This Realm of New Zealand: The Sovereign, the Governor-General and the Crown* (Auckland, Auckland University Press, 2017).

Palmer, GWR, and Palmer, MSR, *Bridled Power: New Zealand's Constitution and Government*, 4th edn (Melbourne, Oxford University Press, 2004) chs 2 and 3.

Electoral Commission website (www.elections.nz).

Government House website (www.gg.govt.nz).

5

Executive

Introduction – Cabinet Government – Prime Minister and Ministers – Public service – Wider State Sector – Public Finance and Managerialism – Conclusion

I. INTRODUCTION

THE EXECUTIVE IS what people usually mean when they refer to 'the government'. The body that directs the executive, the Cabinet, is the product of the government formation processes outlined in the previous chapter. Once the Cabinet is formed, the executive governs by carrying out, operating or 'executing' the law and its policies. These operational activities are the core function of government. But, in doing so, the government constantly faces calls for changes to the law and its policies. So another core function of executive government is reform of law and policy. Compared with the other branches of government, the executive is action oriented. The momentum for action by, and change in, the whole of government comes from the executive branch.

This chapter focuses on how the three parts of the core of the New Zealand executive work in reality: the Cabinet collectively, ministers individually and the public service. We examine the conventional underpinnings of executive government along with the statutory overlay which provides the legal and financial parameters of government action. We also outline the wider state sector machinery and system of financial management which is also part of executive government.

New Zealand has a history of strong executive power. New Zealand's constitutional history since the 1980s has largely consisted of attempts to rein in, or 'bridle' executive power. The mixed-member-proportional (MMP) electoral system has probably had the most effect to date and has increased the power of Parliament, through political parties, to check the executive. But the executive is still the most powerful branch of government in New Zealand. It is at the core of New Zealand's system of government and constitution. Much of the rest of the constitution can be understood as a system of checks on the power of the executive branch, which is the driving force of New Zealand government.

II. CABINET GOVERNMENT

A. Cabinet

Cabinet is the most important institution of executive government. But it has the least basis in law. No law establishes Cabinet. It is a creature of constitutional convention. Cabinet's formal counterpart, the Executive Council (comprising the Governor-General and ministers), carries out formal acts of executive government. But the executive branch of government's decisions of real power are really made by Cabinet. In form, Cabinet does not exercise legal powers. In reality, little in executive government escapes Cabinet's direction.

Cabinet normally consists of around 20 ministers. There are also a number of ministers outside Cabinet. Cabinet's size is determined by the Prime Minister. In a coalition government, that is likely to be the subject of negotiations between the coalition partners. Cabinet usually meets every Monday, in the Cabinet room at the top floor of the Beehive (the Executive Wing of Parliament Buildings that houses most ministers). Ministers outside Cabinet can currently attend meetings of full Cabinet when their items are up for discussion.[1] Cabinet makes decisions by consensus, as summed up by the Prime Minister and reflected in Cabinet minutes issued by the Cabinet Office.

Much of Cabinet's work is done in advance in a system of Cabinet committees. The structure of Cabinet committees is designed by each administration, led by the Prime Minister, to reflect its priorities. There are usually some key committees, which might be labelled, for example, the Strategy Committee or Priorities Committee. There is usually an expenditure-oriented committee. All draft government bills go through the Legislation Committee and government appointments are considered by the Appointments and Honours Committee. Cabinet committees meet every week or second week and these meetings are where a lot of

[1] Cabinet Office, *Cabinet Manual 2017*, [2.29] but see also Cabinet Office, 'Labour-New Zealand First Coalition, with Confidence and Supply from the Green Party' (15 December 2017) CO (17) 10.

Cabinet decisions are worked through. Ministers outside Cabinet often are members of Cabinet committees. Public servants are invited to attend Cabinet committee meetings, though different administrations have different views about how often. Individual ministers put papers to Cabinet committees which make decisions on them, reflected in Cabinet committee minutes. Committee minutes are confirmed – or sometimes not – by the full Cabinet. They are not effective until they are confirmed by Cabinet.

B. Cabinet Manual and Cabinet Office

When a new administration is sworn in, one of its first items of business is to endorse the Cabinet Manual. The Cabinet Manual is the most authoritative source of information about how Cabinet works. It is grounded in constitutional conventions as they relate to Cabinet but also includes less formal statements of expectations. A statement in the Manual does not itself change a convention but it can reflect or trigger a change in underlying practice which, if sustained over time, constitutes a change in convention.[2] Ultimately, the Prime Minister is the final arbiter of Cabinet procedure and of the application of the Manual in individual instances.

The first edition of the Cabinet Manual, in 1979, consolidated 'the rules, precedents, conventions and procedures that have evolved since 29 January 1948 when the Secretary to Cabinet was first admitted to the Cabinet Room and a systematic record of the proceedings of Cabinet became possible'.[3] The Manual was released to all public servants in 1991 and publicly in 1996. The Manual is put before each new administration at its first Cabinet meeting for adoption. It is supplemented by the CabGuide, providing more detailed guidance about Cabinet procedures for ministers and public servants, and by Cabinet Office circulars.

The Cabinet Manual has an important role in constitutional practice. For example, modifications to the Cabinet Manual played a particularly important role in the adjustment to MMP. Cabinet and its Committee on the Implementation of Proportional Representation considered recommendations by an Officials Committee. They were reflected in modifications to the Cabinet Manual adopted in 1996,

[2] E McLeay, 'What is the Constitutional Status of the New Zealand Cabinet Office Manual?' (1999) 10 *Public Law Review* 11. See ch 1, section III.B, (a).

[3] Cabinet Office, *Cabinet Office Manual 1979*.

two months before the first MMP election. This stated, in advance, how the principles of Cabinet decision-making would work in the event of coalition, minority and caretaker governments. When the United Kingdom was faced with a similar prospect in 2010 it used New Zealand's Cabinet Manual as a model for developing its own.

The comprehensiveness of the Cabinet Manual also reflects the highly developed nature of the processes and institution of New Zealand's Cabinet Office. The Cabinet Office, staffed by politically neutral public servants, is part of the Department of the Prime Minister and Cabinet (DPMC). It is headed by the Secretary of the Cabinet who is also directly responsible to the Governor-General as Clerk of the Executive Council. The Cabinet Office provides the staff and maintains processes for meetings of Cabinet and Cabinet Committees to occur, for papers to be circulated ahead of time, and for minutes to be produced afterwards.

Most importantly, the Cabinet Office drafts, and distributes throughout government, the Cabinet minutes which record the decisions of Cabinet and Cabinet committees. Minutes have traditionally been printed on green paper and are informally known as 'Cabinet greens'. These decisions are what ministers and public servants are required to implement, as the product of collective Cabinet decision-making. The efficient systems and processes of the Cabinet Office mean all ministers and public servants know, or should know, exactly what Cabinet has decided. Cabinet minutes have an authoritative status that approaches the effect of law as far as ministers and public servants are concerned.

C. Collective Responsibility

We explained the confidence element of the constitutional convention of collective responsibility in Chapter 4: executive government must maintain the confidence of the House of Representatives. This is what gives Parliament ultimate power over the executive. The House expresses confidence in the government as a collective entity. There are two other elements of the convention of collective responsibility: unanimity and confidentiality. They also have material effects on the functioning of executive government.

i. Unanimity and its Exceptions

The unanimity element of the convention of collective responsibility provides that all ministers must support Cabinet decisions. The Cabinet

Manual states, with important exceptions explained below, '[o]nce Cabinet makes a decision, Ministers must support it … regardless of their personal views and whether or not they were at the meeting concerned'.[4] In other words, Cabinet speaks with one voice.

The constitutional dimension of unanimity has been doubted by some, who suggest Cabinet unity is only a political ideal and is not a constitutional convention in itself.[5] We disagree. We consider the constitutional function of unanimity is under-appreciated and vital. Collective responsibility applies to Cabinet decisions about matters within a minister's own portfolio. It therefore effectively aggregates to Cabinet, as a collective entity, all the powers of all ministers, if Cabinet collectively wants to exercise them. This is what creates Cabinet government and supports the confidence element to ensure that Cabinet's responsibility is genuinely collective. Cabinet Manual guidance has been consistent since at least 1991 in saying that, '[a]s a general rule, Ministers should put before their colleagues the sorts of issues on which they themselves would wish to be consulted'.[6] That guidance is generally followed. And once a decision is made by Cabinet, it falls on all ministers to ensure it is implemented, regardless of whether they personally supported the decision within Cabinet. If a Cabinet decision requires action within a minister's individual ministerial portfolio, the minister must give effect to the Cabinet decision. Ministers must also give effect to the decisions of Cabinet when advising the Governor-General in Executive Council. This aspect of Cabinet unanimity is perhaps so basic that it is easy to overlook. But we have no doubt that unanimity of this kind is fundamental to New Zealand's system of government. Collective responsibility, including the element of unanimity, well merits its status as a constitutional convention.

The strength of collective responsibility in New Zealand has historically been reinforced by public expectations of party unity and the relatively small size of the 120-member House of Representatives and, accordingly, of governing parties. Disunity in opposition parties is similarly reflected in opinion polls. But with multi-party government under MMP, the pressure for unanimity across parties within a cabinet has come under pressure. This was vividly seen in the first government formed under MMP in 1996. The National-led government was in coalition with

[4] Cabinet Office, *Cabinet Manual 2017*, [5.25].

[5] For example, PA Joseph, *Joseph on Constitutional and Administrative Law*, 5th edn (Wellington, Thomson Reuters, 2021) 294.

[6] Cabinet Office, *Cabinet Manual 2017*, [5.11].

New Zealand First, with a highly specified coalition agreement. The coalition broke up in 1998, when Prime Minister Jenny Shipley advised the Governor-General to dismiss the leader of New Zealand First, Winston Peters, for challenging the applicability of, and breaching, the convention of collective responsibility.[7]

Since then, there has been some adaptation of the strictness and enforcement of Cabinet's one public voice principle, especially for ministers from support parties in multi-party governments. Each political party has electoral incentives to maintain their own political identity. Now that more than one political party often makes up a Cabinet, or has ministers, new safety valves for differences of view have evolved. That has been particularly important for smaller parties that otherwise face the prospect of their electoral identity being swallowed up by a government led by, and identified with, a larger party. But the mechanisms which condone the expression of dissent are still collectively agreed.

The first mechanism is agree-to-disagree provisions adopted in coalition and support agreements.[8] Cabinet as a collective can permit the public expression of dissent on a particular matter by a support party. Such a provision was first seen in the Labour-Alliance coalition in 1999. The Alliance Party voted against the Singapore Closer Economic Partnership Agreement in 2000. Every successive administration has followed suit in proclaiming the ability to agree to disagree. But instances of this mechanism being actually exercised have been relatively rare, especially after a second mechanism allowing dissent developed.

The second mechanism is selective or targeted unanimity, where ministers from support parties are only subject to unanimity within their allocated portfolios.[9] In 2005, Labour negotiated confidence-and-supply agreements with New Zealand First and United Future on the basis of this constitutionally novel proposition, that a minister outside Cabinet could be part of the government for some purposes and not others. Ministers appointed from those two smaller parties were only bound by the unanimity principle in relation to matters within their own portfolios, not in relation to any other matters. This meant they were free to criticise government decisions outside their portfolios. So, while Winston Peters was Minister of Foreign Affairs (but not Minister of Trade), his New Zealand First party opposed government legislation for a free trade

[7] A Stockley, 'Constitutional Law' [1999] *New Zealand Law Review* 173.
[8] Cabinet Office, *Cabinet Manual 2017*, [5.27]–[5.28].
[9] Ibid [5.29].

agreement with China in 2008. Likewise, in 2017, ACT and United Future voted against the Resource Legislation Amendment Bill because the portfolios of the parties' ministers were not engaged. Notably, this ability to dissent is only usually available to ministers outside Cabinet from support parties – not ministers from within the lead party of government or parties which form a coalition government with the lead party. And dissent is not possible on a parliamentary vote that is a matter of confidence without risking bringing down the government. The unanimity element of collective responsibility supports, and does not override, the confidence element of collective responsibility.

This model of selective unanimity has proved flexible and pragmatic. The parameters of dissent are collectively mandated via government formation negotiations and the boundaries of portfolios allocated to ministers from support parties who are entitled to otherwise criticise the actions of the government. The model has been followed by each successive administration and reflected in successive versions of the Cabinet Manual. It is now an established aspect of New Zealand's constitutional arrangements. After these dissent mechanisms first appeared, the expectations about unanimity recorded in the Cabinet Manual were amended to recognise them. And the Manual no longer says ministers must first resign before they publicly disassociate themselves from a Cabinet decision, as it did in 1996.[10] Since 2001, it has simply said '[a]ny public dissociation from Cabinet decisions by individual coalition Ministers outside the agreed processes is unacceptable'.[11]

The enforcement of a penalty for breach of the convention has always been a matter of political judgement for the Prime Minister, rather than part of the constitutional convention itself. The variety of circumstances is too great for sanction of breach of the convention to be governed by a rule rather than discretion. There have been periodic resignations and sackings for public expressions of dissent.[12] And ministers have always been able to stake out their own personal positions by making known their views before Cabinet makes a decision, or by surreptitious leaks to the media, without being seen to breach the unanimity element of the convention.

The balance between powers exercised by Cabinet and by individual ministers has always differed over time and between administrations.

[10] Cabinet Office, *Cabinet Office Manual 1996*, [3.5].

[11] Cabinet Office, *Cabinet Manual 2017*, [5.28] ('coalition' was added in 2017).

[12] For example, P Joseph, 'The Honourable DF Quigley's Resignation Strictly Political – Not Constitutional' (1982) 1 *Canterbury Law Review* 428.

Around the margins, the strength of enforcement of the unanimity element appears to vary with the personality of the Prime Minister, the form of government and the degree of central direction in the administration's culture. For example, the National administrations of Jim Bolger (1990 to 1998) and John Key (2008 to 2017) tended to keep individual ministers on a looser leash than did the Labour administration of Helen Clark (1999 to 2008).

ii. Confidentiality

The confidentiality element of collective responsibility boils down to: 'what is said in Cabinet stays in Cabinet', unless otherwise decided by the Prime Minister. The element protects the confidentiality of what is said in Cabinet and Cabinet committees. This reinforces both the unanimity and confidence elements of collective responsibility. Only the Prime Minister is supposed to speak publicly on behalf of Cabinet. The Prime Minister's regular post-Cabinet press conference each week is emblematic of this role. However, like other conventions, its force is sometimes coloured by the particular dynamics of multi-party administrations. In the lead up to an election, for example, minor coalition partners might be more prepared to reveal insights into party positions around the Cabinet table.

The confidentiality element no longer makes all documents put before Cabinet, or its decisions, secret. The Official Information Act 1982, explained in Chapter 8, made significant inroads into Cabinet confidentiality in relation to most Cabinet documents. Unusually amongst freedom of information regimes, Cabinet papers and minutes have no special status. The Act provides that it is the information in documents held by government, rather than classes of documents, that must be assessed for release. They are assessed against a presumption of release unless certain specified grounds are satisfied. The information in them is as available for release as any other government information.

Before 1982, Cabinet minutes were secret and would sometimes contain a record of the different positions adopted by ministers in discussion, especially in Cabinet committees. Since then they tend only to record decisions – what was agreed or noted. Cabinet agendas are still not released before a meeting. Section 9(2)(f) of the Official Information Act explicitly provides that maintaining the constitutional conventions of collective and individual ministerial responsibility and the confidentiality of advice tendered by ministers constitutes good reason for withholding information. But even this exception only applies if not 'outweighed by other considerations which render it desirable, in the public interest, to make that information available', under section 9(1).

The presumption in favour of release of official information has affected the attitudes of New Zealand governments. It seems likely to be no coincidence that the legal doctrine of public interest immunity over Cabinet material lost much of its force in New Zealand before other Westminster democracies. For many years, Cabinet papers have been released publicly and sometimes proactively made available on government websites. Indeed, the Ardern administration decided that, from January 2019, Cabinet papers and associated minutes must be released proactively, within 30 working days, unless there is good reason not to do so.[13] Individual ministers are responsible for implementing the policy and papers are posted on departmental websites.

III. PRIME MINISTER AND MINISTERS

A. Ministers

The Prime Minister is just that – the first and most important minister.[14] Their appointment is symbolic of representative and responsible government and reflects Parliament's mandate in them and their ministers. The Prime Minister chairs Cabinet, leads executive government and advises the Governor-General. Other ministers are appointed or dismissed by the Governor-General on advice from the Prime Minister. The only legal constraint on appointment – required by section 6 of the Constitution Act 1986 and reflecting the Westminster tradition – is that a minister must be a member of Parliament. Most Prime Ministers appoint some ministers as associate ministers, working to a lead minister, creating an interlocking network of portfolios. This can be a particularly useful way of ensuring coherent collective decision-making in a coalition government. Associate ministers assist the lead minister, are constrained by the scope of their delegated authority, and are otherwise subject to being overruled by the lead minister. Parliamentary under-secretaries can also be appointed to assist ministers and are bound by Cabinet collective responsibility, though they do not attend Cabinet, are not members

[13] Cabinet Office, 'Proactive Release of Cabinet Material' (23 October 2018) CO(18)4.
[14] Cabinet Office, *Cabinet Manual 2017*, [2.2]–[2.12].

of the Executive Council in their own right, and are not asked oral or written parliamentary questions.

The political practices for appointment of ministers are different in different political parties. Subject to coalition dynamics, a National Party Prime Minister chooses who to appoint as a minister, what their portfolio(s) will be, and whether they will be inside or outside Cabinet. In a Labour-led government, the Labour caucus initially selects Labour Cabinet ministers by secret ballot and the Prime Minister then allocates all the portfolios and appoints ministers outside Cabinet, Associate Ministers and undersecretaries (although it is understood that in recent times Prime Ministers have signalled their preferences for ministers).

The role of ministers reflects the role of collective Cabinet government, and has both collective and individual dimensions. Ministers 'take significant decisions and determine government policy collectively, through the Cabinet decision-making process'.[15] Within that collective context, ministers individually 'exercise statutory functions and powers under legislation within their portfolios' and 'determine both the policy direction and the priorities for their departments'.[16]

Ministers make a wide variety of decisions, of differing character. A lot of decisions relate to administrative governance, steering the direction and operation of the public service, as we explain further below. Some decisions are adjudicative or quasi-judicial, where ministers determine applications relating to individuals and corporate bodies – everything from licensing of medicines, to permission for overseas companies to operate locally, to suspension of deportation of overstayers on humanitarian grounds. As well as being politically accountable for these decisions, ministers' decisions are frequently scrutinised by the courts on judicial review and through other processes.

Some decisions are legislative, where ministers make rules in the form of regulations or other secondary legislation, under powers delegated to them by Parliament. Delegating such law-making to ministers is usually justified for combined reasons of competence and capacity: ministers are better placed than the legislature to settle the complex minutiae of operational, and often technical, rules and can do so in conjunction with affected communities and industries. But there are dangers associated with delegating discretionary law-making powers to ministers, as

[15] Ibid [2.22(c)].
[16] Ibid [2.22(d)] and [2.22(e)].

this leads to rules being made without the usual democratic and quality controls that come with parliamentary law-making.

Two examples are especially emblematic. First, the power under the Public Safety Conservation Act 1932 to make regulations to prohibit any act 'injurious to the public safety' was used during the 1951 waterfront industrial dispute to outlaw striking, censor the press, and prohibit the giving of food and aid to striking workers.[17] Secondly, in the late 1970s and early 1980s, the Muldoon administration promulgated all sorts of regulations under the Economic Stabilisation Act 1948, including a nationwide price and wage freeze.[18] Both examples are now seen as instances of egregious executive law-making and dark moments in New Zealand constitutional history. As a consequence, there is usually caution about granting ministers extensive and unfettered powers to make regulations and other secondary legislation – more so than in the United Kingdom and elsewhere.[19] And Parliament today retains relatively strong oversight of ministerial law-making, through the Regulations Review Committee and associated regulation disallowance procedures.[20]

It is also important to remember that ministers must be MPs and therefore are politicians too. To develop the metaphor running through this book, ministers, like all politicians, speak the language of politics: negotiating, compromising, doing deals, achieving the possible. The perspectives they bring to issues reflect that experience and function. They pursue policies and look for political advantage consistent with their electoral interests which will manifest in an election which is never more than three years away. But ministers also direct and interact with policy advisers in the public service. That is much of how they transact the business of executive government. To do that, they have to be bi-lingual – they need to speak the language of policy as well.

And, finally, a legal point is important. The law often treats the Crown, whether represented by a minister or a department, as having the legal powers and obligations of a natural person. Or sometimes its powers are, instead, referred to as deriving from a 'third source', after

[17] Waterfront Strike Emergency Regulations 1951; M Bassett, *Confrontation' 51* (Wellington, Reed, 1972).

[18] GWR Palmer, 'Muldoon and the Constitution' in M Clark (ed), *Muldoon Revisited* (Wellington, Dunmore Press, 2004) 167.

[19] See generally DR Knight and E Clark, *Regulations Review Committee Digest*, 7th edn (Wellington, New Zealand Centre for Public Law, 2020), especially ch 4.

[20] See Legislation Act 2019, Part 5; *Standing Orders of the House of Representatives 2020*, SOs 326–333.

statute law and the royal prerogative.[21] We consider that approach has much the same effect in substance. The important point is that the residual ability of the Crown or government to act – through ministers and departments – is subject to law and is no greater than anyone else's ability to act unless the law says so.

B. Individual Ministerial Responsibility

The doctrine of individual ministerial responsibility allocates the power of the executive to individual ministers. Collective responsibility then aggregates those powers to Cabinet, as noted above. The doctrine of individual ministerial responsibility is one of the most fundamental and misunderstood principles regulating the distribution of power within New Zealand government. It is supported by the conflicting conventions of public service loyalty, neutrality and provision of free and frank advice. Individual ministerial responsibility and its public service corollaries are reinforced by statute.

The convention of individual ministerial responsibility can be understood as having three elements: responsibility to explain; responsibility to remedy; and culpability.[22] They tell us who is responsible, for what and to whom. The essence of ministerial responsibility, and its function, is to make clear to whom political responsibility is allocated for a matter within the executive branch of government. It is the minister who is responsible for all those matters of policy or operation that occur within their portfolio. Without that, political accountability would be much less clear, as it is in the United States.[23]

A portfolio of responsibility encompasses policy issues and stances, administration of specific legislation and regulations, administration of funding voted by Parliament to that minister's portfolio for specified purposes, direction of the operation of government departments, purchase of 'outputs' (operational or regulatory services or policy advice) from non-departmental organisations with money voted by Parliament for that purpose, and monitoring of the government's 'ownership'

[21] BV Harris 'The "third source" of authority for government action' (1992) 108 Law Quarterly Review 626.

[22] C Turpin, 'Ministerial Responsibility' in J Jowell and D Oliver (eds), *The Changing Constitution*, 2nd edn (Oxford, Clarendon Press, 1989) 55.

[23] MSR Palmer, 'Towards an Economics of Comparative Political Organization' (1995) 11 *Journal of Law, Economics and Organization* 164.

interest in organisations. Individual portfolios of ministers span the entirety of the Crown's activity. And, as a matter of law, the Crown in New Zealand has the rights and powers of a natural person. So a minister may direct any act or omission that is ordinarily within the law, which could even extend to the establishment of a government department.[24]

If there is a gap in the activities of the Crown not covered by a specific portfolio, it is covered by the overarching responsibilities of the Prime Minister. However, ministerial portfolios span the activities of the Crown not the activities of all executive government. As explained further below, Crown entities are part of executive government but not (legally) part of the Crown.

i. Responsibility to Explain and Remedy

The responsibility to explain and remedy involves speaking on behalf of the executive branch of government about matters within the portfolio and fixing them if they go wrong. If something of interest happens (or doesn't happen) within a minister's portfolio of responsibility, it is up to the minister to know or find out about it and explain to the House and the public what happened (or didn't happen) and why. In the language of accountability, this is the rendering of account that lies at the heart of any accountability obligation. As well as explaining, a minister is responsible for remedying problems. If something bad happens (or something good doesn't happen) within a minister's portfolio, it is up to the minister to ensure that it is put right. Because of the responsibility to explain, the minister must explain how they are attempting to do that.

A minister's responsibility to the House is facilitated through the system of oral and written parliamentary questions, select committee questioning of ministers directly and indirectly through their officials, ministerial sponsorship of legislation and ministers' participation in parliamentary debates concerning their portfolios, as we explain in the next chapter. The way in which Parliament examines, comments, debates and decides on an issue is founded fundamentally on an individual minister's responsibility for that issue.

There are limits to a minister's individual responsibility. The law may specify that a minister is not responsible for some matter they otherwise would be. For example, section 54 of the Public Service Act 2020

[24] Legislation Advisory Committee, *Departmental Statutes and Other Legislation Relating to Departments* (Department of Justice, 1988).

insulates decisions of chief executives about individual employees from ministerial direction. Statutory independence is conferred on the powers or functions of particular government officials, such as the Government Statistician, the Solicitor-General, the Commissioner of Police and the Commissioner of Inland Revenue. And statutes can provide for other, more specific, instances of statutory independence. It is important to ensure that political considerations, which must be expected to affect ministerial decisions, do not and are not seen to impinge on these decisions. With these instances of statutory independence, Parliament has decided someone other than a minister should be responsible.

The convention of collective Cabinet responsibility effectively means an individual minister's decision can be overridden by a collective Cabinet decision. If Cabinet makes a decision, even one inconsistent with an individual minister's view, that decision will prevail. But this overriding ability is itself limited by the law. If legislation assigns a statutory power of decision to an individual minister, that minister must be the decision-maker. Decisions that are legally reserved to an individual minister may still be routinely routed through the collective Cabinet decision-making machinery. A minister may – and, as a matter of convention, often must – take into account the views of their Cabinet colleagues as relevant considerations. However, as a matter of administrative law, Cabinet or other ministers must not substitute their own decision for that legally reserved to an individual minister. The Cabinet Manual reflects how this uncomfortable marriage of political reality and legal principle works when it says: 'Cabinet cannot make, or appear to make, a decision that the statute requires a Minister to make.' The Manual spells out the practical requirements that support that requirement.[25]

ii. Culpability

There is a tendency for opposition politicians and commentators, across all administrations, to invoke the doctrine of ministerial responsibility for the proposition that a minister must resign in certain circumstances. But we suggest this misunderstands the nature of the convention. The culpability element of the convention of ministerial responsibility is less functionally important than the allocation of responsibility itself effected by responsibility to explain and remedy.

[25] Cabinet Office, *Cabinet Manual 2017*, [5.34]–[5.36].

Indeed, the circumstances in which a minister usually resigns, or is dismissed, are not necessarily part of the constitutional convention itself – even if there might be some patterns in the circumstances where resignation or dismissal have arisen in the past. A minister in New Zealand does not now usually resign for errors committed only by that minister's officials; vicarious ministerial responsibility has long since waned. Perhaps there is a pattern of ministers being required to step down when there is a prima facie case of personal impropriety to be investigated. And perhaps impropriety that relates closely to a minister's portfolio tends to be more directly connected to resignation. But there are a wide range of circumstances and considerations bearing on what is taken to constitute personal impropriety and whether a minister who steps down returns in the future.

We consider the most salient feature of the culpability element of individual ministerial responsibility is its political nature and connection with confidence. The convention of individual responsibility allocates power to ministers and identifies them as responsible to the House of Representatives for the exercise of that power. That includes the Prime Minister's responsibility for decisions about the removal of ministers. Similarly, the convention of collective responsibility constitutes the power of the Cabinet as a collective entity and makes the Cabinet responsible to the House, depending on the confidence of the House for its very existence. There is no suggestion there are or should be rules about when Parliament must lose its confidence in a Cabinet. The point of the convention is to hand the authority to make that decision to the House, which will decide on a case-by-case basis in the light of the political, economic, social and cultural circumstances of the time. The sanction is allocated to the discretion of an identified decision-maker rather than defined according to a rule.

We consider reason and practice suggest the same is true of the convention of individual ministerial responsibility. The circumstances in which an individual minister resigns are not determined in advance by a rule, but by the Prime Minister, at the time an issue arises. It is no easier to specify in advance the circumstances in which an individual minister should resign than it is to specify when a government collectively should resign. We consider the convention of ministerial responsibility does not extend to prescribing a rule about what sanction is levied on what behaviour. Rather, the proper formulation of the culpability element of the convention is that a minister must resign when they lose the confidence of the Prime Minister. Where there is a coalition Cabinet, in practice, the

Prime Minister will usually make a decision after discussions with the leader of the relevant coalition party.

An individual minister's political stocks rise and fall with their performance. Sometimes, a minister's mistakes can affect the political stocks of the government as a whole. During the nine-year Clark administration, from 1999 to 2008, 10 ministers were dismissed, stood down or resigned. Three were cleared by investigations and reinstated. Two were not reinstated, having each been cleared of one accusation but suffering other embarrassments. Five were not cleared and not reinstated. During the nine-year Key/English administration from 2008 to 2017, eight ministers were dismissed, stood down or resigned from at least one portfolio. Three were cleared by investigations and reinstated. Five were not cleared and not reinstated.

IV. PUBLIC SERVICE

While ministers and Cabinet are firmly in charge of directing executive government, it is the public service and state sector agencies which they direct. Public servants, or officials, led by departmental chief executives, are responsible for the day-to-day operation of government, in accordance with ministerial direction and priorities.[26] These duties include supporting ministers with free-and-frank advice, developing policy and strategy, implementing policies and decisions made by ministers, and monitoring governmental activities within their domains.[27]

Ongoing reform has been a feature of institutional arrangements in the public sector. The first big reform era for the public service began in 1912, when political neutrality and merit-based appointments became key organising principles following the report of the Hunt Royal Commission and the passage of the Public Service Act 1912.[28] The second big reform was in 1986–1989 with the passage of the State-Owned Enterprises Act 1986, the State Sector Act 1988 and the Public Finance Act 1989. Permanent heads of departments became chief executives, leading a slimmed down public service for fixed terms with the rhetoric of managerial autonomy. There have been a series of

[26] Cabinet Office, *Cabinet Manual 2017*, [3.7].
[27] Ibid [3.9].
[28] Hunt Royal Commission, 'The civil service in New Zealand' (4 September 1912).

attempts to tweak the State Sector Act 1988. The most thorough-going recent reform of the legislation came with the Public Service Act 2020 which emphasised and enabled the collective interests and working of government more explicitly. Time will tell whether the reality will match the reform.

The machinery of executive government can be drawn in different ways. In a formal sense, the government distinguishes between three concentric circles of government organisation:[29]

- The core 'public service' is composed of more than 30 public service departments and departmental agencies which are, legally, part of the Crown. Their employees are public servants. The size of the public service has varied over time, being around 70,000 (permanent) public servants in 1986,[30] down to around 36,000 in 1993, and rising again to around 54,000 in 2019.[31]
- The 'state services' are composed of: the public service as above; other government departments of the Crown (such as the Police and New Zealand Defence Force); four categories of Crown entity; and other public organisations and companies.
- The widest category, the 'state sector', is composed of: the state services as above; Parliamentary organisations and offices of Parliament; tertiary education institutions; State-Owned Enterprises (SOEs); and Mixed Ownership Model Companies.

Today, public servants speak the languages of policy and management. Policy advisors are trained and experienced in the discipline of policy analysis. They formulate general objectives, identify issues, analyse options and make recommendations for generic policy and legislative reform. This is a deductive, abstract perspective which emphasises empirical social science data rather than anecdotes and looks to the future rather than the past. But, since the management reforms of the 1980s, senior managers in the public service are often better versed in the discipline of management than policy. They emphasise systems and procedures and focus on efficiency and outputs. We tend to think that the language of management has been rather too loudly spoken, at the expense of the language of policy, in recent years.

[29] Cabinet Office, *Cabinet Manual 2017*, [3.3]–[3.5].
[30] State Services Commission, '100 Years of Public Service' (April 2013) 22.
[31] State Services Commission, 'Workforce Data' (2019).

A. Departments

The primary units of the apolitical executive are *government departments*. Departments can be created simply by a Cabinet decision and being formally added to a schedule to the Public Service Act 2020 by Order in Council. Some are explicitly called 'departments' and others (frequently with significant policy functions) are called 'ministries'. In law, they are all departments of the Crown, which is one legal entity. As clarified by legislation in 2013, public servants acting in pursuance of their legal duties, functions and powers, in good faith, are immune from personal civil liability.[32] In reality, especially since the reforms of the 1980s, each department has tended to operate separately, under separate chief executives, unless otherwise directed by Cabinet, the minister or the chief executive. A public servant transferring from one department to another changes their employer. The culture of departments can be very different and does not necessarily include a spirit of collaboration or service across organisational boundaries.

Chief executives lead government departments and channel the key relationship of their departments with ministers. Broadly, they are charged with, and responsible to their minister, for working collectively across public service agencies; responding to the collective interests of government; stewardship of the department; performance of functions and duties as required by the minister and legislation; providing free-and-frank advice to their minister; the integrity and conduct of their employees; and the efficient and economical delivery of their goods and services.[33] This relationship between chief executive and minister often now tends to be coloured by managerialism.[34] Ministers identify desired outcomes and commission chief executives – and, through them, their departments – to deliver the outputs needed to achieve them, as we explain in more detail below. Chief executives are appointed to head departments for fixed terms (usually of five years, with the possibility of extension). They are appointed by the Public Service Commissioner.

The Public Service Commissioner (formerly the State Service Commissioner) oversees the sector as a whole and exercises a number of independent powers in relation to these organisations. The position of

[32] Public Service Act 2020, s 104; formerly State Sector Act 1988, s 86.

[33] Public Service Act 2020, s 52; Cabinet Office, *Cabinet Manual 2017*, [3.11].

[34] J Boston and J Halligan, 'Political Management and New Political Governance' in H Bakvis and MD Jarvis (eds), *From New Public Management to New Political Governance* (Montreal, McGill-Queen's University Press, 2012) 204.

Public Service Commissioner is usually filled by a senior and experienced career public servant appointed by the Governor-General in Council on the advice of the Prime Minister. Importantly, they appoint chief executives of departments. They are also responsible for promoting transparent accountability and standards of integrity and conduct across the sector. If necessary, they have independent statutory powers of inspection and investigation. As chief executive of the Public Service Commission (formerly the State Services Commission), the Commissioner provides advice to the Minister of State Services on the machinery of government.

The Commissioner almost always appoints chief executives after conducting an advertising and interview process which includes consultation with the relevant minister. This is an important manifestation of the principle that appointments in the public service are based on merit, which is one of the five public service principles in section 12 of the Public Service Act 2020. In 2018, the Commissioner twice used an alternative transfer procedure under the Act, rather than advertising. One of those processes, which transferred five existing male chief executives to new positions, was not generally seen as constructive. The gender diversity of chief executives has since increased markedly, and at the time of writing is equally split between men and women. In addition to appointing chief executives, the Commissioner also formally reviews their performance and decides whether they should be reappointed.

B. Conventional Public Service Duties

The constitutional position of the New Zealand public service is best understood in terms of three conventions that are corollaries to the convention of ministerial responsibility: loyalty, neutrality and the requirement to provide free and frank advice. The last of these, which derives from the first two, is significant enough that we consider it should replace the outdated corollary of public servants' anonymity. Together these principles are now part of constitutional convention and the basis on which the Public Service Act 2020 is premised.

i. Duty of Loyalty

The public service must be loyal to the government of the day. Public servants must carry out their duties competently and to the best of their ability, as the minister directs. This is what gives the doctrine of individual ministerial responsibility much of its power; public servants have to do what ministers say. This completes the chain of democratic accountability of the executive, which runs from the electorate to the House of Representatives, to Cabinet, to individual ministers and to the public service.

A public servant is an emanation of the minister. For example, even when giving advice to a select committee, the constitutional accountabilities require public servants' advice to go through the minister. Public Service Commission guidelines provide that officials appearing before select committees do so 'in support of Ministerial accountability', are 'ultimately answerable to the Minister of the agency' and have 'an obligation to manage risks and spring no surprises on the Minister'.[35]

The law can and does provide for exceptions to public servants' duty of loyalty. For example, section 54 of the Public Service Act 2020 requires chief executives to make decisions independently in relation to individual public servants' employment. And particular public servants have significant statutory responsibilities legally required to be exercised independently of ministers. These are functions into which Parliament has decided there is good reason why politics should not intrude. There are a number of examples of this, including independent law enforcement and constitutional functions of the Solicitor-General, Commissioner of Police, Commissioner of Inland Revenue and Government Statistician.

ii. Political Neutrality

The most important countervailing force to the duty of loyalty to the minister, other than laws to the contrary, is political neutrality. Political neutrality is just as important as the duty of loyalty in both theory and practice. But the two combine to form a peculiar sort of 'partisan neutrality' which can be as uncomfortable in practice as it sounds in theory.[36] A public servant has to discharge the same standard of loyalty to a current minister and government as they would, and would be seen to, discharge to future governments. The public servant has to do what the minister says, within the law and appropriations, unless it impinges on the public servant's ability to be trusted by a future minister of a different political persuasion. For example, a public servant should strive to fulfil requests by a minister but should not work for a political party, even at the request of the minister, because a future minister of a different party may then have difficulty trusting the public servant.

[35] State Services Commission, 'Officials and Select Committees' (August 2007) 5.

[36] R Shepherd, 'Is the Age of Civil Service Neutrality Over?' (1987) 65 *Public Administration* 69.

This requirement of political neutrality has been a key feature of New Zealand's constitutional system since 1912, including in the principle that appointments of public servants are based on merit. It is taken very seriously in practice. Since 2013, the legislation governing the public service has explicitly recognised the importance of the purpose of political neutrality. The Public Service Commission stresses that the requirement public servants be apolitical when carrying out their duties, functions and powers is 'an established constitutional convention in New Zealand' and 'underpins the continuing employment status of State servants' enabling them 'to provide consistent services (including policy development) for the government of the day'.[37]

One group of public servants who are excepted from political neutrality are political advisors in ministers' offices, who are appointed specifically because they are not politically neutral. Until recently, their position was unsatisfactorily vague. Since 2017, they have been governed by a code of conduct, which provides that ministerial staff are expected to meet the same standards of integrity and conduct as other state services staff and to comply with policies and procedures issued by their employing department, except in respect of political neutrality.[38] Though the advice they offer may have a political element, it must still be robust and complete.

The shift to MMP in 1993–1996 directly affected public servants. There has always been significant pressure on senior public servants in their interactions with the political process. But in an FPP environment, the bipolar political spectrum was simply divided in two. It was clear the direction political opposition would come from.

In an MMP environment, governing parties face competition and attack from a variety of points on the political spectrum. Ministers became alert to the threat of political attacks from any perspective and more sensitive to the possibility of political embarrassment from disclosure of advice from public servants. Combined with the more publicly identifiable role of public servants under the state sector reforms, political sensitivity to public servant statements, advice and decisions increased appreciably from around 1998. Opposition parties saw opportunities to attack governing parties through their public servants. Government ministers have had incentives to seek to control more closely public

[37] State Services Commission, 'Political Neutrality Guidance' (April 2010) 1.

[38] State Services Commission, 'Code of Conduct for Ministerial Staff' (September 2017); State Services Commission, 'Acting in the Spirit of Service' (September 2017).

servant actions, advice and decisions. Some ministers have even criticised public servants publicly themselves.

This has raised concerns about politicisation of the public service. In 1999, the chief executive of the Department of Work and Income, Christine Rankin, became the target of political attack by opposition Labour MPs for corporate excess. She fell out with the incoming Labour minister. Unlike the faceless public servants of yesteryear, she took legal proceedings in the Employment Court against the State Services Commissioner. The Minister, State Services Commissioner and Chief Executive of the Department of the Prime Minister and Cabinet gave evidence about their views of her performance and personal attributes. The challenge was dismissed, but this was an extreme case of tensions between ministers and public servants playing out publicly and without the anonymity traditionally expected of public servants.

Internally, during the 2000s, there was a growing increase in responsiveness, and sometimes perhaps over-responsiveness, by public servants to the political concerns of ministers. There was also a tendency to appoint senior public servants, including chief executives, for their management ability rather than their subject matter expertise or ability to give free and frank advice about substantive matters. We consider these trends started under the Shipley administration in 1998, continued under the Clark government from 1999 to 2008, and levelled off under the Key and Ardern administrations. Since 2016, there have been welcome signs of leadership from the Public Service Commission and DPMC to uphold the political neutrality of public servants and their duty to give ministers free and frank advice. The Public Service Act 2020 enshrines political neutrality as the first of five public service principles.

iii. Free and Frank Advice

Traditionally, public servants have been expected to be free and frank in their advice to ministers, which means they should give full advice and should speak frankly in doing so. That should make for better government decision-making. A minister is not required to accept a public servant's advice. Ministers govern, not public servants. But public servants must provide ministers with their best advice. Ministers must receive and consider the best advice available, and they are then responsible for their decisions.

The provision of free and frank advice by public servants is expected by the better ministers and is the proud product of the better public servants. Since 2013, the capacity to offer free and frank advice to successive governments has been explicitly identified in legislation as a principal responsibility of public service chief executives. But our perception is that the freeness and frankness of policy advice declined from the late 1990s. Much of New Zealand departmental activities are operational. Increased responsiveness to what ministers wanted with regard to management of the operations of government was both necessary and legitimate. But policy advice is different. If policy managers are overly responsive to what ministers want – telling them only what ministers want to hear – policy advice and government decision-making is diminished in quality.

Research into the frankness of policy advice from the public service has found evidence that blunt, wide-ranging advice has been offered less easily in the mid-2000s than previously.[39] Nicola White concluded in 2007, based on qualitative interviews, that written documents tended to stick to a safe middle ground, and delicate or difficult issues tended to be dealt with orally. White considered that avoiding the 'front page of the Dominion test' – a common reference to significant unwanted publicity – was becoming a public service norm equal in status to 'no surprises for the minister'.[40] There may have been an effect on attraction and retention of senior policy staff.

The need to maintain the provision of free and frank advice to (or between or by) ministers is explicitly provided as a reason for withholding official information, under section 9(2)(g)(i) of the Official Information Act 1982. It may be outweighed by other considerations which render it desirable, in the public interest, to make that information available. The enforcement of the official information regime has lain primarily in the hands of the Ombudsman, to whom complaints can be directed. Successive Ombudsmen have taken an admirably strict view of what is necessary to withhold from the public to maintain a convention, in the interests of freedom of information. But the rest of the system of government has struggled to cope with the political implications of releasing free and frank advice publicly. The result has been tension between departments and ministers' offices, some pulling of policy punches and non-compliance with the Official Information Act.

There is no doubt that fear of untimely disclosure of information under the Act can lead to undesirable behaviour by both officials and

[39] N White, *Free and Frank* (Wellington, Institute of Policy Studies, 2007) 271.

[40] The Dominion, now called the Dominion Post, is the morning daily paper in Wellington.

ministers. Officials may give advice orally rather than in writing or in 'draft' or be pressured not to give advice at all when it is warranted. If only oral advice is given, it may never be discovered and is likely to be less coherent and less cogent than if it were in writing. Ministers may refuse to receive or note written advice or, more perniciously, demand that it be withdrawn or rewritten in a particular way.

There have been welcome developments. First, in 2018 the Ombudsman issued new principles-based guidance, which distinguishes between four different phases of advice to ministers, and suggests advice will be more likely to require protection from disclosure at the early stages.[41] Hopefully, the Ombudsman's guidance will lead to better compliance with the Official Information Act. Secondly, in 2018 the chief executive of DPMC and the Chief Ombudsman published a joint article that expressed commitment to free and frank advice and offered more certainty as to the Office of the Ombudsman's treatment of official information requests for such advice.[42] Thirdly, in 2019, the State Services Commissioner issued guidance about the need for public servants to give free and frank advice, 'as central to our system of government'.[43] It includes guidance that advice should be honest and clear, 'delivers any hard truths in the most constructive way possible' and that '[t]he convention also means ensuring the advice is understood, which may include repeating the advice if necessary'.[44] Fourthly, the commitment to the public service providing free and frank advice to ministers is reflected in the Cabinet Manual and in formal expectations for chief executives. The 2017 Cabinet Manual states ministers have 'a duty to give fair consideration and due weight to free and frank advice provided by the public service'.[45] Finally, the recently enacted Public Service Act 2020 explicitly includes free and frank advice as one of five public service principles.

iv. Anonymity

The anonymity of public servants used to be identified as a third corollary to individual ministerial responsibility, related to the duties of loyalty and political neutrality. According to Westminster theory, public servants

[41] Office of the Ombudsman, 'The OIA and the public policy making process' (Office of the Ombudsman, March 2018).

[42] A Kibblewhite and P Boshier, 'Free and Frank Advice and the Official Information Act' (2018) 14(2) *Policy Quarterly* 3.

[43] State Services Commission, 'Acting in the Spirit of Service' (2019).

[44] Ibid 2.

[45] Cabinet Office, *Cabinet Manual 2017*, [3.8].

did not speak publicly themselves, even to the point of not answering criticism. Rather, ministers spoke publicly and defended public servants, if attacked, in the course of exercising ministerial responsibility. There was good reason behind this. If public servants were grey and faceless, they were at less risk of generating an independent public profile in the media. Such a profile carries an inherent risk of the official being separated from the minister's views or expressing other views – something which can easily lead to questions about the official's loyalty or political neutrality.

But the anonymity of senior public servants, particularly chief executives, is no more. It can no longer be said to be part of a constitutional convention in New Zealand. No doubt some of the contextual reasons for that are changes in societal expectations of transparency, accountability and responsiveness in the age of the internet. There was obvious unfairness in visiting vicarious responsibility on a minister for problems to which they did not contribute or were even aware. And the state sector reforms and the advent of MMP have produced pressures and accountability mechanisms on chief executives that militate against facelessness. The public-facing role of the Director-General of Health during the coronavirus pandemic was a good example of that. But, even apart from these developments, the Official Information Act has contributed directly to the public identification of public servants.

V. WIDER STATE SECTOR

While the departments of the Crown all constitute one juristic entity, Crown entities and other organisations in the 'wider state sector' have separate legal personality. Each is a legally separate entity with (usually) a chief executive and a board established by its own Act. Their employees are not public servants, though they share many of the same obligations by legislative requirement. Crown entities have greater insulation from direction by ministers than do public servants in government departments.

A Crown entity is subject to different sets of accountability arrangements provided by the Crown Entities Act 2004:

- *Crown agents* are the closest to the Crown. Their board members can be dismissed by the responsible minister entirely at the minister's discretion and they must give effect to government policy when directed by the responsible minister. These include institutions such as the Accident Compensation Corporation and the New Zealand Transport Authority.

- *Autonomous Crown entities* are at some distance from the Crown. Their board members can only be dismissed by the responsible minister, for any reason that in the minister's opinion justifies removal. They must have regard to government policy when directed by the responsible minister. These include the Guardians of New Zealand Superannuation and the New Zealand Symphony Orchestra.
- *Independent Crown entities* are the most independent from the Crown. Their board members can only be dismissed 'for just cause' by the Governor-General on advice of the responsible minister given after consultation with the Attorney-General. They are not subject to government policy. The Commerce Commission, Electoral Commission, Financial Markets Authority, Health and Disability Commissioner, Human Rights Commission and the Law Commission are examples of independent Crown entities.
- *Crown entity companies* are also defined to be Crown entities as well as being incorporated under the Companies Act 1993.

School boards of trustees (elected by the parents of school children) and tertiary education institutions are also Crown entities with their own accountability arrangements.

There are a variety of other largely independent entities subject to their own public-sector accountability regimes. The creation of SOEs in 1986 was the first step in the 1980s reform of New Zealand's public sector. The commercial functions of government were separated out into separate legal entities. SOEs are formed as companies, under ordinary company law, and subjected to an additional public-sector accountability framework by the State-Owned Enterprises Act 1986. SOEs are directed to be successful businesses, especially being profitable and efficient, acting as a good employer and exhibiting a sense of social responsibility. They are subject to the Official Information Act 1982 and the complaints jurisdiction of the Ombudsmen as well as to a public-sector accountability system of planning and reporting involving shareholding ministers and the House of Representatives. A number of SOEs were subsequently privatised in the early 1990s, in order to pay down government debt. And, in 2012, four SOEs were partly privatised as Mixed Ownership Model companies, which is a hybrid between full state-ownership and full privatisation, where ministers maintain at least 51 per cent ownership on behalf of the Crown. The SOE model has proved a stable organisational form for commercial functions in government ownership.

VI. PUBLIC FINANCE AND MANAGERIALISM

The reforms of the late 1980s were intended to introduce a sea change in attitudes within the public service. Those parts of the public service thought to operate commercial activities were transferred to SOEs. The State Sector Act 1988 sought to introduce more efficiency incentives into the stultified centralised bureaucracy of the core public service. The rhetoric of the reforms explained that this provided the opportunity for managers, not ministers, to manage their employees and other resources.[46] Chief executives would be freed up to do that which was efficient.

Our impression is that the management of operational functions of public service departments is now appreciably more efficient than it was before the reforms. The reform of the relevant law did not quite match its rhetoric, though. Legally, and as a matter of constitutional convention, ministers continue to be able to direct chief executives in relation to policy, management and operations. Chief executives' legal powers over the management and operation of departments are not legally excepted from their duty of loyalty to their minister, despite the 1980s rhetoric of empowering managers to manage. The generic exception from ministerial direction in section 54 of the Public Service Act 2020 is confined to employment matters relating to individual public servants. Ministers, and Cabinet, still have the legal power to direct chief executives in relation to the operation of their departments. But, at least initially, rhetoric was reality. The late 1980s and early 1990s saw an increase in private sector corporate team-building techniques, leadership styles and bonus pay arrangements introduced to the public sector.

The effect of public finance on government behaviour remains underappreciated. Much of what ministers, chief executives, individual public service managers and public servants do is constrained and channelled by how much money they have to do it. In reality, the public finance and public management regime is one of the most significant influences on the power of executive government in any nation. Parliament's control over the executive's budget and the power to tax is fundamental to a Westminster system of government, including New Zealand's.

[46] J Boston and others, *Public Management* (Auckland, Oxford University Press, 1996).

The budget takes the form of estimates of expenditure presented by the executive to Parliament every year in the form of an appropriation bill, as explained in Chapter 6. The second reading of an appropriation bill, which goes to the essence of the bill, is so fundamental to a government's programme it constitutes an automatic vote of confidence.

The Public Finance Act 1989 put all government finances onto an accrual accounting basis, measured against generally accepted accounting practice, professionally and independently defined. So, expenditure must be accounted for when a commitment to spend money is made rather than when the money is actually spent. This makes it difficult to hide or escape the real financial consequences of decisions.

Modern managerial accounting separately identifies 'inputs', 'outputs' and 'outcomes'. These are injected into planning and reporting processes in order to provide key indicators for accountability for both ministers and public servants. Ministers are responsible for outcomes and contract with chief executives for the delivery of certain outcomes. Chief executives and their departments determine the inputs that should be commissioned in order to efficiently and effectively deliver the required outputs.

The Act involves a cascade of financial delegations, reporting and accountability from Parliament, to Cabinet, to ministers, to the public service. The application of the usual public finance regime is modified for non-executive officers of Parliament, to recognise their different constitutional accountabilities. It is reflected in the format of the annual Appropriation Bills and the Act's reporting requirements on all individual government departments, other government entities and the annual financial statements of government as a whole.

The Act was premised on the fundamental Westminster principles of the executive proposing, and Parliament determining, the government's budget. Relatively unnoticed in 2005, though, Parliament repealed by summary process the requirement of the Constitution Act 1986 that any bill for the appropriation of public money must be recommended by the Crown.[47] Instead, Standing Orders provide for executive government to have a financial veto over any bill which it considers would have more than a minor impact on the government's fiscal aggregates.

The Fiscal Responsibility Act 1994 represented a further, constitutionally novel, attempt to solidify norms of fiscal restraint into government

[47] MSR Palmer, 'New Zealand Constitutional Culture' (2007) 22 *New Zealand Universities Law Review* 565, 594–96.

behaviour. Its provisions, now in an amended Public Finance Act 1989, require governments to pursue their policy objectives in accordance with the principles 'of responsible fiscal management' set out in section 26G. These principles concern debt reduction; maintenance of net worth; prudent management of fiscal risks; specified revenue and fiscal strategy objectives, and effective and efficient management of Crown resources. The government is explicitly allowed to depart from the principles of responsible fiscal management provided the departure is temporary and the Minister of Finance states the reasons for the departure, the intended approach to return to the principles, and how long they expect the departure to take. The legislation also contains a detailed reporting regime for fiscal strategy, fiscal position and periodic economic and fiscal updates, prepared independently by the Treasury. This approach to fiscal restraint has become accepted by both major parties which have led governments since then. The fiscal responsibility provisions, along with the rest of the public sector financial management regime effected by the Act, represent a direct constitutional constraint on government.

New Zealand's reforms to its public finance regime in the 1980s and 1990s were world-leading. Deriving from a combination of accounting and economic theory, the reforms subjected the public sector to similar accounting standards as the private sector, in the interests of transparency and accountability. The comprehensive accounting and reporting regimes applying to departments, Crown entities and other public sector organisations make it difficult to hide corruption. Much of the rest of the world has caught up to New Zealand's public finance regime.

Another significant leap seems now to be in the process of being taken. For several years the Treasury has mused about measuring economic success in terms of a broader set of objectives and measures than only financial and economic.[48] In the 2018 budget, the Minister of Finance, Grant Robertson, announced the traditional financial capital dimension of the budget process would be broadened to add natural capital, human capital and social capital together with financial and physical capital.[49] The first Well-Being Budget, in 2019, was formulated on the basis of five inter-generational well-being budget priorities agreed by Cabinet: taking mental health seriously; improving child well-being; supporting Māori and Pasifika aspirations; building a productive nation; and

[48] Treasury, 'Working Towards High Living Standards for New Zealanders' (New Zealand Treasury Paper 11/02, May 2011).

[49] G Robertson, 'Budget 2018' (New Zealand Government, 14 December 2017), 7 and 9.

transforming the economy.[50] This was reinforced by the requirement of the Child Poverty Act 2018 for government to report on progress towards child poverty targets. The 2020 budget was somewhat diverted by the huge economic and social shocks associated with fighting the coronavirus pandemic. The 2021 Well-Being budget is dedicated to 'securing our recovery' from the economic consequences of the pandemic, with some attention given to climate change, child poverty and housing affordability.[51]

New Zealand's traditional public sector financial management system has succeeded in ensuring government financial policies and effects are coherently and consistently reported and, therefore, formulated. It will be interesting to see if the wellbeing financial reforms have a similarly transformative effect sustained over successive administrations. If so, it would represent further significant constitutional change of a sort which is often not recognised as constitutional.

VII. CONCLUSION

MMP has meant that the executive branch of government is often controlled by more than one political party. But it is still the executive which is the most active branch of government, formulating and reformulating public policy and legislative proposals, operating the mechanisms of government and defending its record of so doing. It is relatively streamlined and efficient, compared to other versions of Westminster government and other forms of democratic government. And much of the rest of New Zealand's constitution can be seen as a system of checks and balances on the power of the executive.

FURTHER READING

Cabinet Office, *Cabinet Manual 2017*.

McLeay, E, *The Cabinet and Political Power in New Zealand* (Auckland, Oxford University Press, 1995).

Palmer, G, 'The Cabinet, the Prime Minister and the Constitution: the Constitutional Background to Cabinet' (2006) 4 *New Zealand Journal of Public and International Law* 1.

[50] G Robertson, 'The Wellbeing Budget 2019' (New Zealand Government, 30 May 2019).

[51] New Zealand Government, 'Wellbeing Budget 2021: Budget at a Glance' (20 May 2021).

Palmer, MSR, 'What is New Zealand's Constitution and Who Interprets It? Constitutional Realism and the Importance of Public Office-holders' (2006) 17 *Public Law Review* 133.

Quentin-Baxter, A, and McLean, J, *This Realm of New Zealand: The Sovereign, the Governor-General and the Crown* (Auckland, Auckland University Press, 2017).

6

Parliament

Introduction – Parliamentary Institutions – Parliamentary Functions – Parliamentary Dynamics under MMP – Legislative Supremacy and Its Limits – Conclusion

I. INTRODUCTION

PARLIAMENT, COMPRISING THE House of Representatives and the Sovereign, is New Zealand's legislature. Parliament makes the primary form of law, known as statutes, legislation or Acts of Parliament. The House of Representatives also provides governments, holds the government to account, and is a forum for the party-political contest. Parliamentary procedures and institutions reflect these functions, including the particularly well-developed role of select committees. In theory, Parliament is entirely unconstrained in its power to make laws. In reality, there are political incentives that constrain what laws it makes. Parliament is significantly directed by the executive, which springs from and is responsible to Parliament. New Zealand's Parliament used to be described as an 'executive paradise' because of the extent of executive domination.[1] However, the mixed-member-proportional (MMP) electoral system MMP has lessened the executive's ability to get its own way in the people's assembly.

II. PARLIAMENTARY INSTITUTIONS

A. Parliament

New Zealand has a unicameral legislature, unlike its Westminster counterpart: there is only one house. The legislature, Parliament, is made up

[1] L Zines, *Constitutional Change in the Commonwealth* (Cambridge, Cambridge University Press, 1991) 47.

of the House of Representatives together with the Sovereign in right of New Zealand (Constitution Act 1986, s 14). When first established as a colonial legislature, Parliament was originally styled as the General Assembly and included the Governor (later Governor-General), House of Representatives and the Legislative Council.[2] The Legislative Council was abolished in 1950, as explained in Chapter 4.

B. House of Representatives

The House of Representatives is recognised in the Constitution Act 1986, including its historic genesis under the New Zealand Constitution Act 1852 (Imp) (s 10(2)) and its continuing existence since, even when Parliament is dissolved (s 10(1) and (3)). The House is made up of 120 elected members of Parliament (sometimes more). Electoral mechanics revolve around three-yearly elections under MMP, as explained in Chapter 4.

The House sits as an assembly of all MPs in a debating chamber within Parliament Buildings in the capital city, Wellington. The chamber is modelled on the House of Commons in Britain: a tight horseshoe with the Prime Minister and Leader of the Opposition sitting face-to-face across the chamber table from each other. Unlike the House of Commons, there is room for all MPs and each has a desk. While other seating is allocated as best as possible to reflect the multi-party government and politics that come with MMP, the physical layout has not been altered from its adversarial, two-party origins under FPP.[3]

The proceedings of the House reflect its Westminster origins as a debating chamber, governed by standing orders adopted by the House itself.[4] Standing orders provide primary – indeed, constitutional – rules regulating how the House goes about its business.[5] Standing orders apply unless suspended or amended by the House, and may be supplemented by temporary sessional orders. The Speaker chairs proceedings and is charged with enforcing standing orders.[6] The House's usual sitting days are Tuesday, Wednesday and Thursday, for around 30 weeks of the year

[2] New Zealand Constitution Act 1852 (Imp) 15 & 16 Vict c 72, s 32.

[3] N Roberts, 'Grand Designs' (2009) 61 *Political Science* 75, 84.

[4] Standing Orders of the House of Representatives 2020.

[5] See generally M Harris and D Wilson (eds), *McGee: Parliamentary Practice in New Zealand*, 4th edn (Auckland, Oratia Books, 2017) 12.

[6] The role of the Speaker is discussed in section II.C.

(the Business Committee recommends an annual sitting programme). The House sits from 2–6 pm and 7–10 pm on Tuesdays and Wednesdays and 2–5 pm on Thursdays but this schedule changes from time to time. Sittings may be extended if the Business Committee or the House agrees to extended sitting hours for any particular day.

An urgency motion may also be passed, requiring the House to complete particular business, in precedence to all other House business, before it adjourns. Transacting business under urgency sometimes proves to be controversial.[7] Provision was made for extended sitting hours in 2011, designed, in part, to provide the government with alternative, less controversial, means of progressing business than under urgency.

The House's principal agenda is the Order Paper, prepared each sitting day by the Clerk. It sets out the business for the House, such as the bills and other matters set down for debate, in the order the government wishes them to be progressed on any particular sitting day. Different ordering arrangements apply for private, local and members' bills, which take precedence over government business for one day every two sitting weeks. On any sitting day, before progressing the business on the Order Paper, the House deals with general business and other transactional matters not on the Order Paper. Questions for oral answer are the most high-profile form of general business, with questions being put to ministers for about an hour each sitting day, soon after 2 pm. General debates – either a weekly general debate or, with the Speaker's permission, a debate on a matter of urgent public importance – follow.

The standard way the House addresses its business is by motion, debate and vote. In other words, an MP moves that a particular proposition be considered, MPs debate the proposition by making speeches, and the House then votes on that proposition (or amendments to that proposition). Thus, we can see the character of the House and Parliament as a debating chamber. Standing Orders regulate the various aspects of this process, including the nature and form of motions, the length and formats of debates, the manner of speaking and content of speeches, and the means of voting.

Consistent with democratic principle, a proposition ('question') is passed by the House if a simple majority vote in favour of the question. The exception to this rule is where the provisions reserved under the Electoral Act 1993 require an alternative procedure about the 'manner

[7] C Geiringer and others, *What's the Hurry?* (Wellington, Victoria University Press, 2011).

and form' for amending some legislation, such as a 75 per cent majority vote. Tied votes are lost; the Speaker does not have a casting vote.

C. Speaker and Clerk

Two key officeholders are charged with ensuring the smooth and effective operation of the House: the Speaker of the House of Representatives; and the Clerk of the House of Representatives.

The Speaker is the House's most senior officeholder and is ranked third in the country's order of precedence, after only the Governor-General and the Prime Minister. Elected by the House, the Speaker plays a pivotal role in the House's day-to-day business, charged with regulating its affairs in an impartial manner. The Speaker is supported in this role by a Deputy Speaker and up to two Assistant Speakers. The Speaker has three main roles: constitutional, arbitral and administrative.[8] The Speaker is expected to act in a non-partisan manner, despite continuing to serve as an MP and remaining a member of a political party. The Speaker continues to have an ordinary vote, which is usually cast by their party when a party vote is called for. Unlike some other legislatures, the Speaker does not now have a casting vote.

In the *constitutional* role, the Speaker has a variety of functions ranging from ceremonial formalities to essential practices that protect and maintain the foundations of New Zealand's liberal democracy. The Speaker represents and embodies the House as an institution. The Speaker speaks for, and reports matters to, the Sovereign on behalf of elected representatives (hence the historical derivation of the title of 'Speaker'). The Speaker lays claim to, and zealously protects, the House's right to freedom of speech in debate. In this role, the Speaker intervenes in court proceedings if it appears that the House's proceedings, parliamentary privilege or MPs' freedoms are threatened or called into question.[9] Intervening and representing the House maintains the constitutional dialogue between the legislature and the other branches of government. It also ensures that the inherent powers of the House are

[8] P Roycroft, 'The Ayes Have It' (2017) 15 *New Zealand Journal of Public and International Law* 353, 356.

[9] Bill of Rights 1688 (UK) 1 Will and Mar c 2, art 9. See eg *Attorney-General v Taylor* [2017] NZCA 215, [2017] 3 NZLR 24, [110]–[146].

protected and the principle of comity between the branches of government is recognised and upheld.

In the *arbitral* role, the Speaker chairs the sittings of the House and keeps order during proceedings and debates in the House's main debating chamber. As part of this role, the Speaker adjudicates on the meaning and application of the House's Standing Orders (delivering binding Speakers' Rulings). The Speaker may sanction MPs for breaches of Standing Orders. The Speaker also chairs important House committees, including the Business Committee (which deals with House business and governance).

Finally, the Speaker performs an important *administrative* role in relation to parliamentary departments and offices, as well as being responsible for administrative functions in relation to the House itself. The Speaker acts as the responsible minister for parliamentary departments including, for example, the Parliamentary Service and the Office of the Clerk, as well as the officers of Parliament: the Auditor-General, the Ombudsmen and the Parliamentary Commissioner for the Environment. The Speaker's responsibilities for these departments and offices vary but generally the Speaker has a role in securing funding and rendering account for matters which may arise. The Speaker chairs the Parliamentary Service Commission, a statutory committee charged with advising the Speaker on the nature of services to be provided to the House, MPs and parties, and on the appropriate funding for this administrative support. The Speaker also acts as landlord for the parliamentary estate. In doing so, the Speaker is the effective gatekeeper to the forecourt, grounds and gardens of Parliament – an important site in New Zealand for civic expression and protest.

The Clerk of the House of Representatives is the senior permanent officer of the House, appointed by the Governor-General on the advice of the Speaker. They undertake various statutory and administrative functions necessary for the House to function efficiently and effectively. While the House is sitting, the Clerk sits in front of the Speaker's chair and, amongst other things, provides procedural advice to the Speaker and other MPs. Maintaining records of the proceedings of the House is a key responsibility of the Clerk. They are required to note the proceedings of the House and its committees (recording motions, decisions and other items of business, published as the *Journals of the House of Representatives*) and maintain an official report of the proceedings (verbatim reports of debates, known as *Hansard*). The Clerk also leads an office which provides operational support for the House and its committees. The Clerk has also assumed responsibility for some other functions such as public broadcasting of proceedings and public outreach on behalf of the House.

D. Committees

The House relies on a range of committees to provide a more convenient means of considering certain business.

The House frequently reconstitutes itself as a committee, known as the *Committee of the Whole House*. About a quarter of the House's sitting time is spent sitting as a Committee of the Whole mainly for detailed scrutiny of bills but also for some debates related to appropriations and departmental reviews. When sitting as a committee, the House continues to sit in the main debating chamber and all MPs are entitled to speak as members of the committee, but the Committee of the Whole House is chaired by a chairperson, not the Speaker. While most of the House's rules about order continue to apply, the Committee of the Whole House is subject to some different rules for MPs' contributions – usually shorter and more frequent speeches.

The House enlists *select committees* to undertake much of its detailed work, especially close scrutiny of legislative business, accountability of departments and officials, and consultative processes. A select committee is a group of MPs appointed by the House to consider legislative or other parliamentary business and report back. Typically, only non-executive MPs sit and vote in select committees, except for select committees with special mandates like the Privileges Committee. Although there is no formal provision in the standing orders that prevents ministers from sitting and voting in a select committee, it is now conventional that Cabinet ministers do not do so. Select committees may be established, disestablished or have their focus changed by resolution of the House. Currently, there are 12 subject-specific select committees, which consider bills and other business within their subject area as we discuss further below.[10]

In addition to the subject select committees, there are a number of specific committees with special mandates which assist the House in the performance of its general functions.

The Business Committee is an all-party committee, chaired by the Speaker, designed to assist in managing parliamentary business.[11] It has

[10] Standing Orders of the House of Representatives 2020, SOs 185 and 189.
[11] Standing Orders of the House of Representatives 2020, SO 77.

the power to determine a wide range of matters including sitting times, the size and membership of select committees, arrangements for parliamentary business, time allocations for debates, allocation and order of oral questions and any other matters delegated to it under the standing orders. The Business Committee operates on the basis of unanimity or 'near unanimity'. Its determinations take effect once circulated and apply despite any standing order to the contrary. It therefore has a very powerful and influential role in shaping the deliberations of the House, freeing up the need for the House itself to debate many administrative matters.

The Privileges Committee is charged with investigating matters of 'privilege'.[12] Privileges are powers and immunities established over time that enable the House to function as a legislature. Key privileges include the freedom of speech and debate, exclusive control over proceedings, reportage and parliamentary precincts, any questions about qualification to sit and vote in the House, regulation of parliamentary conduct and the power to punish for contempt of Parliament.[13] Potential issues regarding matters of privilege are usually raised with the Speaker, who determines whether a matter of privilege is involved; matters can also be raised by motion or petition. The Privileges Committee considers and determines matters of privilege, and then issues a report to the House with its findings and recommendations. The House retains the power to finally determine whether a breach of privilege or contempt has occurred and any sanctions, such as imprisonment, fines, censure, or suspension from the House. Findings of contempt are relatively rare in recent years.[14]

The Regulations Review Committee is a standing select committee charged with scrutinising secondary legislation and the delegation of legislative functions by Parliament.[15] Established in the mid-1980s, it has traditionally been chaired by an Opposition MP. The committee scrutinises regulations and other specified forms of secondary legislation; it looks at all new regulations, as well as hearing complaints about regulations and other instruments. When reviewing regulations and other

[12] Standing Orders of the House of Representatives 2020, SO 409.

[13] See generally Harris and Wilson (n 5), chs 44–47.

[14] See eg Privileges Committee, 'Question of privilege on the action taken by TVNZ in relation to its chief executive, following evidence he gave to the Finance and Expenditure Committee' (interim report, April 2006) (fine imposed and apology required for adverse treatment of select committee witness).

[15] DR Knight and E Clark, *Regulations Review Committee Digest*, 7th edn (Wellington, New Zealand Centre for Public Law, 2020).

instruments, the committee assesses them against grounds mandated in Standing Orders.[16] The grounds focus the Committee on norms of good law-making – rather than the policy of the regulations, with the latter remaining a matter for the executive. The Committee also scrutinises regulation-making powers in bills and will often advise that such powers be sharpened or circumscribed in order to avoid the misuse of delegated legislative power. The Committee occasionally investigates other matters in relation to delegated legislation and issues occasional reports on thematic topics. The Committee only has the power of report and recommendation but its expert and apolitical character means its views are usually taken seriously by ministers and other select committees. Regulations or draft bills are often amended to take account of its recommendations. The committee also has a special role in triggering the House's disallowance procedures in relation to regulations, although this nuclear option is rarely used.

There are also (a) a committee responsible for reviewing Standing Orders; (b) a committee for the appointment and oversight of officers of Parliament; (c) a committee responsible for receiving and coordinating considerations of petitions; and (d) a statutorily-constituted Intelligence and Security committee responsible for overseeing intelligence agencies.

III. PARLIAMENTARY FUNCTIONS

The functions of Parliament and the House of Representatives are not formally defined but they revolve around making law and holding the executive government to account. They include:[17]

- making law through the passing of statutes;
- providing government;
- controlling public finances;
- holding the executive to account;

[16] Standing Orders of the House of Representatives 2020, SOs 326(1) and 327(2); key grounds include inconsistency with general objects and intentions of empowering legislation, undue trespass on personal rights and liberties, unmandated retrospectivity or exclusion of review, unusual or unexpected use of powers, inappropriate use relative to parliamentary enactment, and failure to conduct prescribed consultation.

[17] GWR Palmer, 'What is Parliament for?' [2011] *New Zealand Law Journal* 378; D McGee, *Parliamentary Practice in New Zealand*, 3rd edn (Wellington, Dunmore Publishing Ltd, 2005) 1–5.

- acting as a forum for party political contest; and
- being a symbol of representative government.

A. Law-making

Parliament's primary function is law-making, with one product: an Act of Parliament. This function is explicitly recognised in section 15(1) of the Constitution Act 1986. Primary legislation requires the sanction of both of Parliament's constituent bodies. First, the House of Representatives signals its agreement to proposed laws by passing a 'bill' through its legislative stages and presenting it to the Governor-General for assent. Secondly, the Governor-General signals agreement by signing a copy of the bill so presented. On rare occasions, the Sovereign herself discharges the assent function.

The House is responsible for the generation of proposals for laws, as bills are introduced and passed through its legislative process. Considering and deliberating on bills is one main function of the House and occupies about half its time. The most common type of bill is a government bill, which is a bill addressing a matter of public policy introduced by a minister. Although law-making power lies with the House and Parliament, the reality is that the vast majority of bills that are passed into law are initiated, developed and shaped by the executive. Proposing new legislation and navigating them through the House's processes is one of the privileges of executive government and one of the most tangible ways an administration can give effect to its political priorities. Importantly, the need to seek approval from Parliament in order to undertake many of the activities of executive government – to obtain legal authorisation to do things – is one way to ensure parliamentary control of government.

There are other types of bills:[18]

- a member's bill: addressing a matter of public policy, drawn from a ballot when the legislative programme allows, and introduced by a member who is not a minister;
- a local bill: affecting a particular locality only, promoted by a local authority;
- a private bill: for the particular interest or benefit of a person or body of persons, promoted by that person or body.

[18] Standing Orders of the House of Representatives 2020, SO 257.

The usual process of preparing a government bill involves a minister taking a paper to a Cabinet committee. If agreed to by Cabinet, the sponsoring department then issues drafting instructions to the Parliamentary Counsel Office. Despite its name, the Parliamentary Counsel Office is an instrument of the Crown and a separate statutory office responsible to the Attorney-General, under the Legislation Act 2012. They are essentially the executive's professional legislative drafters and have relatively tight control over the drafting, printing, publication and revision of government legislation (except for tax legislation, which is drafted by Inland Revenue officials).

The House, through its standing orders and customs, determines the requirements that must be met. The general rule is that a bill must be 'read' three times, as well as considered by a select committee and committee of the whole House. However, standing orders allow expedited procedures for a few types of bills and the House may expedite the procedure for individual bills through 'urgency' or the suspension of standing orders. The standard progress of a bill through Parliament is illustrated in Figure 6.1.

Figure 6.1 Progress of a Bill through Parliament

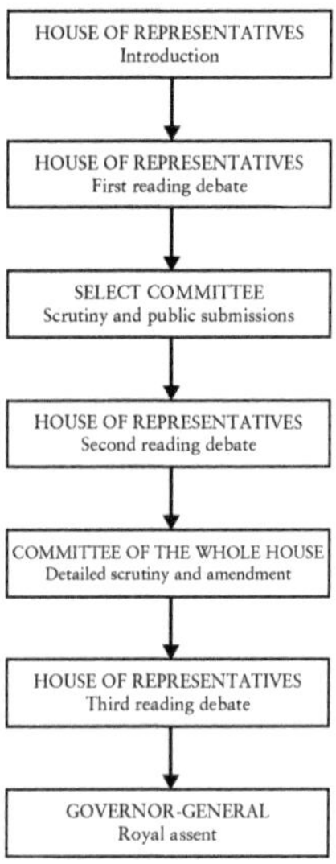

A bill is introduced and usually receives its first reading a few days later. The first reading debate allows the House to debate the general policy of the bill.

Following the first reading, bills are usually referred to a select committee for close scrutiny and consideration. About 95 per cent of bills are referred to select committee for consideration, public consultation and report – a practice systemised since 1979.[19] There are two main exceptions: (a) appropriation and imprest supply bills; and (b) bills progressed under urgency (unless the urgency motion allows for select committee consideration). Select committees examine bills to determine whether they should be passed, along with proposing amendments. When examining a bill, committees usually invite written submissions from the public and hear oral evidence from submitters. While the committee is not bound by any of the public's submissions, the process allows for direct public engagement with the legislative process, allowing the House to assess the level of support. Committees also receive briefings and advice from departmental officials, other advisors appointed by the committee, and, occasionally, the minister in charge of the bill. Ultimately, the committee issues a report, with marked up proposed amendments to the bill, along with a commentary on the key issues. Minority views, if any, can also be recorded in the committee's report. Select committee reports on bills are recommendatory only. The House decides whether to proceed with a bill at its second reading in light of the committee's report and considers whether to adopt the committee's recommended amendments.

Select committee scrutiny of bills is a cherished part of the New Zealand legislative process because it provides members of the public with some ability to influence the shape of laws. Yet its significance should not be overstated. First, like other participatory processes, the legislative process can suffer from apathy, fatigue, capture, logistical overload and so forth. Some bills attract little attention; others generate overwhelming numbers of submissions, making it difficult to give members of the public a meaningful opportunity for input. Submissions from people or bodies with special expertise or interests are often impactful but the small size of democracy in New Zealand means it is easy for some to dominate the participatory process. Secondly, while select committee scrutiny is treated seriously by opposition and backbench government MPs, the process is not free from executive influence. Government MPs often promote the executive's position and may not agree to recommended amendments unless they find favour with the sponsoring minister. If the government has a majority on the select committee, the views of the government on

[19] Harris and Wilson (n 5) 405.

the bill will usually dominate the committee's report. And, if departmental officials are advising a select committee, they do so on behalf of their minister. Thirdly, sometimes substantial or important amendments will be made to a bill during the Committee of the Whole stage, by a supplementary order paper (SOP). These changes need not be subject to public consultation or select committee scrutiny.

Next is the second reading debate, where the House considers the report of the select committee and votes to accept any amendments the committee has proposed. The House then engages in its own detailed scrutiny of the wording of the bill, reconstituting itself as a Committee of the Whole House. It considers and votes on any amendments proposed by SOPs or ad hoc amendments lodged with the Clerk during the debate. The third reading debate allows the House to debate the finalised bill and its underlying policy for a final time. Once a bill receives its third reading, it is treated as being passed by the House.

The Clerk of the House then directs that a copy of the bill be printed and authenticates two copies for royal assent, confirming that the printed bill represents the bill as passed by the House. The Clerk facilitates the presentation of the bill to the Governor-General, in conjunction with the Prime Minister (or other senior minister) and Attorney-General. The Prime Minister formally advises the Governor-General to assent to the bill and the Attorney-General confirms that there is no reason why the bill should not receive royal assent. The Governor-General signals agreement by signing a copy of the bill, as a token of royal assent in accordance with section 16 of the Constitution Act 1986.[20]

B. Provider of Government

It falls to the House of Representatives to determine who should be appointed Prime Minister and lead executive government, as we outlined in Chapter 4. The Prime Minister and their ministry must be drawn from, and maintain the confidence of, the House. So, the House is the 'provider' of a government and election of government in New Zealand is 'indirect'.[21] The Prime Minister and their ministry are usually appointed before the House first meets following an election. The House's formal

[20] On the reserve power to refuse royal assent, see ch 3.

[21] Harris and Wilson (n 5) 3–4; PA Joseph, *Joseph on Constitutional and Administrative Law*, 5th edn (Wellington, Thomson Reuters, 2021) 366–67.

involvement in effect merely ratifies the appointment of Prime Minister, as and when a confidence vote subsequently arises. In contrast, as also explained in Chapter 4, a vote in the House may formally trigger the death of a government and the need for a new political settlement.

C. Control of Public Finances

Parliament and the House control the purse strings of government. Following Westminster constitutional understandings, parliamentary approval, through an Act of Parliament, is required for the government to raise money through taxes, borrow money or spend money (Constitution Act 1986, section 22).[22] The requirement for parliamentary consent to expenditure of public money helps ensure a government's programme has a democratic mandate. This need for financial authorisation is intertwined with the other ways in which Parliament ensures a government and its activities have a mandate through expressing confidence (constitutional entitlement to govern) and passing laws (legal authorisation to undertake certain activities).

Proposed income and expenditure are subjected to scrutiny in the course of the budget process. The centrepiece of the budget process is the passage of an appropriation bill which sets out proposed government expenditure for the forthcoming year commencing on 1 July. The budget statement, usually given around May, is the Minister of Finance's speech moving the second reading of the main appropriation bill. The appropriation bill itself summarises the proposed expenditure by vote, type or scope of activity, amount and period (if a multi-year appropriation). A 'vote' is a way of describing an appropriation or a group of appropriations that is the responsibility of a designated minister or ministers and is usually administered by one department. For example, Vote Building and Construction is the joint responsibility of the Minister for Building and Construction, the Minister of Housing, and the Minister for Greater Christchurch Regeneration, and is administered by the Ministry of Business, Innovation and Employment. The appropriation bill is supported by more detailed information, including the *Estimates of Appropriations for the Government of New Zealand*, a

[22] See also Public Finance Act 1989, ss 4(1) and 5 (legislative approval required to 'incur expenses or capital expenditure' and 'spend public money' respectively).

comprehensive document which is subjected to detailed scrutiny by the House and its committees.

The appropriation bill is usually passed in August or September after parliamentary scrutiny has been completed, and within three or four months of the original budget statement. Because the government's programme of spending is often finally approved by Parliament after the financial year has started, the government seeks interim authority to spend money in an imprest supply bill, passed on an expedited basis before the commencement of the new financial year. During the course of the financial year, the authorisation of expenditure is usually updated by a further imprest supply bill and supplementary appropriation bill. There is also provision for unauthorised spending to be validated retrospectively by a specific appropriation bill.

Taxation must also be authorised by Parliament by or under legislation. If a tax is levied without this specific authority, the courts may order the tax be returned to taxpayers.[23] Taxes include direct taxes such as income tax, indirect taxes such as Goods and Services Tax and duties which are compulsory, for public purposes, and are legally enforceable. Fees and levies, where the amount charged is no more than the reasonable cost of providing the service to which they related, do not constitute a tax and are treated differently.[24]

D. Holding the Executive to Account

The House operates as an essential check on executive government, holding ministers responsible and calling them to account for the matters within their ministerial portfolios. Responsible government is built on the notion that the government is responsible and accountable to the Parliament and thus the people. The dynamics of the democratic assembly and the processes specifically developed by the House enable it to scrutinise and control the actions of executive government. There are numerous processes where MPs are able to directly require ministers to answer for actions either they or government officials within their portfolios have taken.

[23] *Waikato Regional Airport Ltd v Attorney-General* [2002] 3 NZLR 433 (CA).

[24] Regulations Review Committee, 'Inquiry into the Constitutional Principles to Apply when Parliament Empowers the Crown to Charge Fees by Regulation' [1989] I *Appendix to the Journals of the House of Representatives* 16C.

i. Ministerial Questions

The most prominent form of accountability is 'question time'. Question time enables MPs to ask ministers oral questions about government policy, the performance of public agencies, the management of their portfolios, and their conduct in office. A dozen oral questions are scheduled each sitting day, with the questions being allocated to parties in proportion to each party's number of non-executive members, in a rotating pattern determined by the Business Committee. MPs may direct their question to any minister on any matter within that minister's portfolio responsibility. There is no set schedule of ministers taking questions. Customarily the Prime Minister is available for questions on Tuesdays and Wednesday but rarely on Thursdays. If a minister is absent, another minister answers the question on their behalf. Questions are lodged with the Office of the Clerk and are vetted by the Clerk and Speaker to ensure they are in order and within a minister's portfolio responsibility.

Ministers are given notice of the primary question they will be asked, usually by 11 am, giving their departments and offices a short period to prepare information, statistics and strategy before the House sits at 2 pm. Ministers are not, however, given any notice of what 'supplementary' questions MPs may ask to elucidate further information. The only restriction on supplementary questions is that they must relate to the primary question or its answer in some way. Ministers must 'address' the question, unless doing so would be contrary to the public interest. Whether they have done so is for the Speaker to judge.[25]

Question time, by its very nature, is one of the more adversarial political accountability mechanisms in the House. These exchanges are often heated and dynamic. Wide-ranging questions demand immediate answers and justification from ministers but also allow for political points-scoring from both sides of the House. Despite sometimes theatrical overtones, question time is fundamental to our representative democracy: elected MPs can hold ministers to account on the public's behalf. It is an important constitutional tool used to obtain information and bring to light perceived abuses of governmental power or influence.[26] Consistent poor ministerial performance in question time can raise doubts about the future of a minister or even, more broadly, a government.

[25] Standing Orders of the House of Representatives 2020, SO 396.

[26] See K Coghill and A Hunt, 'Reforming Question Time' (1998) 12 *Legislative Studies* 36, 36.

MPs may also ask ministers written questions. Written questions are less publicised than oral questions and the question time process. But they serve an important, if more technical, function. They can be used to seek more detailed answers that require a higher-level of departmental involvement and research. The information obtained through the written questions process is often used by the Opposition to gather statistics on unreported or little-known actions, processes or policies within government, with a view to raising matters later in question time, debates or in the media. There is no restriction on the number of written questions that may be lodged. Like oral questions, written questions are vetted to ensure they are in order and within a minister's portfolio responsibility. A minister has six working days to answer each written question. The Office of the Clerk displays all questions and their answers online for the public to see.

ii. Debates

The House has a number of opportunities for MPs to debate the performance of executive government generally or in relation to specific matters which arise. First, a general debate – on 'miscellaneous business' – is held every Wednesday after question time and is a wide-ranging political debate. It gives MPs an opportunity to speak on current issues facing the government and the electorate. Opposition MPs use this opportunity for a 'free for all' style debate to criticise and scrutinise the government's actions without the general topic restrictions imposed during question time. While often unscripted and sometimes petty, the general debate is a useful accountability mechanism in that it gives MPs the freedom to speak very broadly and subject a range of ministerial actions to scrutiny from the media and the public.

Secondly, MPs may request a debate on matters urgently arising, if any event involving ministerial responsibility has recently arisen. The Speaker considers whether the event justifies interrupting the House's usual programme of business and rules on whether debate on it should be allowed. Typically, such a debate is only occasionally allowed.

Thirdly, the performance of the government is often raised in debates ancillary to other business. For example, debates on bills may provide opposition MPs with the opportunity to debate the executive's priorities and its stewardship of government generally.

iii. Select Committees

Holding the executive to account is a key function of the select committee system, though scrutiny of bills is the most well-known function and most of the workload of subject select committees.[27] While scrutiny of bills is primarily a component of the law-making process, it also allows select committees to hold the executive to account for its priorities, policy formulation and legislative design.

Select committees also hold the executive to account when undertaking other tasks, including financial reviews, inquiries, considering petitions and even reviewing international treaties. As well as examining proposed spending as part of the budget process, select committees also review the performance of government departments, Crown entities and state-owned enterprises in the previous financial year. This review follows the presentation of the department's or entity's annual report in September and October. The Finance and Expenditure Committee allocates the reports to the subject select committees to conduct the annual review. The annual review is a wide-ranging opportunity for examination and accountability, given it may raise any aspect of a department or entity's activities over the previous year. Chief executives, senior officials and sometimes the responsible minister are questioned by the committee. The committee issues a report, which is subsequently debated in the House.

Select committees can initiate inquiries or receive briefings on any matter within their subject area. This allows select committees to investigate any aspect of the executive's activities. While briefings on a wide range of issues are commonplace, formal inquiries are relatively infrequent, despite the hope that this means of accountability would be reinvigorated under MMP. More routinely, select committees consider and report on petitions (including a recently established Petitions committee, which oversees and coordinates the petitions process). Some petitions may raise matters relating to executive governance and priorities, allowing further parliamentary scrutiny of the executive. And most international treaties are presented to the House and examined by a select committee before they are ratified or finally agreed to by the executive, as we explain in Chapter 11. Following consideration of a petition

[27] Harris and Wilson (n 5) 280.

or examination of an international treaty, the select committee issues a report. These reports may be debated by the House although, in practice, such debates are uncommon.

E. Forum for Party-Political Contest

The House provides a forum for party-political contest: a crucible for parties to battle over policies, priorities, performance and personalities. Sometimes people speak dismissively about these political exchanges, especially when they turn ugly. But party politics fuels the engine of democracy and the House has an essential role in supporting these contests. The party-political contest that occurs throughout the electoral cycle represents the competition of different policy and ideological positions for popular support, using emotion and personality as well as rational debate.

F. Symbol of Representative Government

Parliament stands as an emblem of representative government, providing a link between the community and those governing. It ensures that everyone has a stake in the business of government and the state. This representative function provides the community with the opportunity to participate through the election of their delegate. Other processes give the public the ability to inject their priorities and preferences into the deliberative mix or to raise grievances. As the elective part of Parliament, the House gives voice to the people. The quid pro quo of this voice and representation is (deemed) consent to be bound by the actions of Parliament and subject to the laws it passes.

IV. PARLIAMENTARY DYNAMICS UNDER MMP

MMP has had a significant impact on Parliament's internal business and functions, over and above its role in regulating the election of representatives to sit in the House. The underlying theme of party proportionality is central to MMP and is reflected in several processes and institutions within the House. For example:

- membership in the House is roughly proportional to the party vote gained by each political party;

- membership of select committees is determined on a proportional basis;
- the calling of MPs in debates reflects the proportion of seats the party holds in the House; and
- oral questions are allocated to parties on the strength of their membership in the House.

Political parties have become more prominent in the House's proceedings under MMP, as discussed in Chapter 4. Emblematic of this change was the adoption of party votes in 1996, in a suite of reforms updating standing orders and House proceedings when MMP was adopted. Most contested questions in the House are resolved by a party vote, which is usually called for after an initial voice vote. Under a party vote, the Clerk calls on each party – by name, in descending order of size – to cast their votes. A representative of each party, usually the whip, announces the number of votes for or against the question on behalf of their MPs. A party usually votes as a block but, in rare cases, it may cast a split vote – with votes for and against a question. Personal votes, where individual MPs cast their vote in the traditional Westminster fashion by passing into the Ayes or Noes lobby and declaring their vote to a teller, remain possible. But they are restricted to circumstances where personal voting might be material such as issues of conscience. Each party decides what issues its MPs will be allowed to vote according to their consciences.

MMP has, to a fair degree, moderated executive power within the House. Under FPP, an executive comprised of a single political party was able to dominate the House's proceedings and business, leading to the characterisation of the system as an 'elective dictatorship' or 'unbridled power'. In contrast, MMP has fragmented executive government, through the need for multiple political parties to form the executive, and opened up the day-to-day business of government to more contestation.[28] Governing parties must bargain and negotiate with each other – or, sometimes, with opposition parties – in order to progress their agenda. The policy and law-making process under MMP is more dynamic because it requires political support for initiatives to be negotiated outside one single party. Some of that support may be secured through governance arrangements like coalition or confidence-and-supply agreements, either explicitly for particular initiatives or generically through agreed policy

[28] R Malone, *Rebalancing the Constitution* (Wellington, Institute of Policy Studies, 2008).

processes. Other support may need to be negotiated on a case-by-case basis, often requiring concessions or compromise by government parties.

While these negotiations take place away from the House itself, they shape the House's proceedings. The government's agenda is no longer a fait accompli and smooth progression cannot be guaranteed. The progress of a bill might reflect the extent of support and time needed to garner that support. For example, a government bill might be delayed until the executive is assured of the necessary numbers to pass it but, once secured, the bill then proceeds quickly through the various stages in the House. Alternatively, sometimes support (or opposition) parties agree to support the introduction of a bill in the House and public consultation via select committee; once returned to the House, the bill may sit on the order paper for some time until further negotiations are completed and support for further progression is secured.

Overall, the move to MMP has generated a more dynamic political environment within the House and the law-making process than was the case with the typical two-party majoritarian settings under FPP.

V. LEGISLATIVE SUPREMACY AND ITS LIMITS

We return to Parliament's primary function: law-making. The end product – an Act of Parliament – is at the top of the hierarchy of New Zealand laws. Acts of Parliament override *any* other law to the contrary. This includes all regulations, the common law, exercises of the royal prerogative, or any earlier Act that is, in its terms, inconsistent with the later Act. That Acts of Parliament are 'supreme' is an ultimate, but legally controversial, fact of New Zealand's constitutional system. This principle is known interchangeably as legislative supremacy or parliamentary sovereignty. We prefer the former because it is the legislation that is supreme, rather than the institution which creates it. It reflects New Zealand's longstanding attachment to representative democracy. The will of the people is transferred to their representatives in Parliament, and Parliament can enact that will in any way whatsoever. Or so the theory goes.

Expressed to its fullest, legislative supremacy means, first, a duly enacted Act of Parliament overrides any other law to the contrary and, secondly, that there is no law that Parliament cannot make, unmake or amend.[29] It captures ideas about the hierarchy of law (the force of

[29] AV Dicey, *Introduction to the Study of the Law of the Constitution*, 10th edn (London, MacMillan, 1959) 39–40.

primary legislation) and the omnipotence of the legislature (the unrestrained authority of Parliament to make laws). The principle of legislative supremacy colours much of New Zealand's constitutional settings and practice. The principle is expressed in the continuing recognition of Parliament's 'full power to make laws' (Constitution Act 1986, section 15(1)).[30] But the force of the principle is a product of years of historical contest between civic institutions and actors, in both the United Kingdom and New Zealand. And, even with its predominance, the nature and potential limits on the principle are still subjected to continuing debate, albeit that the debate is largely theoretical and rarely arises for determination in practice.

A. Origins

The origins of legislative supremacy lie in British political history.[31] The principle arose from a lengthy power struggle by the British Parliaments, predominantly over the seventeenth century, to wrest power from successive monarchs and to subject the royal prerogative to parliamentary control. There was no singular and explicit grant of supreme legislative power to the Parliament. Rather, Parliament's omnipotence arose from its accumulation of authority in a series of such assertions, such as the Bill of Rights of 1688.

With the assertion of British sovereignty in New Zealand following the signing of te Tiriti o Waitangi / the Treaty of Waitangi in 1840, the British established civic institutions mimicking their homeland. The settlers instinctively relied on British constitutional traditions and conventions, as they understood them in the mid-nineteenth century. A colonial Parliament was established and granted limited law-making power by its British parent. Legislative authority was originally conferred on the Legislative Council, made up of the Governor and appointed members.[32] With the establishment of representative government in 1854, legislative authority was vested in the General Assembly, then comprising the Governor, an appointed Legislative Council and an elected House of Representatives, under the New Zealand Constitution Act 1852 (Imp).

[30] See also Senior Courts Act 2016, s 3(2) ('continuing commitment' to the sovereignty of Parliament and the rule of law).

[31] See P Leyland, *The Constitution of the United Kingdom* (Oxford, Hart Publishing, 2007) 9–13; J Alder, *Constitutional and Administrative Law* (London, Palgrave, 2007) ch 4.

[32] New South Wales Continuance Act 1840 (UK) 3 & 4 Vict c 62; Letters Patent issued on 16 November 1840, known as The New Zealand Charter.

Interestingly, that followed passage of an 1846 New Zealand Constitution Act which never came into force, due to representations by colonists and Governor Grey.

After the 1852 Act was passed by the British Parliament, with provisions for elections, New Zealand had its own struggle for responsible government, with the House of Representatives insisting to the Governor that his advisors be drawn from its ranks and be responsible to it. Law-making authority was initially restricted to matters which were necessary for the peace, order and good government of the colony.[33] Particular limits were also imposed. The legislature was prohibited from making laws that were repugnant to the laws of England or laws which purported to have extra-territorial effect. Any laws passed outside the scope of authority granted to the colonial legislature were subject to invalidation by the courts. In addition, laws passed were subject to scrutiny by British ministers. Assent for bills could be withheld, reserved (referred by the Governor to the Sovereign for assent) or refused; Acts could be disallowed.[34] These powers were a means by which Britain exercised some control over New Zealand legislation. From 1856 to 1910, 13 bills were blocked in these ways.[35]

These restrictions were refined and narrowed over time, as the British Parliament gradually modified the terms on which the law-making power was granted to the colonial legislature, enlarging the law-making power of New Zealand's Parliament.[36] This eventually culminated in the adoption of the United Kingdom's Statute of Westminster 1931 and the transfer of full authority to amend colonial legislation from the British Parliament to the New Zealand Parliament.[37] New Zealand waited 16 years to pass the Statute of Westminster Application Act 1947, at which time New Zealand also requested authority to amend the 1852 Act itself. The New Zealand Parliament passed the New Zealand Constitution Amendment (Request and Consent) Act 1947 (NZ) and the British Parliament obliged by passing the New Zealand Constitution (Amendment) Act 1947 (UK). This signalled the point at which New Zealand's

[33] New Zealand Constitution Act 1852 (Imp) 15 & 16 Vict c 72, s 18.

[34] JE Martin, 'Refusal of Assent' (2010) 41 *Victoria University of Wellington Law Review* 51.

[35] Ibid 55–56.

[36] New Zealand Constitution (Amendment) Act 1857 (Imp); Colonial Law Validity Act 1865 (UK).

[37] B Harris, 'The Law-Making Power of the New Zealand General Assembly' (1984) 5 *Otago Law Review* 565.

Parliament possessed full authority over the constitutional instruments regulating its law-making authority. The original 'peace, order and good government' and other restrictions on legislative authority were eventually removed by the New Zealand Constitution Amendment Act 1973 (NZ). With the patriation of constitutional instruments under the Constitution Act 1986, legislative authority continues to be expressed in omnipotent terms by section 15(1): 'The Parliament of New Zealand continues to have full power to make laws.'

B. Nature

Professor Dicey's nineteenth century explanation of legislative supremacy is commonly still taken as the leading account:[38]

> Parliament thus defined has … the right to make or unmake any law whatever; and, further, … no person or body is recognised by the law … as having a right to override or set aside the legislation of Parliament.

This explanation was adopted in the landmark constitutional case of *Fitzgerald v Muldoon*.[39] Parliament makes law through the legislative process, whether making a new law or unmaking an existing law. Parliament may unmake law in two ways: (a) expressly, by explicitly providing for the repeal or change of an existing law in legislation; or (b) impliedly, by making a new law that is inconsistent with an existing law. In the case of implied repeal, the courts will usually treat the new law as overriding the existing law to the extent there is an irreconcilable inconsistency.[40]

Read to its fullest extent, the principle of legislative supremacy gives rise to a number of propositions. First, Parliament can legislate, without restriction, on any subject matter.[41] That is, Parliament can make or change *any* law. And any such law must be complied with by other civic actors. 'Any Act of Parliament, or any part of an Act of Parliament, which makes a new law, or repeals or modifies an existing law', as Dicey explained, 'will be obeyed by the courts'.[42] In principle, this could

[38] Dicey (n 29) 39–40.
[39] *Fitzgerald v Muldoon* [1976] 2 NZLR 615 (SC), 622.
[40] *Ellen Street Estates Ltd v Minister of Health* [1934] 1 KB 590 (CA); *Henderson Borough Council v Auckland Regional Authority* [1984] 1 NZLR 16 (CA).
[41] But see below section V.C.
[42] Dicey (n 29) 40.

mean Parliament can make laws requiring all blue-eyed baby boys to be killed – a hypothetical example commonly recited in law schools to capture the breadth of Parliament's law-making power.

Secondly, no other branch of government, entity or body can cancel the provisions of a duly enacted act of Parliament. In other words, under the fullest form of legislative supremacy, neither the courts nor the executive have the power to invalidate, suspend or disapply legislation. A famous example of this was the case of *Fitzgerald v Muldoon*.[43] The Prime Minister, Robert Muldoon, announced in a media statement that compulsory contributions to the national superannuation scheme, operating under the New Zealand Superannuation Act 1974, were to be suspended and contributions were to cease immediately. A civil servant covered by the scheme challenged the announcement, on the basis that the announcement was unlawful under art 1 of the Bill of Rights 1688 ('the pretended power of suspending of laws, or the execution of laws, by regal authority, without consent of Parliament, is illegal'). Wild CJ ruled that the media statement amounted to an 'unequivocal pronouncement that the compulsory requirement for employee deductions and employer contributions were to cease as stated' and thus breached article 1. Adopting Dicey's explanation of parliamentary sovereignty, he said: 'Parliament had made the law' and therefore it followed that 'the law could be amended or suspended only by Parliament or with the authority of Parliament.'[44] Executive suspension of the legislation was declared to be unlawful, although the judge did not grant further relief and left time for Parliament to pass legislation retrospectively dismantling the scheme.

Thirdly, primary legislation trumps the common law. In the event of an irreconcilable conflict between a rule in an Act and the common law, the Act prevails over the common law. Similarly, Parliament may legislate to overturn the effect of a court decision. For example, in *Ngāti Apa* in 2003, the Court of Appeal ruled that, on the law as it then stood, Māori had the ability to apply to the Māori Land Court for a determination as to entitlement to customary ownership of the foreshore and seabed.[45] A year later, the Foreshore and Seabed Act 2004 reversed that decision, providing that no one could own the foreshore or seabed. Subject to the debate outlined below, the courts cannot 'strike down' legislation for

[43] *Fitzgerald v Muldoon* (n 39). See also S Kós, 'Constitutional collision' (2014) 13 *Otago Law Review* 243.

[44] *Fitzgerald v Muldoon* (n 39) 622.

[45] *Attorney-General v Ngāti Apa* [2003] 3 NZLR 643 (CA).

inconsistency with the common law or principles of fundamental justice. Put simply, what Parliament says, goes.

Fourthly, Parliament may change even constitutional rules by ordinary legislation. Formally, there is no hierarchical distinction between ordinary laws and those laws considered constitutional or fundamental. All Acts are treated as having the same status and force, regardless of their subject-matter, and can be changed through ordinary law-making processes. In practice, though, as we explain in Chapter 9, occasionally the courts suggest some laws have greater constitutional significance. Parliament as a sovereign legislature, as de Tocqueville said, is 'at once a legislative *and* constituent assembly'.[46] The corollary of this proposition is that laws are not void and cannot be struck down for unconstitutionality. Similarly, the adoption of statutory human rights protections does not undermine the force of legislative supremacy. The New Zealand Bill of Rights Act 1990 directs that the courts must not invalidate, disapply or treat as impliedly repealed any legislation by reason only of inconsistency with the Bill of Rights Act.

Finally, Parliament cannot, by legislation, bind its successors. Under the older orthodox and fullest form of legislative supremacy, it is not possible to entrench laws or protect them from later amendment – either absolutely or by requiring enhanced law-making procedures.[47] As Parliament's law-making power is absolute, it follows that a future Parliament can change any existing law, regardless of whether the existing law purported to prevent such change. The courts will give effect to the most recent law, consistent with their obligation to obey any law passed by Parliament. So, it is possible to argue that the only restriction on Parliament's law-making authority is that Parliament cannot seek to limit its law-making authority.

These propositions reflect the orthodox expression of legislative supremacy, which treats Parliament as supreme and legally omnipotent to take any course of action it so desires. The force of the principle is firmly embedded in the constitutional culture of New Zealand.[48] We look next at possible glosses and limits on this full-throttled Diceyan version of legislative supremacy.

[46] A de Tocqueville, *Democracy in America* (London, Saunders and Otley, 1835), 169 (emphasis added).

[47] *Ellen Street Estates Ltd v Minister of Health* (n 40). But see later at section V.C.

[48] MSR Palmer, 'New Zealand Constitutional Culture' (2007) 22 *New Zealand Universities Law Review* 565.

C. Possible Limits

Two different types of legal restrictions have been argued to limit Parliament's omnipotent legislative power.

i. Procedural Restrictions: Manner and Form Entrenchment

It is now expected that the courts will enforce 'manner and form' provisions, that is, enhanced procedural requirements beyond the standard obligation that a bill be passed, by a simple majority, through the various stages of the House.[49] The orthodox understanding of legislative supremacy would not contemplate such a restriction; doing so would amount to an impermissible attempt by one parliament to bind its successors and would undermine its perpetual sovereignty. But this form of procedural entrenchment is no longer regarded as legally objectionable.

The only instance of this form of entrenchment in New Zealand is the handful of reserved electoral provisions, identified in Chapter 4, for which a 75 per cent parliamentary majority or simple majority in a public referendum is needed to amend or repeal them.[50] When originally passed the intention was to engender a constitutional convention, rather than an enforceable legal rule, because the then prevailing view was that the latter was not constitutionally possible. By and large, that proved to be the case, as the enhanced procedure has at least assumed conventional force.[51]

The shift in mood about the legal enforceability of manner and form entrenchment can be seen in the Supreme Court's decision in *Ngaronoa v Attorney-General*.[52] In a challenge to legislation disenfranchising prisoners, the Attorney-General conceded in argument that the courts could invalidate legislation not passed in accordance with the entrenchment clause. The Court did not need to resolve that question because it ruled prisoners' voting rights were not protected on the terms of section 268. However, while leaving the point for full argument in later cases, the majority noted that it seemed 'the pendulum has swung in

[49] On the rationale for entrenchment, see NW Barber, 'Why Entrench?' (2016) 14 *International Journal of Constitutional Law* 325.

[50] See ch 4 and E McLeay, *In Search of Consensus* (Wellington, Victoria University Press, 2018).

[51] Royal Commission on the Electoral System, 'Towards a Better Democracy' (December 1986), [9.182].

[52] *Ngaronoa v Attorney-General* [2018] NZSC 123, [2019] 1 NZLR 289.

favour of [legal] enforceability'.[53] This shift in attitude is not attributable to a single legal event. It is a product of a series of factors in the New Zealand experience which have modified constitutional culture and traditions, along with developments in thinking around the world. Judicial openness to quashing improperly passed statutes in jurisdictions with colonial legislatures with limited legislative authority fuelled some of the rethink.[54] So too did an emerging distinction between procedural and substantive restrictions, along with stronger articulation of the cherished role of courts to declare non-compliance with law.[55]

The willingness of courts to enforce entrenched provisions might depend on whether there was widespread support for their adoption – 'practical sanctity', as Lord Cooke described it.[56] Notably, too, Parliament's own procedures for entrenchment now insist that any proposed manner and form provision be passed by the same elevated majority it seeks to impose.[57]

ii. Substantive Restrictions: Inviolable Fundamentals

More controversial is the question of whether there might be some laws which lie beyond the competence of Parliament. In other words, are there some laws that are so egregious or inconsistent with higher order norms that the courts might refuse to apply them? Our view is that the circumstances in which the courts might be called on to disapply legislation are unlikely to arise in New Zealand. Realistically, were they to arise, we would be deep in crisis and our current constitutional traditions and understanding would inevitably require modification in some way.

The debate about the possibility of substantive limits on the law-making authority has been largely extrajudicial and abstract. Lord Cooke was the standard-bearer, especially in the 1980s, for those

[53] Ibid [70] and [159].

[54] See eg *Attorney-General for New South Wales v Trethowan* [1932] AC 526 (PC); *Taylor v Attorney-General of Queensland* (1917) 23 CLR 457; *Bribery Commissioner v Ranasinghe* [1965] AC 172 (PC); *Harris v Minister of the Interior* 1952 (2) SA 428 (AD). See *R v Fineberg* [1968] NZLR 119 (SC) for similar obiter comments.

[55] *Westco-Lagan v Attorney-General* [2001] 1 NZLR 40 (HC), [91]–[95]; *Jackson v Attorney-General* [2006] 1 AC 262 (HL), [81] (Lord Steyn). See also the continuing power under the Declaratory Judgments Act 1908 to grant a declaration about the 'construction or validity of any statute'.

[56] R Cooke, 'Practicalities of a Bill of Rights' in WK Hastings (ed), *FS Dethridge Memorial Addresses 1977–1988* (Wellington, Maritime Law Association of Australia and New Zealand, 1989) 23.

[57] Standing Orders of the House of Representatives 2020, SO 270.

suggesting the law-making power might be limited in this way. In a well-known speech, 'Fundamentals', he pointed to 'two complementary and lawfully unalterable principles', namely, 'the operation of a democratic legislature and the operation of independent courts'.[58] He suggested that if Parliament passed legislation that were to 'undermine either of them to a significant extent', then the courts would be obliged to 'say so' and, if then ignored, to resign.[59] Lord Cooke also raised the possibility that some fundamental human rights might be similarly protected, at a time when rights were not then explicitly recognised in a statutory bill of rights. He argued that the concept of a free democracy must carry with it some limitation on legislative power; in other words, there might be some infringements of human rights that were so grave that 'they will not be recognised as law at all by us'.[60]

These themes, especially the possibility that some common law rights might be inviolable, had been earlier seeded in remarks in judgments that were not essential to their outcome. For example, in *Taylor v New Zealand Poultry Board*, when dismissing a challenge to a regulation requiring people possessing eggs to answer questions about where those eggs came from, Cooke J (later Lord Cooke) said: 'I do not think that literal compulsion, by torture for instance, would be within the lawful powers of Parliament. Some common law rights presumably lie so deep that even Parliament could not override them.'[61] These words have the character of warning shots. The New Zealand courts have shown no enthusiasm for serious deployment of any power to strike down or refuse to enforce legislation.[62] But those warnings persist today. For example, Francis Cooke J in *New Zealand Council of Licensed Firearms Owners Inc v Minister of Police* recently suggested it is 'strongly arguable' Parliament could not override some principles of New Zealand's unwritten constitution such as by abolishing Parliament or the courts.[63]

The objections to judicial power to invalidate or refuse to apply legislation on substantive grounds include concerns that it would be

[58] R Cooke, 'Fundamentals' [1988] *New Zealand Law Journal* 158, 164.

[59] Ibid 164.

[60] Ibid 164.

[61] *Taylor v New Zealand Poultry Board* [1984] 1 NZLR 394 (CA), 398. See also *New Zealand Drivers' Association v New Zealand Road Carriers* [1982] 1 NZLR 374 (CA), 390.

[62] *Westco-Lagan v Attorney-General* (n 55); *Cooper v Attorney-General* [1996] 3 NZLR 480 (HC); *Shaw v Commissioner of Inland Revenue* [1999] 3 NZLR 154 (CA).

[63] *New Zealand Council of Licensed Firearms Owners Inc v Minister of Police* [2020] NZHC 1456, [37]. For similar recent warnings abroad, see *R (Privacy International) v Investigatory Powers Tribunal* [2019] UKSC 22, [2019] 2 WLR 1219 (Lord Carnwath) [119]–[131].

undemocratic and aggregate power to unelected and unaccountable judges. Doubts have also been raised about whether any such redefinition of legislative supremacy is the sole preserve of the courts, absent any contribution from other civil institutions and the community.[64] And New Zealand's system of government has also changed a fair bit since Lord Cooke's article on constitutional fundamentals, including measures to reduce executive domination in Parliament and to better enshrine and protect human rights.

Perhaps this unresolved theoretical debate has more important cultural side-effects, though. It generates inter-branch tension, counselling restraint on the part of both law-makers and judges, and the legal speculation influences constitutional culture. The value of suggested inviolable fundamentals is in their contingency – the potential for their use if New Zealand's constitution comes under extreme stress. This potential reinforces the external and internal pressures which encourage Parliament to use its law-making power carefully. As highlighted throughout this book, democratic politics usually restrains law-making in New Zealand, including through the potential political cost of electoral reaction to heinous laws. Signals from, and dialogue with, other institutions and bodies (including both domestic and international bodies) also encourage legislative modesty. The recent formalisation of judicial declarations of inconsistency under the Bill of Rights Act, which we discuss in Chapter 9, is one form of this dialogue. And, as we also outline in Chapters 7 and 9, the courts employ a range of techniques and methods that soften the impact of legislative power. Whether these restraints on legislative supremacy are sufficient will no doubt be a matter of ongoing constitutional dialogue and debate.

VI. CONCLUSION

Parliament works in tandem with the executive to ensure the democratic operation of government. The House supplies the political leadership of executive government from amongst its members and expresses its confidence (or lack of confidence) in them. And it continues to hold the Prime Minister and their ministry to account on an ongoing basis, interrogating their stewardship in government in a variety of ways. Parliament

[64] T Bingham, 'The Rule of Law and the Sovereignty of Parliament?' (2008) 19 *King's Law Journal* 223.

also sets the main boundaries of government action: through its law-making powers, it sets the parameters of what can be done and whether it is funded.

Legislative supremacy gives Parliament a monopoly over the making and unmaking of primary legislation. New Zealand's legislature has, in theory, acquired omnipotent law-making power. But this power is not exercised to its fullest extent in practice and seems unlikely to be. As we see in the next chapter, it is the function of the courts to interpret the resulting legislation.

FURTHER READING

McLeay, E, *In Search of Consensus: New Zealand's Electoral Act 1956 and its Constitutional Legacy* (Wellington, Victoria University Press, 2018).

Parliament's website (www.parliament.nz).

Harris, M, and Wilson, D (eds), *McGee: Parliamentary Practice in New Zealand*, 4th edn (Auckland, Oratia Books, 2017).

Knight, DR, and Clark, E, *Regulations Review Committee Digest*, 7th edn (Wellington, New Zealand Centre for Public Law, 2020).

Malone, R, *Rebalancing the Constitution: The Challenge of Government Law-Making under MMP* (Wellington, Institute of Policy Studies, 2008).

7

Judiciary

Introduction – Rule of Law and Forms of Law – Judiciary as an Institution – Judicial Independence and Accountability – Conclusion

I. INTRODUCTION

THE JUDICIAL BRANCH of government decides what the law means and how it applies to any particular case brought to court. In doing that, judges make law: the 'common law'. That simple description indicates what is different about the judicial function compared with the legislative and the executive functions. The power of interpreting law, and creating common law, can be significant. But the judiciary's powers are exercised in the specific context of individual cases. The judges do not initiate cases; they judge the cases brought to court. They must give reasons for, and put their names to, each decision. A court's decision is always subject to at least one appeal as of right, and the senior appellate courts are composed of panels of judges. As we saw in the last chapter, court decisions can be overridden by legislation if Parliament chooses.

In this chapter, consistent with our emphasis on function over form, we start with the adjudicative function of judges and the rule of law. We then turn to the judiciary as an institution within New Zealand's constitutional system, including its structure and processes, as well as the daily practice of what judges do. Finally, we canvass aspects of the reality of judicial independence and judicial accountability in New Zealand.

II. THE RULE OF LAW AND FORMS OF LAW

The question 'what is law' is as old as law itself. In simple terms we think of it as publicly stated rules about human behaviour that are enforced by state-imposed sanctions. In reality there is a continuum of sorts. There are many sources of expectations of human behaviour, including those formed and expressed by the evolution of social norms and explicitly demanded by different groups within a society. Here, we look at the different ways the courts determine the nature and meaning of law in the course of adjudication. First, we explain the rule of law as a constitutional principle in New Zealand.

A. The Rule of Law

Whole books have been written about the rule of law without encouraging much consensus about its meaning. This is a world-wide issue and we do not canvass it in depth here. Professor Brian Tamanaha, for example, groups the different rule of law traditions thematically into interrelated conceptions:[1]

Formal conceptions of the rule of law focus on the necessary conditions or precepts for a law and a legal system, without passing judgement on the content of the law generated within the legal system. A thin conception of the rule of law stands for the basic idea that governors, officials and citizens alike should comply with the law. Government under the rule of law therefore means ministers, officials and public bodies must operate through, and within, law when executing their functions. A thicker conception, sometimes called formal legality, contends that laws must be capable of being obeyed by those subject to them. It follows that laws should be publicly promulgated, prospective, certain and stable, and the legal system should ensure there is congruence between laws as enacted and laws as applied. An even thicker conception, combining formal legality and democracy, suggests that the obligation to comply with law arises from actual or implied consent from those subject to those laws. Democracy provides the means by which that consent is proffered. It follows that laws should also be passed through processes which are democratic in nature.

Substantive conceptions of the rule of law focus on the morality of laws passed over-and-above their formal character. In other words, substantive conceptions also condemn laws that fail to respect human or

[1] B Tamanaha, *On the Rule of Law* (Cambridge, Cambridge University Press, 2004). See also T Bingham, *The Rule of Law* (London, Allen Lane, 2010).

fundamental rights. Different substantive conceptions of the rule of law speak differently about the nature of rights that should be respected and which organs of government should primarily be responsible for their observance.

One of us has offered a relatively thin conception of the rule of law based on core elements common to most other accounts that appear to be accepted in New Zealand.[2] This means it is more likely to be widely accepted and can be simply and coherently stated and applied. This conception centres on certainty and freedom from arbitrariness in the law. It involves taking seriously the words of the phrase 'the rule of law' and attempting to hone in on the functional purpose of the rule of law in constitutional design. It marries both text and purpose. It suggests the phrase 'the rule of law' itself indicates there is some distinctly separate or objective meaning to law that is independent of human interests. It is law itself that rules and that *should* rule. In other words, this definition of the rule of law requires that the meaning of a law as it is applied is:

- independent of the interests of those who made the law; and
- independent of the interests of those who apply the law; and
- independent of the interests of those to whom it is applied; and
- independent of the time at which it is applied.

This formulation emphasises that the rule of law is an ideal. It seeks to remove, as far as practical, the influence of the interests of particular human actors.

Ultimately, the meaning of the rule of law continues to be a contested ideal in New Zealand and elsewhere. Some care must therefore be taken when resorting to the rule of law in legal argument or political debate. But, whatever it means, the rule of law is important in New Zealand's constitution as a key constitutional principle, evidenced in part by the number of occasions on which people and institutions say it is important. The Senior Courts Act 2016 contains a provision that states 'nothing in this Act affects New Zealand's continuing commitment to the rule of law and the sovereignty of Parliament'.[3] And the first fundamental obligation of every lawyer in New Zealand, under section 4(a) of the Lawyers and

[2] MSR Palmer, 'Constitutional Dialogue and the Rule of Law' (2017) 47 *Hong Kong Law Journal* 505, 521.

[3] For some controversy about initial proposals not to carry over the reference in reform of court legislation, see J McGrath, 'Final Sitting Speech' (Supreme Court of New Zealand, 6 March 2015).

Conveyancers Act 2006, is to 'uphold the rule of law and facilitate the administration of justice in New Zealand'.

In performing their adjudicative function, judges interpret and apply the law, including these and other statutory provisions. They also develop the common law and recognise tikanga Māori.

B. Statutory Interpretation

i. Judges Determine the Meaning of Legislation

Legislation usually states generic rules and general expectations of behaviour and establishes procedures and institutions to administer and enforce those rules and expectations. Most law in New Zealand is, now, legislation.[4]

The primary function of the judiciary is to interpret and apply law to specific cases where there is a dispute about the result of the application of the law. The parties to the dispute put their arguments to a court which interprets and determines the meaning of the provision in order to apply the law to the specific factual context of the dispute. Interpretation is necessary when there is argument about what a particular statutory word or phrase means or how different statutory provisions reconcile with each other. That might be because of difficulties in the wording used in the statute or because they are being applied to factual circumstances that had not been anticipated by Parliament.

Putting it like this, it is obvious that judges look at the law through a very different prism than do legislators. Legislators formulate general rules governing behaviour. Judges focus on whether the general rules stated in legislation apply or do not apply to a particular situation. They test the general rules by examining their possible meanings in particular circumstances. The court's decision resolves the dispute; it gives the parties an answer. And the conclusion a court reaches about the meaning of a legislative provision also becomes the officially sanctioned meaning – it becomes the law itself. In this way, a court makes law. It can only be changed by a more senior court or by Parliament.

[4] J Burrows, 'Common Law among the Statutes' (2008) 39 *Victoria University of Wellington Law Review* 401.

ii. Purposive Statutory Interpretation

There are a variety of possible ways in which courts can approach the task of interpreting statutes. The current practice in New Zealand is to adopt a purposive interpretation, rather than more literal methods.

For a long time, New Zealand courts, influenced by nineteenth century English courts, used what is known as a 'literal' approach. This involved attending primarily to the 'plain meaning' of the words of the statute, rather than their context, whether or not that led to odd or unjust results. The standard New Zealand text on statutory interpretation, *Burrows and Carter*, gives an example of an English statute which made it an offence to 'impersonate a person entitled to vote'.[5] In 1868, an English court held that did not cover voting in the name of a dead person, because a dead person was not entitled to vote.[6]

The purposive approach to statutory interpretation has long since eclipsed the literal approach in New Zealand. As early as 1851, the Interpretation Ordinance provided that 'the language of every Ordinance shall be construed according to its plain import and, where it is doubtful, according to the purpose thereof'.[7] And, today, New Zealand courts routinely adopt a purposive approach to interpreting statutes.[8] While the court starts with the ordinary meaning of the words of the statute, it reads those words in context in order to give effect to Parliament's purpose in passing it. This is now a well-established interpretative principle, arrived at through constitutional dialogue.

Section 5(j) of the Interpretation Act 1924 said every Act 'shall receive such fair, large, and liberal construction and interpretation as will best ensure the attainment of the object of the Act and of such provision or enactment according to its true intent, meaning, and spirit'. Judges increasingly adopted a purposive interpretation during the twentieth century. In 1990, the Law Commission recommended a bill updating the 1924 Act to reinforce the approach of purposive interpretation by saying: 'The meaning of an enactment is to be ascertained from its text in the light of its purpose and in its context.'[9] Eventually, in 1997, the executive branch introduced the Interpretation Bill which omitted the

[5] R Carter, *Burrows and Carter Statute Law in New Zealand*, 5th edn (Wellington, LexisNexis NZ Ltd, 2015) 217.

[6] *Whiteley v Chappell* (1868) LR 4 QB 147.

[7] Legislative Council, *Interpretation Ordinance* (2 July 1851).

[8] Carter (n 5) 216.

[9] Law Commission, 'A New Interpretation Act' (NZLC R17, 1990) x.

last four words as too 'imprecise' and potentially leading to interpreted meanings that 'might well go beyond the approach of the Courts currently'.[10] The Justice and Law Reform Committee of the House of Representatives endorsed the provision as introduced, which was enacted as section 5(1) of the Interpretation Act 1999. But by this time, the judiciary was well settled in its view that context matters to the meaning of words; the omission of the words 'and context' by Parliament in section 5 made little difference.[11] In 2017, the executive tried again. Cabinet agreed that the Attorney-General David Parker should introduce a Legislation Bill. The resulting Legislation Act 2019 directs that '[t]he meaning of legislation must be ascertained from its text and in the light of its purpose and context' (section 10). Interestingly, by mid-2021, it had still not been brought into force.

The approach taken by the judiciary to statutory interpretation is constitutional, according to our perspective of constitutional realism, because it directly affects the generic exercise of public power in New Zealand. It is one of the most important, but underappreciated, constitutional contributions of the judiciary. And the way the approach has evolved has been through an iterative process of constitutional dialogue between the institutions of government.

The context used by courts in statutory interpretation includes the context of other provisions in the Act, the scheme of the Act and other Acts, as well as the economic, social and cultural context to the passage of the Act. One aspect of context that has been routinely and explicitly consulted since the 1980s is the legislative history of a bill leading to its enactment. Parliamentary debates and select committee reports on bills are commonly referred to by courts. Sometimes, even Cabinet papers or departmental discussion documents might be referred to.[12] Law Commission reports which result in legislation are particularly influential.

There has been debate about the extent to which courts should have regard to parliamentary history in interpreting legislation. In the twenty-first century, the United Kingdom Supreme Court has retreated somewhat in its stated willingness to do this. Lord Steyn expressed concern that the

[10] Interpretation Bill 1997 (90-1) (explanatory note) 3.

[11] See eg *Commerce Commission v Fonterra Co-operative Group Ltd* [2007] NZSC 36, [2007] 3 NZLR 767, [22].

[12] *Taylor v Attorney-General* [2017] NZCA 215, [2017] 3 NZLR 24, [132]–[135].

practice might lead legislators to tailor their parliamentary speeches in order to influence the meaning of a bill through judicial interpretation when they cannot influence it through parliamentary means.[13] No doubt that opportunity exists but most New Zealand legislators are more focused on the politics or policy of the draft statute in front of them. Officials may sometimes have the courts in mind when drafting speeches for sponsoring ministers.

In adopting a purposive approach, the courts are not determining the meaning of a statute based solely on the meaning envisaged by parliamentarians. Legislative history is usually used to confirm an interpretation and is rarely used to justify a different interpretation. There would be problems in doing so. Should primacy be given to the sponsoring Minister's stated views when they are part of the executive as well as Parliament? Should opposition views be discounted? What of the position of members of parties which support but do not form the government? In reality, much of the time, there is little in parliamentary debates that elucidates the particular issue arising in a case before the courts. Where there is such material, a court will bear that in mind, but this material will not determine the case. The words of a statute are still primary, consistent with the requirements of the rule of law. Judicial understanding of Parliament's purpose in enacting legislation crucially informs, but does not substitute for, judicial interpretation of the legislative words Parliament enacted.[14] And what the court is doing in considering Parliament's purpose is examining the context in which a bill was passed to see whether that illuminates the meaning of the words Parliament used. As any student of literature knows, and as courts often repeat, words take their meaning from the context in which they are uttered. Parliamentary debates are just part of that context.

Another important aspect of statutory interpretation is how it is approached when fundamental human rights are at issue. We explain these interpretative techniques in more detail in Chapter 9. For present purposes, it is sufficient to observe that, when human rights are engaged, the courts' methodological approach may shift gears, giving extra weight, or intensity, to the protection of rights.

[13] J Steyn, '*Pepper v Hart*' (2001) 21 *Oxford Journal of Legal Studies* 59, 69.

[14] The purpose can act as a cross-check for the meaning of the text: *Commerce Commission v Fonterra Co-operative Group Ltd* [2007] NZSC 36, [2007] 3 NZLR 767, [22].

C. Common Law

Much of what the courts now do involves statutory interpretation. But their method of statutory interpretation is essentially the method courts have used for centuries in England to develop 'the common law' when there were no relevant statutes. The common law was originally customary in nature, as courts reflected the customs and practices 'common' to various localities in England in their decisions. It has been built up over time by courts resolving particular cases by reference to decisions in previous cases. A court's decision in each case represents the law in relation to the particular set of facts at issue there. Later, another court decision will consider whether the law is the same or different if the facts are different in another particular case. And so on. The effect is somewhat like painting a pointillist picture. The courts paint each point by deciding an individual case, determining what the law is. As more and more points are decided, the shape of the law becomes clearer. Only by standing back from the individual decisions does the full picture become apparent.

The common law, made only by the judiciary, sits as a foundation under legislation. Common law is overridden by legislation. And large chunks of it have been modified or abolished by legislation. But there is more common law in force in New Zealand than most New Zealanders probably appreciate. The law of contract, torts, equity and judicial review have each been impacted by legislative reform in various ways but are all, in essence, still bodies of New Zealand common law. With regard to common law, there can be no dispute that judges make law.

New Zealand inherited the common law when it was colonised. In 1840, when Britain asserted sovereignty in New Zealand, courts were established. In 1847, the Supreme Court (the equivalent to the current High Court) affirmed the application of English laws from the establishment of the colony.[15] By the English Laws Act 1858, the New Zealand Parliament confirmed that English law (which implicitly included common law) was part of the law of New Zealand from 14 January 1840, so far as applicable to the circumstances of New Zealand. This derivative application of English common law to New Zealand continued to apply under successor statutes in similar form. Currently, section 5 of the Imperial Laws Application Act 1988 provides that 'the common law of England (including the principles and rules of equity), so far as it

[15] *R v Symonds* (1847) NZPCC 387 (SC).

was part of the laws of New Zealand immediately before the commencement of this Act, shall continue to be part of the laws of New Zealand'. So, in a way, the continuing legal relevance of at least pre-1840 English common law still turns on statutory language adopted in New Zealand in 1858. But, as New Zealand courts have applied the common law in local circumstances, it has naturally become New Zealand common law, adapting to local conditions and attitudes. This was an explicit reason given by the Court of Appeal, upheld by the Privy Council, in departing from English precedent in a case of negligence in the construction and inspection of a house in the early 1980s.[16] One area of current adaptation of New Zealand common law with constitutional flavour relates to tikanga, Māori customary law, to which we next turn.

D. Tikanga

For Māori, tikanga provided a legal framework for behaviour in New Zealand before Europeans arrived and has continued to govern Māori behaviour after that.[17] When English common law was applied in colonies, it developed to accept that the laws of the indigenous peoples survived. This represented a pragmatic adaptation to new circumstances. There are examples of overly-emphatic judicial rejection of the existence of Māori customary law, such as in *Wi Parata v Bishop of Wellington* in 1877.[18] That was overruled in 1901 by the Judicial Committee of the Privy Council, a decision confirmed again by the Court of Appeal in 2003.[19] There have been periodic cases of judicial acceptance that Māori custom could be recognised by the courts if it did not conflict with statute and was 'reasonable'.[20] Today, a variety of New Zealand statutes are explicit in their recognition of tikanga in particular spheres of law, particularly in the contexts of Māori land, customary rights to the foreshore and seabed, and resource management decision-making.

[16] *Invercargill City Council v Hamlin* [1984] 3 NZLR 513 (CA); *Invercargill City Council v Hamlin* [1996] 1 NZLR 513 (PC).

[17] HM Mead, *Tikanga Māori*, 2nd edn (Wellington, Huia Publishers, 2016); Waitangi Tribunal, 'He Whakaputanga me te Tiriti' (Wai 1040, 2014) ch 2; C Jones, *New Treaty, New Tradition* (Vancouver, UBC Press, 2016) ch 2.

[18] *Parata v Bishop of Wellington* (1878) 3 NZJur (NS) 72.

[19] *Nireaha Tamaki v Baker* [1901] AC 561 (PC); *Attorney-General v Ngāti Apa* [2003] 3 NZLR 643 (CA).

[20] See eg *Arani v Public Trustee* [1920] AC 198 (PC); *Huakina Development Trust v Waikato Valley Authority* [1987] 2 NZLR 188 (HC).

Recently, the courts have also begun to recognise the role of tikanga more fully. For example, *Takamore v Clarke* was a case about competing cultural views regarding the burial of a deceased. The Court of Appeal held that Māori custom should be integrated into the common law where possible.[21] The majority of the Supreme Court did not engage with that question directly but held that the common law 'requires reference to the tikanga, along with other important cultural, spiritual and religious values and all other circumstances of the case as matters that must form part of the evaluation'.[22] Issues of tikanga relating to the burial of a deceased person were relevant considerations to an executor exercising a common law discretion.[23] In her minority decision, Chief Justice Elias said 'Māori custom according to tikanga is therefore part of the values of the New Zealand common law'.[24] She also stated that what constitutes tikanga in a particular case is a question of fact for expert evidence or reference to the Māori Appellate Court.[25]

Takamore opens the door to a conversation, perhaps even a constitutional dialogue, about the nature and role of tikanga in New Zealand.[26] The Supreme Court has considered argument (but not yet released its reasoning) about whether Māori customary views about the endurance of mana beyond death affects the ability of a deceased Pākehā litigant's case to continue.[27] In *Trans-Tasman Resources* in 2020, the Court of Appeal held it to be axiomatic that 'the tikanga Māori that defines and governs the interests of tangata whenua in the taonga protected by the Treaty is an integral strand of the common law of New Zealand'.[28] Just what this means is still in the process of clarification. But we expect the increasing recognition of tikanga by New Zealand common law, as well as statute, will be one of the more important legal developments in the twenty-first century.

[21] *Takamore v Clark* [2011] NZCA 587, [2011] 1 NZLR 573 at [254].
[22] *Takamore v Clark* [2012] NZSC 116, [2013] 2 NZLR 733, [150] and [164].
[23] Ibid [156].
[24] Ibid [94].
[25] Ibid [95].
[26] See N Coates, 'The Recognition of Tikanga in the Common Law of New Zealand' [2015] *New Zealand Law Review* 1.
[27] *Ellis v R* [2020] NZSC 89.
[28] *Trans-Tasman Resources Ltd v Taranaki-Whanganui Conservation Board* [2020] NZCA 86, [2020] NZRMA 248, [177] (as at mid-2021, awaiting outcome of appeal).

III. THE JUDICIARY AS AN INSTITUTION

A. Court Structure and Processes

The New Zealand court structure is reasonably straightforward and is illustrated in Figure 7.1.[29]

Figure 7.1 The structure of the court system in New Zealand

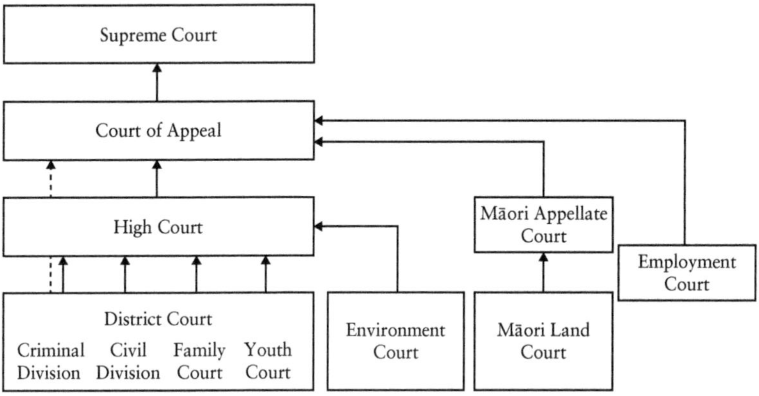

In terms of process, each court has its own set of rules which govern procedure.[30] There is a constant tension between rules being prescriptive, comprehensive and somewhat restrictive, and being principle-based, discretionary and somewhat unclear. The balance shifts from time to time.

i. The Senior Courts

There are three senior Courts in New Zealand which make law: in ascending order, the High Court, the Court of Appeal and the Supreme Court.

[29] See Courts of New Zealand, 'Structure of the court system' (www.courtsofnz.govt.nz).

[30] For the courts of general jurisdiction, see: Supreme Court Rules 2004; Court of Appeal (Criminal) Rules 2001; Court of Appeal (Civil) Rules 2005; High Court Rules 2016; District Court Rules 2014.

The High Court is the senior trial court of inherent and general jurisdiction.[31] It conducts trials of the most serious criminal and civil cases. Applications for judicial review of administrative actions are heard in the High Court. It also hears appeals from the less senior trial court established by statute, the District Court. As at the mid-2021, there are 39 High Court judges, as well as seven Associate Judges who have a more constrained jurisdiction. They are based in the three main centres of Auckland, Wellington and Christchurch, which each have circuits in other areas. One High Court judge usually sits on a case but a 'full court' of two or three judges can sometimes be convened for particularly significant cases.

The Court of Appeal's role is largely to correct errors made by the courts below. Most decisions of the High Court and lower courts can be appealed as of right to the Court of Appeal, though certain categories require leave. Most Court of Appeal decisions can be appealed to the Supreme Court, but not all. There are 10 Court of Appeal judges, who are mostly based in Wellington. The Court of Appeal sits in panels of three. There are also 'divisions' of the Court of Appeal which deal with less significant (and more numerous) appeals of criminal and civil cases. Divisional courts are composed of one member of the permanent Court of Appeal and two High Court judges.

The Supreme Court's role is to guide the development of the law of New Zealand. Appeals to it can only be taken if the Supreme Court gives leave on the ground that it is necessary to do so in the interests of justice.[32] That is legislatively defined to be satisfied if it involves a matter of general or public importance, which is defined to include a significant issue relating to the Treaty of Waitangi; a miscarriage of justice may have occurred or may occur; or it involves a matter of general commercial significance.[33] From 2015 to 2020 the Supreme Court gave leave to appeal to an average of about 26 cases or so each year.

It is a historical curiosity that the Supreme Court was established by statute only in 2003. Until then, New Zealand's highest court was the Judicial Committee of the Privy Council, which sat in London in the United Kingdom. It was composed of members of the House of Lords and the occasional visiting New Zealand appellate judge. New Zealand

[31] Before 1980, the High Court was known as the Supreme Court: Judicature Amendment Act 1979, s 2.

[32] See generally P Blanchard, 'The Early Experience of the New Zealand Supreme Court' (2008) 6 *New Zealand Journal of Public and International Law* 175.

[33] Senior Courts Act 2016, s 74.

retained its appeals to the Privy Council longer than most similar Commonwealth nations, even though the Privy Council began to defer, in some situations, to local courts in cases involving local circumstances. In 1996 a National government introduced a bill to abolish the right to appeal to the Privy Council, and leave the Court of Appeal as the highest court, following recommendations made by the Solicitor-General.[34] The lack of another tier of appeal caused controversy. Some Māori opposed the proposal out of concerns that judges in the United Kingdom might have less of a 'settler' stake in New Zealand society, and out of respect for the link to the Crown in te Tiriti o Waitangi. Sections of the business community opposed the proposal on the basis of the perceived quality of the House of Lords' commercial decisions. The Bill did not proceed as a result of coalition negotiations between National and (ironically, given the name) the New Zealand First party after the 1996 election. In 2002, the Labour government introduced a different bill based on the report of an advisory group to the Attorney-General. Parliament passed the bill in 2003, and it became the Supreme Court Act 2003. The Supreme Court was created to replace the Privy Council.

The Supreme Court has heard appeals since 1 July 2004 and, since January 2010, sits in a purpose-designed courtroom in the civic precinct in the capital city, Wellington. The Court sits as a court of five members, with the Chief Justice presiding. Legislation allows up to six permanent members of the Court, which assists to manage conflicts of interest. Otherwise, retired Supreme Court judges or senior judges from the Court of Appeal may sit as temporary judges or the Court may sit as a bench of four judges.

ii. The Less Senior Courts

The District Court is the busiest court in New Zealand, hearing the vast majority of criminal cases, over 130,000 a year.[35] Whereas a High Court judge would often do fewer than 10 sentencings a year, a District Court judge can do 15 sentencings in a day. While most will be far less serious, they can include lengthy sentences for crimes such as rape or aggravated robbery. The civil jurisdiction covers disputes worth up to $350,000. There are 182 District Court judges in 22 permanent locations throughout New Zealand, although they travel to other courts on circuit. One District Court judge usually sits on each case.

[34] Solicitor-General, 'Appeals to the Privy Council' (10 March 1995).

[35] See District Court of New Zealand, 'About the Court' (www.districtcourts.govt.nz).

There are a number of specialist courts, established by statutes, which form part of, or sit alongside, the District Court: Family Court; Youth Court; Environment Court. The specialist Employment Court sits alongside the High Court, hearing appeals from the Employment Relations Authority. Te Kooti Whenua Māori (the Māori Land Court) and the Māori Appellate Court provide specialist forums resolving claims and other disputes in relation to Māori land. The District Court has also been highly creative in recognising the need for other specialist approaches to particular sorts of cases and litigants. District Court judges have effectively created a series of additional specialist courts by drawing on international examples of best practice. For example, the Rangatahi courts operate in the same way as the Youth Court but sit on marae nationwide, in the presence of kaumātua and kuia (elders) to hear cases of young people who have admitted the charges they are facing. Te Kooti o Timatanga Hou (the New Beginnings Court) in Auckland, and the Special Circumstances Court in Wellington, deal with homeless offenders. The Alcohol and Other Drug Treatment courts, which treat addiction issues underlying offending, have been evaluated and are being extended. The Court ensures that the necessary social and health supports are provided to address the underlying causes of the offending, while also holding offenders accountable and ensuring issues for victims are addressed.

There are many other examples of specialist courts. These are largely judicial initiatives, where the practices adopted are within the powers and jurisdiction, but not the traditional convention, of the court. The sexual violence courts have been evaluated and were described as successful, in that the stakeholders 'experienced the intended outcomes of improved timeliness and improved practices in case and trial management'.[36] Also in 2020, Chief District Court Judge Heemi Taumanu announced a new vision for all District Courts: Te Ao Marama.[37] It incorporates elements of practice of the specialist courts, including avoiding legal jargon, greater involvement of the local community including iwi, and a greater emphasis on understanding the context of those before the courts.

In addition to the courts, there are some tribunals which 'borrow' a District Court judge to be their chair. There are also specialist judicial

[36] Ministry of Justice, 'Evaluation of the Sexual Violence Court Pilot' (June 2019), 2.

[37] H Taumanu, '… mai te po ki te ao marama … the transition from night to the enlightened world … Calls for transformative change and the District Court response', Norris Ward McKinnon Annual Lecture 2020 (12 November 2020).

bodies: (a) coroners; (b) the Land Valuation Tribunal; and (c) the Liquor Licensing Tribunal. In Chapter 8, we outline what we call 'administrative tribunals'. But some tribunals have a more judicial, rather than administrative, character. For example, as Chapter 9 explains, the Human Rights Review Tribunal has judicial functions in determining alleged breaches of the Human Rights Act 1993. So does the Waitangi Tribunal, regarding alleged breaches of te Tiriti o Waitangi, although it is formally established as a commission of inquiry.

B. Judges and the Judiciary

i. The Face of the Judiciary

Judges are people too. To a realist, it is important to remember that a judge brings to bear on their job all the experiences, training, perspectives and preconceptions that they have developed, suffered and enjoyed over the course of their life; just like anyone does. As any lawyer knows, the identity of the judge affects the likely result, to some extent. This reflection of the effect of humanity is not always consistent with a thin conception of the rule of law but it is inevitable.

One aspect of training, and at least some experience, that all judges share is that they must be lawyers. Only a person who has held a New Zealand practising certificate for at least seven years as a barrister, or barrister and solicitor, may be appointed as a judge.[38] This is generally accepted as a natural pre-condition for being a judge. But we think it has important implications for the culture of the judiciary that should not be under-estimated. In previous chapters we have explained different perspectives using the analogy of those in different institutions speaking different languages. In this sense, judges speak the language of the common law:[39]

> Paradigmatically, common lawyers and judges approach an opinion, an argument or a judgment by identifying the issue, identifying the material facts, outlining the relevant law, examining the arguments from both (ie, two) sides and applying the law to the facts. This is an inductive form of reasoning – from the particulars of individual cases towards the general rule. It pays

[38] Senior Courts Act 2016, s 94; District Court Act 2016, s 15. The Attorney-General, after consultation with the Chief Justice, appoints Queens' Counsel who are generally seen as the leading barristers.

[39] Palmer (n 2) 518.

attention to specific factual context of the particular cases. It looks to past precedents for guidance.

This is a very different cultural perspective, or language, from that of politicians or public servants, as outlined previously. The effect is to add piquancy and point to the judiciary's cross-checking of the application of general legislative principles in particular factual contexts. Not only are the constitutional functions of legislature, executive and judiciary different, but so are their cultures. No doubt culture is influenced by function; but function is also influenced by culture.

What more do we know about New Zealand judges? Most of them have had a legal practice that involved appearing in court, which means they understand the courtroom environment and are inculcated with how things have been done there. As at mid-2021, around half of the senior court judges had practised as barristers or Queen's Counsel before their appointment to the bench. About half had practised as solicitors, in law firms, before appointment. One judge had also been New Zealand's permanent representative to the United Nations when New Zealand was on the Security Council. Another had been Inspector-General of Intelligence and Security. Judges are more likely than practitioners to have post-graduate law degrees and the proportion of judges with post-graduate degrees increases through the hierarchy of the courts. As at mid-2021, two of the six current Supreme Court judges have doctorates (from Cambridge and Oxford) and two others have LLMs from Canada. Five of the 10 Court of Appeal judges have master's degrees, another has a doctorate and another was a Rhodes Scholar. Of the 46 High Court judges and Associate Judges, 19 have master's degrees and three have doctorates.

New Zealand judges do not fully mirror the diversity amongst the New Zealand community:

- Only a small minority of senior court judges are appointed when they are under the age of 50, though the proportion is significantly greater for District Court judges. As at 2019, the average age of all senior court judges was 61.
- Women make up 40 per cent of senior court judges and 43 per cent of District Court judges.
- Only one judge on each senior court bench identifies as Māori. Significantly larger numbers of Māori have been appointed to the District Court, particularly in recent years.
- Only one senior court judge publicly identifies as gay.

These statistics, in part, reflect the fact that women and minorities are under-represented in the senior reaches of the legal profession, from which judges are drawn. As Chief Justice Winkelmann has stated, a fully diverse judiciary is important to judicial legitimacy not only in reflecting a democratic ideal but also in affecting the quality of substantive law in channelling current understandings of New Zealand society.[40]

While all judges are created equal in terms of independence, some are more equal than others in terms of administrative responsibilities. The Chief Justice is the head of the judiciary as a whole (and also stands in for the Governor-General on occasion, as seen in Chapter 3). Administrative decisions relating to each individual bench are made by the relevant 'head of bench'. That is the Chief Justice for the Supreme Court, and the President of the Court of Appeal, Chief High Court Judge and Chief District Court Judge for the courts of general jurisdiction. Heads of Bench are statutorily responsible to the Chief Justice for ensuring the orderly and efficient conduct of the business of their courts. Each legislatively established specialist court also has its own head of bench.

ii. The Selection and Appointment of Judges

Formally, the judicial appointment process in New Zealand is relatively unreconstructed for the modern age. The Attorney-General advises the Governor-General on appointment of all senior court judges (other than the Chief Justice) under section 100 of the Senior Courts Act 2016. The Governor-General accepts the advice and makes the appointment 'in the name and on behalf of Her Majesty'. The Chief Justice is also appointed by the Governor-General but on the advice of the Prime Minister. New Zealand still holds on to both the theory and the practice of judicial appointments being non-political, even though the Attorney-General is a politician who usually sits in Cabinet. The Attorney-General will usually advise the shadow Attorney-General of appointments, but they are not debated in public, in Parliament or in Cabinet. Each individual Attorney-General will have their own inclinations as to the sort of people they wish to appoint but appointments have not been decided on a party-political basis.

Successive Attorneys-General have adopted a process of consultation and advice, run by the Solicitor-General in accordance with a Judicial

[40] H Winkelmann, 'What Right Do We Have?' [2020] 2 *New Zealand Law Review* 180–81.

Appointments Protocol. The protocol includes criteria for appointment, such as legal ability, qualities of character, personal and technical skills and reflection of society. Expressions of interest are called for, by public advertisement, every three years. The names of those who express interest and are eligible for appointment are kept on a register maintained by an appointments unit within the Ministry of Justice. When a vacancy arises, the Solicitor-General reviews the names on the register and consults the Attorney-General, Chief Justice, President of the Court of Appeal, Chief High Court Judge and Secretary for Justice as to whether additional names should be added to the list. The Solicitor-General seeks a rating of the candidates from the Chief Justice, the President of the Court of Appeal and the Chief High Court Judge and consults with the President of the Law Commission, the President of the New Zealand Bar Association, the President of the New Zealand Law Society as well as, potentially, the Criminal Bar Association, the Māori Law Society and women lawyers' associations. Nominations are also sought from the Minister of Justice, the Minister for Women and the Minister for Māori Development and may be sought from the Chair of the Justice and Electoral Committee and the shadow Attorney-General. The process is similar for District Court judges under section 11 of the District Court Act 2016.

A shortlist of no more than three names for a particular vacancy is determined by the Attorney-General with the agreement of the Chief Justice. The Solicitor-General may undertake 'checks on the personal reputation' of those on the shortlist. The Attorney-General may interview or arrange for the Solicitor-General to interview potential candidates. The Attorney-General selects the candidate from the shortlist and recommends that appointment to the Governor-General. The appointment is mentioned in Cabinet before the advice is tendered.

Sometimes District Court judges are appointed to the High Court but that is not routine as the two roles call for different skills and experiences. Appointments to the Court of Appeal are usually made from the High Court and appointments to the Supreme Court are usually from the Court of Appeal. For those appointments, the Attorney-General 'consults with interested persons and bodies' and, with the agreement of the Chief Justice who confers with the relevant head of bench, settles a shortlist of no more than three possible appointees. The Attorney may ask the Solicitor-General to undertake confidential consultations. Then the Attorney-General selects the most suitable candidate from the shortlist, notifies Cabinet and recommends the appointment to the Governor-General.

A bespoke process is adopted for the appointment of the Chief Justice.[41] For the appointment of Chief Justice Winkelmann in 2019, a panel of two distinguished former judges was engaged to produce a short list of candidates, following the development of a long list through consultation. The Prime Minister then consulted with the outgoing Chief Justice and ministerial colleagues in order to determine which candidate the Prime Minister recommended be appointed by the Governor-General.

C. The Daily Practice of Judges and the Judiciary

From the perspective of one of us, as a High Court judge, one of the most salient aspects of the job is the very wide range of issues and aspects of New Zealand society that a judge comes into contact with.[42] Cases arise from high stakes financial clashes within or between corporate boardrooms, and from very physical clashes between gangs or the homeless, and any number of other examples in between. Rather than being isolated from society, as some have thought in past times, most judges see a greater variety of legal issues, factual contexts and ways of life in New Zealand in their courtroom than they did before their appointments.

We think the generalist nature of the role is quite valuable. As one of us has described elsewhere, a typical duty week in the Auckland High Court in 2016 involved dealing with issues in commercial, family, trust, criminal, intellectual property, company, property and procedural areas of law.[43] The effect of dealing with such a variety of issues is that judges see patterns in the law that are not apparent to lawyers specialising in one particular area. The search for underlying principle is inherent in the common law method of legal analysis. Frequently, issues of a similar kind arise in very different areas of law. There is value in the consistency and coherence of the law if these issues are decided on the basis of common principles. The alternative, of greater specialisation, can lead to legal principle becoming inconsistent in different areas of law. There is an argument that this has sometimes happened in tax and resource management law in the past.

[41] J Ardern and D Parker, 'Process underway to appoint next Chief Justice of New Zealand' (6 November 2016) (www.beehive.govt.nz).

[42] MSR Palmer, 'Impressions of Life and Law on the High Court Bench' (2018) 49 *Victoria University of Wellington Law Review* 297.

[43] Ibid 303.

The responsibility of judging can be heavy. Every decision made affects the litigants. At least one party usually loses something. In the most serious cases, an offender loses their liberty, potentially for life. The effect of making such serious decisions regarding the person before them informs all the decisions that judges make. As an illustration, when a judge listens to lawyers point-scoring in a low-level commercial dispute, their perspective may be valuably informed by their experience the previous day sentencing someone to 20 years' imprisonment for murder.

IV. JUDICIAL INDEPENDENCE AND ACCOUNTABILITY

A. Protection of Judicial Independence

Any conception of the rule of law is intimately bound up with the constitutional doctrines of the separation of powers and judicial independence. The separation of powers is a necessary (but not sufficient) condition for the rule of law. If a person who makes or executes law interprets the law, then the meaning of the law is likely to reside in that person's intention at the time it is interpreted for the purposes of a specific case. The lawmaker/executor would be able to retrospectively identify in the law 'what I meant at the time', even if that was not evident in the legal text at the time it was made or the time it was interpreted. This combination of making and applying law would be contrary to the rule of law. The meaning of the law would become that which the maker and executor later deems, potentially arbitrarily, to be correct – rather than a meaning that resides in the law itself. Law would not rule; it would have no independent meaning. The lawmaker and applier would rule, arbitrarily, without independent check by the law itself.

In reality, the doctrine of judicial independence is alive and well in New Zealand. We are not aware of any instance in which the executive or legislative branch of government has attempted to pressure the judicial branch, or any individual judge, in their decision-making.

It is worth pausing on the idea that the principle of judicial independence protects each individual judge. The doctrine of judicial independence applies to protect each judge from pressure from the executive or legislative branches or from any institution. That includes pressure from the judiciary itself. Other than through formal appeals, individual judges should not be influenced in their specific judicial decisions by other judges, whether they are the Chief Justice, heads of bench, or groups of other judges of any bench. Judges can, of course, be provided with information and education. Te Kura Kaiwhakawā, the Institute of Judicial Studies, directed by the judiciary (and currently chaired by one of us), provides for the continuing education of judges, as is required in many professions. But this takes the form only of exposing judges to information, experiences and perspectives that they can decide whether to use to inform their judicial decision-making.

Legally, the principle of judicial independence is reflected in two provisions in Part 4 of the Constitution Act 1986, protecting judges from being removed from office except in prescribed circumstances and preventing their salaries from being reduced by the other two branches of government. The predecessors of these provisions date back to the 1850s. Section 23 protects judges from removal from office except by the Sovereign or Governor-General, acting upon the advice of the House of Representatives 'which address may be moved only on the grounds of that Judge's misbehaviour or that Judge's incapacity to discharge the functions of that Judge's office'. The process for removal is detailed in the Judicial Conduct Commissioner and Judicial Conduct Panel Act 2004, as we see below. Section 24 of the Constitution Act provides that a senior court judge's salary 'shall not be reduced during the continuance of the Judge's commission'. Section 38 of the District Court Act 2016 provides the same for District Court judges. Judges' salaries are paid by way of permanent legislative appropriation. The Remuneration Authority, an independent Crown entity, sets judicial salaries but is not empowered to reduce them, to preserve judicial independence.

Consistent with New Zealand's constitutional structure, these key provisions can be modified or repealed by a simple majority in Parliament. But they are reinforced, culturally, by adherence in practice as well as theory to the principle of judicial independence. Solicitors-General advise executive government about the constitutional importance of protection from removal and salary reduction.

The extent of financial protection of judicial salaries and superannuation is not always free from debate. Judicial salary reduction cannot happen in New Zealand except by legislation and whether such legislation would accord with constitutional principle would depend on its motivation. A discriminatory measure specifically targeting judges would be constitutionally objectionable in New Zealand. But not every reduction in judicial remuneration is unconstitutional. General changes to taxation are not. The Supreme Court of Canada has stated that a reduction would have to be of general application and be recommended by an independent commission, and not be the product of negotiations between the branches of government.[44] In 1921 and 1931, and 2020, legislated pay cuts for ministers and public servants were not applied to judges. In 1991, heads of bench agreed to voluntary salary reductions. In 2001, Chief Justice Elias said she was not convinced a voluntary contribution to a national effort would erode the principle of judicial independence.[45]

B. Judicial Direction and Executive Operation of the Court System

The court system is not operated only by judges. There is a large variety of support staff. Judges' associates and clerks assist judges with administration and research. Registrars and court takers assist judges in court. A significant number of other staff in court registries operate the process of receiving, organising and directing the very large amount of documentation associated with cases. In some jurisdictions, such as the United States federal judiciary and the Australian High Court, the judges are in charge of the operation of the courts and these staff. New Zealand has a more co-dependent system. The judges make judicial decisions and direct the operation of the courts, supported by staff employed by the Ministry of Justice.

The most frequent, though usually low-level, flashpoint between the branches of government concerning judicial independence typically lies in interactions between judges and the Ministry of Justice. Funding for the Ministry, determined by the Cabinet and Parliament, is never as much as judges or Ministry officials would like. So, sometimes Ministry officials are in the unenviable position of having to tell judges that some activity the judges want to undertake in their courts cannot be funded. On other occasions, Heads of Bench have to inform Ministry officials that their favoured policy or legislative proposal is not consistent with the principle of judicial independence because some decisions are for judges, not the executive branch of government.

There are obvious potentials for conflict in this situation. Every judge works with registry officers almost every day. On a day to day, low-level basis, an individual judge and registry officer may make inconsistent decisions regarding the progress of an individual case. It is not unheard of for a registry officer to make decisions that judges should make, such

[44] *Reference re Remuneration of Judges* [1997] 3 SCR 3.

[45] S Elias, 'Discounting Justice' (address to the Legal Research Foundation's Annual General Meeting, Auckland, 25 October 2001), 2.

as adjourning a case, usually out of lack of experience. Because the Ministry of Justice pay rates are relatively low, there is frequent turnover of registry staff. The pressure of business means that judges in the District Court often feel required to hear cases in large numbers and quickly. But, on the whole, relationships between judges and the registry are mutually respectful and harmonious.

While the system remains co-dependent, we consider the harmony of its operation is largely a matter of relationship management and each branch having a shared and clear understanding of the limits of their respective constitutional roles. The judges and the Ministry must seek to understand each other's motivations and incentives and be committed to talking through issues as they arise. This task is made harder by the very different perspectives taken in each institution. Paradigmatically, as we have suggested, the judiciary speaks the language of the common law, instinctively looking to past precedent and doing justice in the individual case. The Ministry speaks a combination of policy and management, looking to general principles and systems and seeking to achieve ministers' objectives. The most flexible and able judges and officials understand and can see the value in each other's perspectives. But this has not always happened in the past.

In 1994, there was an independent review of the Department of Justice's operation of the court system, advocated by the Chief Justice. It recommended that the court-related functions be separated out into a new Department for Courts. A government review, driven by the Treasury, recommended the same for other functions. A new Ministry of Justice was established to focus only on policy advice (and, initially, management of the electoral system). The Department for Courts saw itself as adopting a 'partnership' approach of full information-sharing and the establishment of joint decision-making bodies with both judicial and administrative representatives.[46] The experiment lasted until 2003. At that point, the functions of the Department for Courts were folded back into the Ministry of Justice. The government of the day did not consult the judges when doing that. We understand that executive government became concerned that the stand-alone department had been 'captured' by the judges. Such are the perils of co-dependence.

Relationship management issues have, of course, continued to arise from time to time between the Ministry and the judiciary. A positive

[46] J Lake and JJW Bailey, 'The Development and Implementation of a Constitutional Partnership' (1999) 9 *Journal of Judicial Administration* 37.

development in 2018 was the signing of a memorandum of understanding by the Chief Justice and the Secretary for Justice (the Chief Executive of the Ministry).[47] It identifies the responsibilities of both the Ministry and the judiciary in ensuring the operation of the courts, and formalises the constitutional principles on which their relationship is based.

Nearly 25 years ago, Chief Justice Eichelbaum expressed the hope that a model of judicial autonomy or judicial governance in the administration of the courts would be adopted in due course.[48] Similar judicial hopes have sometimes been expressed since.[49] But there are at least two problems with these hopes. First, most judges, like most lawyers, are not good managers. The language of the common law is not the language of management for good reason. It is not clear that judges would be any more successful than Ministry officials in bidding for or managing a budget. Secondly, if judges are responsible for the administration of the court system, they must be accountable for it. Accountability of the executive branch of government includes political scrutiny by the House of Representatives. When applied to the judiciary, that could open up the possibility that the mechanisms of accountability might potentially undermine judicial independence.

C. Judicial Removal and Accountability

The biggest charge against the legitimacy of the judiciary in New Zealand is that they are not 'accountable'. That usually means judges are not elected and do not face the corresponding political incentives to respond to the electorate. As we canvass in more detail in the next chapter, there are a variety of different facets to executive accountability. Judicial accountability is even more nuanced.

We consider that, in reality, the most constant and important form of accountability for New Zealand judges lies in the public and reasoned nature of what they do. Every judge is required to give reasons for every decision. Every judge's name stands behind those reasons. The reasons and the name are public. Judges have institutional, professional and

[47] New Zealand Law Society, 'Ministry and Judiciary sign MOU' (19 December 2018) (www.lawsociety.org.nz).

[48] T Eichelbaum, 'The Inaugural Neil Williamson Memorial Lecture' (1997) 6 *Canterbury Law Review* 421, 423.

[49] F Miller, 'Reform of Courts Administration in New Zealand' [2019] *New Zealand Law Journal* 232.

personal incentives to take pride in doing a good job. A successful appeal that corrects the reasoning of the judge below can be a salutary form of learning accountability. But the very fact that the reasoning behind a judge's decision has to be spelt out and can be scrutinised by higher courts, lawyers and the public focuses most judicial minds. As the Court of Appeal recorded in 2017, the requirement to give reasons 'expose[s] the parties to the disciplined thought pattern of the specialist adjudicator, thereby dispelling any suggestion of arbitrariness' and 'concentrates the mind' of the adjudicator, meaning the decision is 'much more likely to be soundly based on the evidence than if it is not'.[50] Reasons also play a role in due process, especially allowing disappointed parties to assess whether they should appeal the decision. We think attributed public reason-giving is the most effective day-to-day form of judicial accountability.

The process for removing judges is often seen as a core part of accountability and can be important, at least in theory. As we touched on earlier, the Constitution Act protects senior court judges from removal other than by the Governor-General on an address to the House of Representatives. Under section 29 of the District Court Act 2016, a District Court judge is removed by the Governor-General on the advice of the Attorney-General. A high threshold is required to make out the grounds of removal of a judge: 'misbehaviour' or 'incapacity' in the case of a senior court judge and 'misbehaviour' or 'inability' in the case of a District Court judge. In this context, 'misbehaviour' means, as Solicitor-General John McGrath explained in an opinion in 1997 that was released publicly at the time, 'conduct that is so morally wrong and improper that it demonstrates a judge lacks the integrity to continue to exercise judicial office' and is not confined to conduct could be the subject of a criminal conviction.[51] Remember that the Attorney-General, although a politician, is not supposed to act politically and, in New Zealand so far, has not to our knowledge acted politically in relation to the judiciary.

In reality, no judge has ever been removed by the Governor-General. But the threat of that happening has its own force. The traditional approach, on the rare occasions the question arose, was for the Attorney-General to indicate to a judge the likelihood of removal, leading the judge to resign.

[50] *Ngāti Hurungaterangi v Ngāti Wahiao* [2017] NZCA 429, [2017] 3 NZLR 770, [61]–[62].

[51] Solicitor-General, 'Judge M J Beattie: Section 7 District Courts Act 1947' (1 September 1997).

The Judicial Conduct Commissioner and Judicial Conduct Panel Act 2004 added detail to the removal process. Before the Attorney-General can progress the removal of a judge, a Judicial Conduct Panel must first recommend removal. A Judicial Conduct Panel comprises two judges, former judges or lawyers and a lay member; a panel can only be established by the Attorney-General if the Judicial Conduct Commissioner so recommends.

The Judicial Conduct Act was unexpectedly tested in 2007.[52] The Acting Attorney-General accepted the Commissioner's recommendation to establish a Judicial Conduct Panel to investigate the actions of a Supreme Court judge in relation to the adequacy of disclosures about a conflict of interest. The judge challenged the process by way of judicial review.[53] After having success in the High Court, the judge resigned. This episode highlights that formal processes of removal of a judge may not be straightforward.

Removal is a blunt instrument and is only considered where there is a serious problem. The only generic formal mechanism is the ability of anyone to complain about a judge to the Judicial Conduct Commissioner established under the Judicial Conduct Act. Most complaints are by those dissatisfied with a judge's decision and are weeded out by the Commissioner and no action is taken. But every year a few complaints are found to have substance. In 2019/2020, out of 136 complaints, eight were referred to a Head of Bench, of which one recommendation was made for appointment of a Judicial Conduct Panel.[54]

If the Commissioner considers there is substance to a complaint but it does not warrant establishment of a Judicial Conduct Panel, the Commissioner can refer it to the relevant Head of Bench. The Chief Justice has issued a set of *Guidelines for Judicial Conduct*, last revised in 2019, to make clear to the public and to judges what is expected of judges in terms of impartiality; conduct at court; activities outside the courtroom; issues involving family and relatives; and general matters. The prospect of being the subject of a complaint that is upheld is felt keenly by most judges. A Head of Bench (we understand) is capable of leaving a judge in no uncertainty about what they have done wrong and the need to avoid doing it again. Heads of Bench may also be able to reassign judges, report to the Chief Justice or even make a public statement.

[52] See BV Harris, 'The Resignation of Wilson J' (2011) *New Zealand Law Review* 625.
[53] *Wilson v Attorney-General* [2011] 1 NZLR 399 (HC).
[54] Judicial Conduct Commissioner, 'Report for the Year to 31 July 2020', 2.

V. CONCLUSION

Judges interpret and apply legislation, develop the common law and recognise tikanga. It is important for the health of New Zealand's constitution that they do so independently of the other branches of government, in order to uphold the rule of law. Accordingly, the institutions and procedures that protect their independence, while ensuring their accountability, are also of the highest constitutional importance.

In the longer term, the enduring independence and accountability of the judiciary both depend on their public legitimacy. We consider that the constitutional security of the New Zealand judiciary depends not (so) much on formal legal mechanisms but on the constitutional forbearance of the other branches of government in abiding by constitutional norms, particularly the independence of the judiciary. That long-term forbearance is conditional upon the long-term legitimacy of the judiciary in New Zealand.

The marginal effect of a judicial decision in one particular case is unlikely to figure much in public opinion. But the judiciary can be thought of as having a fund of institutional capital or legitimacy that they can conserve or expend on decisions more or less aligned to public opinion.[55] This is a less short-term, even more nebulous concept of 'the people' than that to which politicians respond. It is more akin to the judgement of history in a society. And judicial perceptions of that are mediated through the language of the common law spoken by judges. But we consider that any 'showdown' between the branches of government in New Zealand would depend on the relative strength of their funds of legitimacy.

Law sits in the background of disputes between individuals who bargain in its shadow, ever conscious its force may be deployed by the other party.[56] In a similar way, we consider that disputes or even dialogues between the branches of government occur in the shadow of their respective public legitimacies.[57] The strength of New Zealand's constitutional norm of representative democracy gives power to the political branches of government. It also enables the judiciary to raise its voice if

[55] JH Choper, *Judicial Review and the National Political Process* (Chicago, University of Chicago Press, 1980).

[56] RH Mnookin and L Kornhauser, 'Bargaining in the Shadow of the Law' (1978–1979) 88 *Yale Law Journal* 950.

[57] MSR Palmer, 'Open the Doors and Where Are the People?' in C Charters and DR Knight (eds), *We, The People(s)* (Wellington, Victoria University Press, 2011) 72–74.

its interpretation of the law does justice in such a way that is valued in the longer-term judgement of the people. The branches of government bargain in the shadow of the people in conducting their constitutional dialogue.

FURTHER READING

Courts of New Zealand website (www.courtsofnz.govt.nz).
District Court website (www.districtcourts.govt.nz).
Palmer, MSR, 'Constitutional Dialogue and the Rule of Law' (2017) 47 *Hong Kong Law Journal* 505.
Palmer, MSR, 'Impressions of Life and Law on the High Court Bench' (2018) 49 *Victoria University of Wellington Law Review* 297.

8

Accountability and Transparency

Introduction – Accountability – Transparency – Conclusion

I. INTRODUCTION

THIS CHAPTER LOOKS at the accountability of ministers, officials and other public bodies for decisions they make, beyond the parliamentary and legal institutions we have already discussed in earlier chapters. We examine the various ways executive government is expected to justify its actions and the important accountability mechanisms, such as judicial review, appeals, administrative tribunals and other supervisory processes, that provide different ways for citizens to raise grievances. Accountability is closely allied to, and fuelled by, transparency. We also explain the expectation – firmly recognised in law – that official information and details of administrative decisions be made public.

We have no doubt that these topics are quintessentially constitutional, even if their treatment elsewhere sometimes sees them relegated to the domain of administrative law. New Zealand, rightly, does not recognise a sharp distinction between administrative law and constitutional law. First, the general doctrines and principles of administrative law reflect constitutional principles such as the rule of law, separation of powers and legislative supremacy. And the way these principles bite in administrative law is also heavily conditioned by the democratic context in which they arise. Secondly, many of New Zealand's landmark constitutional developments have been realised through administrative law's routine accountability mechanisms.[1] Thirdly, constitutional thinking has also encouraged administrative law to be less routine in particular

[1] See for example *Fitzgerald v Muldoon* [1976] 2 NZLR 615 (SC); *New Zealand Maori Council v Attorney-General (Lands Case)* [1987] 1 NZLR 641 (CA).

circumstances. Some aspects of administrative law take on a different character – heightened demands on government and more searching supervisory methodologies – when addressing 'rights' or other constitutional norms, as opposed to its regular appetite of 'public wrongs'.[2] Finally, of course, the constitutional realism we are committed to naturally finds an interest in the exercise of power on-the-ground – both in its expression and control – as much as more rarefied forms of government power.

II. ACCOUNTABILITY

The call for accountability is a common, almost deafening, refrain in systems of democratic government today. Ministers, officials and other public bodies must account – and be accountable – for decisions they make. We can trace the idea of accountability in common law systems back to Anglo-Norman origins, when William I required all property owners to render 'a count' of everything they owned.[3] The resulting Domesday book listed everything in the king's realm, providing a record for taxation and governance. Since then, accountability has become more of a legal and political concept, which is richer than its bookkeeping origins. It has also been transposed from the monarch holding their subjects to account to citizens holding their executive government to account.

Modern government in New Zealand is characterised by multiple, often overlapping, lines of accountability – some formal, some informal; some legal, some political. The state sector reforms of the 1980s sought to sharpen those lines; that is, to refine and concentrate accountability using precise expectations and standards. In doing so, it generated a mass of lines of accountability, much like a spider's web. However, the multiplicity of sharpened lines has tended to atomise accountability, arguably allowing some actors to evade responsibility by pointing to the more direct responsibility of others. A good example of this is the increasingly common response from ministers that a matter is operational and thus falls within the domain of the relevant departmental chief executive to explain.

[2] On the linguistic contrast between 'public wrongs' and 'rights', see M Taggart, 'Proportionality, Deference, Wednesbury' [2008] *New Zealand Law Review* 423.

[3] M Bovens, 'Analysing and Assessing Accountability' (2007) 13 *European Law Journal* 447, 448.

In order to make sense of this chorus of accountability that provides checks-and-balances for executive government, we think it is helpful to think about accountability, as Bovens suggests, as a social relation:[4]

> Accountability is a relationship between an actor and forum in which an actor has an obligation to explain and to justify his or her conduct, the forum can pose questions and pass judgement, and the actor may face consequences.

Accountability is delivered through dialogue. For example, ministerial responsibility sets up an accountability relationship between, amongst others, a minister and the House of Representatives, as we identified in Chapter 5. Ministers are expected to explain and justify matters that have gone on in their portfolios. Other MPs interrogate ministers and make judgements about their stewardship of government office. Ministers may also face consequences, such as public opprobrium, diminished electoral prospects and, if the confidence of their colleagues is sorely tested, loss of office. A contrasting example is the way in which judicial review may expose ministers to an accountability relationship with the courts, as we explain in more detail below. Ministers are expected to respond to such a challenge by explaining and justifying the factual and legal basis of their decision, which is then tested by the courts in the course of the proceedings. The court ultimately judges whether the decision was legally justified and proper. Adverse findings have consequences such as invalidation of the decision and perhaps reputational or political repercussions for the minister.

These accountability relationships take their colour from their different aims. Some accountability relationships are predominantly *legal*, in that they seek formally to curtail the abuse of power and privilege. Some are *political*, in that they seek to ensure government actors are monitored by the public and other democratically legitimised bodies and give effect to views and preferences of the community. Some seek to facilitate *learning*, in that they encourage government actors to be continuously reflexive and to focus on delivering community wellbeing. The dichotomy between legal and political is well known.[5] However, we believe it is also important to be attentive to accountability relationships which encourage learning, consistent with our 'realists' focus throughout this book. While often less conspicuous, our sense is that this learning dimension can play a significant role in improving the quality of decision-making

[4] Ibid 450.

[5] See eg D Howarth, 'The Politics of Public Law' in D Feldman and M Elliott, *Cambridge Companion to Public Law* (Cambridge, Cambridge University Press, 2015) 37.

and promoting good government. In any event, all these dimensions of accountability play crucial roles in animating and controlling public power within our constitutional system.

We explain below some of the key mechanisms which provide accountability for government decision-making, focusing mainly on those which are generic in character. In addition, there are other forums which allow the public to raise grievances and the government to be held account for its actions through investigations and adjudication – too numerous for thorough explication here.

A. Judicial Review

Judicial review is the one of the key formal mechanisms for delivering accountability for decision-making. Judicial review is what it says it is: review of a decision by a judge. But review is focused and concentrated, and examines whether the decision and decision-making process comply with judge-developed norms of good administration. In general terms, judges look at whether the decision-maker understood and applied the law correctly, whether the decision-maker followed the proper process, and whether the decision itself is reasonable. Judges are not supposed to second-guess the 'merits' of the decision; that is, they do not decide a case based on their own view of whether the decision itself is wise or optimal. Judicial review involves the appraisal of a decision against strict legal benchmarks rather than the wholesale revisitation of a decision.

Judicial review has its origins in the ancient prerogative writs – peculiar legal processes and demands that could only be issued by the monarch.[6] Over centuries, these writs have evolved into a means by which the public can request that the courts review public decision-making. While ultimately judicial review is a creature of common law, the procedure for applying for judicial review is now set out in statute and simplified – most recently in the Judicial Review Procedure Act 2016.[7] However, the scope, grounds and other substantive principles of judicial review continue to be sourced in the common law, developed by judges according to conceptions of the rule of law, the

[6] S de Smith, 'Prerogative Writs' (1951) 11 *Cambridge Law Journal* 40.

[7] The procedure for applying for judicial review was first incorporated in statute in the Judicature Amendment Act 1972; see DR Knight, 'Privately Public' (2013) 24 *Public Law Review* 108, 117.

interests of justice and the demands of good administration. The derivative nature of much of New Zealand's common law means English authority continues to be relied on in local cases, though increasingly less often.[8] Another way to test the legality of governmental action is applying for a declaration under the Declaratory Judgments Act 1908. This provides an alternative mechanism for determining 'any question as to the construction or validity' of statutes or various other instruments, although strictly speaking it is not judicial review.[9]

Judicial review is traditionally expected to be 'a relatively simple, untechnical, and prompt procedure', due to its generally circumscribed and legal focus.[10] Applications for judicial review can be made as of right to the High Court. There is no requirement to seek leave or permission to issue proceedings. New Zealand's approach to a person's standing to challenge a decision is relatively generous. One of us has characterised the approach to standing as being 'significantly relaxed' but 'not so relaxed that it is horizontal'.[11] Evidence is almost always restricted to affidavit evidence and permission to cross-examine witnesses is rare.

The scope of judicial review depends on the common law. The core focus of judicial review is decisions of public bodies or of a public nature. However, the precise parameters of judicial review at common law continues to be debated at its margins. One of us considers the scope of judicial review at common law is coextensive with the scope of public law. That is, judicial review is a public law remedy and is only available if the impugned decision or decision-maker has a sufficient degree of publicness.[12] This means, at the margins, whether a decision is amenable to judicial review is sometimes contested, especially in cases where a non-governmental decision-maker is undertaking quasi-public functions, such as a private regulatory body or a private entity delivering services on behalf of the government.[13] The other considers that judicial review represents a more general invocation of the supervisory jurisdiction of the courts as a means of accountability. This perspective suggests that

[8] DR Knight, 'Importation and Indigeneity' in TT Arvind and others (eds), *Executive Decision-Making and the Courts* (Oxford, Hart Publishing, 2021).

[9] Declaratory Judgments Act 1908, s 3.

[10] *Minister of Energy v Petrocorp Exploration Ltd* [1989] 1 NZLR 348 (CA), 353.

[11] *Smith v Attorney-General* [2017] NZHC 1647, [2017] NZAR 1094, [18] (Palmer J).

[12] For example, *Dunne v CanWest TVWorks Ltd* [2005] NZAR 577 (HC); *Phipps v Royal Australasian College of Surgeons* [2000] 2 NZLR 513 (PC); *R (Datafin plc) v Panel on Take overs and Mergers* [1987] QB 815 (CA).

[13] Knight (n 7).

the law of judicial review is not limited only to decisions by public bodies or of a public nature, though they are its core focus. But the courts may also review decisions of other bodies in the name of accountability, such as decisions by incorporated societies or companies that are inconsistent with their rules.[14]

In any case, the Judicial Review Procedure Act 2016 provides a simplified procedure for judicial review of the exercise of 'statutory power'. This is expansively defined to include not just decisions made under statutes but also decisions made by corporate entities under their governing instruments. However, the Act does not in itself enlarge the jurisdiction to review, which continues to be governed by common law limits, whatever they may be.

Even if the courts have jurisdiction to review a particular decision, a court might still decline to review the decision on the basis that the matter is non-justiciable, that is, not suitable for judicial determination for constitutional, practical or other reasons. For example, the Court of Appeal ruled that a decision to disband the air strike force was non-justiciable because it was a matter of high policy without any suitable legal benchmark to assess its propriety and the government would more readily be held to account for the decision at the ballot box.[15] Now, the courts seem less willing than they used to be to treat matters as non-justiciable.[16] Unlike many other jurisdictions, the New Zealand courts cannot generally judicially review Acts of Parliament and judicial review is restricted to administrative action.[17] However, the courts have a declaratory power, which enables them to, for example, declare that legislation is inconsistent with the Bill of Rights Act without invalidating the legislation.[18]

The focus of the courts' supervision is guided by principles of good administration, as mentioned above. In a practical sense, this means the courts will intervene when one of the established grounds of review is made out.[19] The starting point for this appraisal is often a simplified

[14] For example, *Singh v Auckland Co-Operative Taxi Society Ltd* [2019] NZHC 1759 (Palmer J).

[15] *Curtis v Minister of Defence* [2002] 2 NZLR 744 (CA).

[16] *Ngāti Whātua Ōrākei Trust v Attorney-General* [2018] NZSC 84, [2019] 1 NZLR 116; *R (Miller) v Prime Minister* [2019] UKSC 41, [2020] AC 373.

[17] *Attorney-General v Taylor* [2017] NZCA 215, [2017] 3 NZLR 24, [58].

[18] *Attorney-General v Taylor* [2018] NZSC 104, [2019] 1 NZLR 213.

[19] DR Knight, *Vigilance and Restraint in the Common Law of Judicial Review* (Cambridge, Cambridge University Press, 2018) ch 3.

set of tripartite grounds for intervention: illegality; (procedural) unfairness; and unreasonableness.[20] However, the courts have developed more particularised versions of these generalised legality and procedural grounds, such as taking into account irrelevant considerations, failing to take into account relevant considerations, acting with an improper purpose, improper fettering of discretion, breach of natural justice, bias, and so forth.[21]

The unreasonableness ground is traditionally calibrated deferentially – 'so unreasonable that no reasonable authority would make such a decision', as it was put in *Wednesbury* – in part to discourage judges from second-guessing the merits of a decision.[22] However, sometimes the courts have deployed different standards of reasonableness or developed alternative substantive grounds which invite closer scrutiny of the merits of a decision.[23] Those with some degree of currency include reformulated forms of unreasonableness,[24] breach of legitimate expectation[25] and (serious) mistake of fact.[26] Proportionality has not taken off as a general ground of review, except in narrow circumstances such as review of penalties and bylaws.[27] And now and then a few judges have justified their invention on a more generalised threshold ('whether something had gone wrong of a nature and degree which required the intervention of the court').[28] Both of us have expressed concern about this indeterminate and largely discretionary ground of judicial review and its inconsistency with the rule of law.[29]

[20] *New Zealand Fishing Industry Association Inc v Minister of Agriculture and Fisheries* [1988] 1 NZLR 544 (CA).

[21] M Smith, *Judicial Review Handbook*, 2nd edn (Wellington, Thomson Reuters, 2016); Crown Law Office, *The Judge Over Your Shoulder*, 4th edn (Wellington, 2005).

[22] *Associated Provincial Picture Houses Ltd v Wednesbury Corporation* [1948] 1 KB 223, [1947] 2 All ER 680 (CA); *Wellington City Council v Woolworths New Zealand Limited (No 2)* [1996] 2 NZLR 537 (CA).

[23] DR Knight, 'Mapping the Rainbow of Review' [2010] *New Zealand Law Review* 393.

[24] *Wolf v Minister of Immigration* [2004] NZAR 414 (HC); *Kim v Minister of Justice of New Zealand* [2019] NZCA 209, [2019] 3 NZLR 173; *Hu v Immigration and Protection Tribunal* [2017] NZHC 41, [2017] NZAR 508; *Zhang v Minister of Immigration* [2020] NZHC 568.

[25] *Comptroller of Customs v Terminals (NZ) Ltd* [2012] NZCA 598, [2014] 2 NZLR 137.

[26] *Ririnui v Landcorp Farming Ltd* [2016] NZSC 62; [2016] 1 NZLR 1056; *Air Nelson Ltd v Minister of Transport* [2007] NZAR 266 (HC).

[27] *Institute of Chartered Accountants of New Zealand v Bevan* [2003] 1 NZLR 154 (CA); *Carter Holt Harvey Ltd v North Shore City Council* [2006] 2 NZLR 787 (HC), [102].

[28] *Electoral Commission v Cameron* [1997] 2 NZLR 421 (CA), 430; *R (ex parte Guinness plc) v Panel on Takeovers and Mergers* [1990] 1 QB 146 (CA), 159–60.

[29] *AI (Somalia) v Immigration and Protection Tribunal* [2016] NZHC 2227, [2016] NZAR 1471 (Palmer J); DR Knight, 'Contextual Review' [2020] 40 *Legal Studies* 1.

Even amongst these established grounds of review, it is sometimes difficult to generalise about the parameters of judicial review, especially the circumstances in which judicial intervention might be justified. The vast domain of public decision-making subject to judicial review and the diverse contexts in which review takes place means it is dynamic and circumstantial. The doctrine of precedent does not provide the same glue found elsewhere in the common law. The courts find the need to balance the rule of law and interests of individual justice, on the one hand, with caution arising from the separation of powers and judicial humility, on the other. Judges tend to be most confident stepping in to address hard-edged errors on which they have particular expertise such as errors of law and process, or where the matter concerns fundamental human rights. Judges tend to be more circumspect when dealing with more contested matters where executive government might have greater expertise such as matters of policy, factual evaluation and overall judgement.

Remedies in judicial review are discretionary, both as to whether relief should be granted and, if so, what orders should be granted. Typically, proceedings will ask for a decision to be invalidated and, if invalidated, the decision will be sent back to the decision-maker to make the decision again, often with directions about the proper way to do so.[30] This approach does open up the possibility of Pyrrhic victories, where a decision invalidated on judicial review is reconsidered but the decision-maker once again comes to the same decision. Other orders are possible too, such as a declaration that a decision was not made lawfully but without any order invalidating the decision itself.

There is no right in judicial review for compensation for an invalid decision. However, in limited circumstances, invalidation of a decision by judicial review might trigger fiscal consequences in other domains of law.[31] And, in rare cases, decisions declared invalid may give rise to the tort of misfeasance in public office.[32] Finally, if an invalid decision also amounts to a breach of rights under the Bill of Rights Act, a claim for compensation could be made to vindicate the rights breached – although successful claims are relatively rare.[33]

[30] Judicial Review Procedure Act 2016, s 16.

[31] See eg *Attorney-General v Van Essen* [2015] NZCA 22.

[32] See eg *Commissioner of Inland Revenue v Chesterfields Preschools Ltd* [2013] NZCA 53, [2013] 2 NZLR 679.

[33] *Taunoa v Attorney-General* [2007] NZSC 70, [2008] 1 NZLR 429, [255]; *Attorney-General v Chapman* [2009] NZCA 552, [2010] 2 NZLR 317, [106].

Despite their prominence in the suite of accountability mechanisms, applications for judicial review are not very frequent, perhaps no more than a couple of hundred or so applications a year. The influence judicial review has on good governance and administrative justice is under-studied in New Zealand, although adverse findings are taken very seriously by government. More generally, judicial review has an important 'hortatory' character: it generates principles of good administration that ministers, officials and public bodies are expected to comply with in the course of making decisions. And these principles are sometimes co-opted into other accountability and integrity processes, such as the Ombudsman or tribunals. Thus, in reality, the qualitative force of the institution of judicial review resonates beyond any quantitative score of invalidated decisions.

Judges rightly regard judicial review as part of their inherent constitutional function and jealously guard its existence and potency.[34] Emblematic of this defensiveness is the courts' usual nullification of privative or ouster clauses (statutory provisions where the legislature has sought to prevent some decisions being reviewed by the courts).[35] The New Zealand courts followed the lead of the English courts to read down privative clauses to preserve the ability of the courts to scrutinise decisions.[36] 'Judges should be slow to conclude', the Supreme Court says, 'that a statutory provision ousting or limiting access to the courts was intended to preclude applications to the High Court for judicial review alleging unlawfulness of any kind'.[37] In recent decades the courts' approach to privative clauses has become more complicated, with hostility towards legislative attempts to exclude review varying with the particular context. For example, the courts have respected and applied privative clauses in situations where the exclusion of review is teamed with alternative and effective mechanisms for legal accountability such as tribunal or appellate review. In those situations, judicial review is

[34] P Craig, *Administrative Law*, 9th edn (London, Sweet & Maxwell, 2016); PA Joseph, *Joseph on Constitutional and Administrative Law*, 5th edn (Wellington, Thomson Reuters, 2021).

[35] J Pemberton, 'The Judicial Approach to Privative Provisions in New Zealand' [2015] *New Zealand Law Review* 617.

[36] *Anisminic v Foreign Compensation Commission* [1969] 2 AC 147 (HL); *Bulk Gas Users Group v Attorney-General* [1983] NZLR 129 (CA).

[37] *Tannadyce Investments Ltd v Commissioner of Inland Revenue* [2011] NZSC 158, [2012] 2 NZLR 153, [56], repeating *Bulk Gas* (n 36) 133.

preserved as a residual remedy for errors that cannot adequately be addressed through statutory grievance mechanisms.[38]

B. Statutory Appeals

Sometimes administrative decisions are supervised by the District Court and/or High Court in their statutory appellate jurisdiction, rather than through common law judicial review. Some examples include the right to appeal a decision of the Commerce Commission on price-control regulation to the High Court, the right to appeal a decision of a departmental chief executive relating to building consents to the District Court, and the right to appeal the decision of an independent reviewer on accident compensation to the District Court. There is some overlap with the work of administrative tribunals. We focus on appeals determined by the judiciary.

In the case of a statutory appeal, the jurisdiction and powers of the appellate court are defined comprehensively in the relevant legislation providing the right of appeal. Appellate review usually has a wider focus and is more intrusive than judicial review. For example, in *Austin, Nichols & Co Inc v Stichting Lodestar* the Supreme Court cautioned against courts unduly deferring to a decision-maker under review, saying 'it is an error for the [appellate] court to defer to the lower court's assessment of the acceptability and weight to be accorded to the evidence, rather than forming its own opinion'.[39] If the appellate court's conclusion is different from the lower court, the decision under appeal 'is wrong in the only sense that matters'.[40] Differences between judicial review and appellate review should not, though, be overstated. While the source of authority to engage in review is different and the benchmarks applied when appraising a decision may vary, in reality there are strong similarities between each in the way in which the courts scrutinise decisions and test the government's justification.[41]

Judicial supervision through appellate review might be direct, in that the courts hear an appeal directly against the decision of the original

[38] *Tannadyce* (n 37); *McGuire v Secretary for Justice* [2018] NZSC 116, [2019] 1 NZLR 335; compare *H v Refugee and Protection Officer* [2019] NZSC 13, [2019] 1 NZLR 433.

[39] *Austin, Nichols & Co Inc v Stichting Lodestar* [2007] NZSC 103, [2008] 2 NZLR 141, [16].

[40] Ibid [16].

[41] MR Ferrere, 'The Functional Convergence of Appeal and Judicial Review' [2016] *New Zealand Law Review* 157.

governmental decision-maker. In other cases, the appeal may be indirect, in that the court hears an appeal from a body or tribunal which has determined an appeal against the governmental decision-maker. Examples of indirect appeals include the power of the High Court to hear appeals from the Environment Court determining appeals from decisions originally made by local authorities.

C. Administrative Tribunals

Tribunals provide a check on some government decision-making and another mechanism for the public to raise grievances in some domains. Following moves in England, a number of specialist tribunals were established in New Zealand to provide a forum where there was 'need for cheapness, accessibility, freedom from technicality, expedition and expert knowledge of a particular subject'.[42] New Zealand's system of tribunals has never quite matured, is not comprehensive and generally lacks coherence.[43] And tribunals play a less prominent role in the system of administrative law than in many comparable jurisdictions.

There are different breeds of tribunals.[44] Administrative tribunals address grievances arising from executive and other public decision-making. Licensing bodies regulate professions and industries; there is usually a public dimension to such licensing, so these tribunals can also be seen as a subset of administrative tribunals. Other tribunals regulate private transactions and disputes. Some tribunals also have a role in regulatory design, as well as adjudication of associated disputes. Occasionally some tribunals may blend these different functions. There is no legally mandated taxonomy and categorisation is not always straightforward.[45] We focus on administrative tribunals, which provide alternative forms of legal accountability for grievances against government decision-making or other matters of public interest.

Administrative tribunals and their subject matter are diverse, including for example, the Alcohol Regulatory and Licensing Authority (review of local alcohol policies and applications for liquor licences),

[42] Report of the Franks Committee, 'Committee on Administrative Tribunals and Inquiries' (Cmnd 218, 1957), 406.

[43] Law Commission, 'Tribunals in New Zealand' (NZLC IP6, 2008), [1.28].

[44] For a comprehensive list, including administrative tribunals, licensing bodies and private dispute resolution tribunals, see Law Commission, 'Table of all bodies that may be considered Tribunals' (NZLC OP2, 2007).

[45] Law Commission (n 43) ch 2.

Social Security Appeal Authority (appeals against decisions on benefits), and the Immigration & Protection Tribunal (appeals against decisions on visas, deportation and refugee status). Two tribunals are especially important and need particular mention. First, the Human Rights Review Tribunal, as explained in detail below, has the power to determine anti-discrimination complaints (including the power to declare legislation inconsistent with equality protections) and other complaints such as breaches of privacy. Secondly, the Waitangi Tribunal, as explained more fully in Chapter 10, is a standing commission of inquiry that hears claims from Māori about breaches of te Tiriti o Waitangi by the Crown.

The institutional form, jurisdiction, processes and remedies of tribunals are bespoke and are determined by the governing legislation. The Tribunals Powers and Procedures Legislation Act 2018 harmonised some aspects for some tribunals but the character and power of each tribunal is unique. Some general themes emerge. First, tribunals are often made up of adjudicators with special expertise in the tribunal's subject-matter, frequently augmented by adjudicators with legal expertise. Secondly, tribunals are only permitted to address matters that specifically fall within their statutory jurisdiction. Thirdly, in order to give effect to their goal of cost effective, speedy and efficient justice, tribunal procedures are often relatively informal, although their proceedings must still comply with the principles of natural justice. Notably, tribunals are frequently directed to be more inquisitorial and less legalistic; also, sometimes legal representation is not permitted as of right. But a few tribunals, such as the Human Rights Review Tribunal, more strongly emulate the formal character and practice of the courts. Fourthly, tribunals are usually charged with appellate or adjudicative powers that allow them to decide on all matters of law, fact and policy.[46] This means they may overturn decisions they consider are wrong. Fifthly, while tribunals can only grant the particular remedies specified in their governing legislation, the suite of options is normally very broad. In particular, it is common for tribunals to be empowered to substitute their decision for that of the original decision-maker – they need not send the decision back for reconsideration like the courts usually do.[47] Finally, often there is a further right of appeal, to the District Court or High Court, albeit typically restricted to matters of law.[48] Judicial review of a tribunal's procedure and findings also remains a possibility.

[46] P Cane, *Administrative Tribunals and Adjudication* (Oxford, Hart Publishing, 2009).
[47] Ministry of Justice, 'Tribunals Guidelines' (2015), 27.
[48] Ibid 30.

D. Ombudsman

The Ombudsman is an exemplar of non-judicial administrative justice and accountability. Born in the Scandinavian jurisdictions and adopted by New Zealand in 1962, the Ombudsman is designed to provide a readily accessible and relatively informal system for the resolution of grievances. Independence and impartiality is a crucial feature of the office and is assured in various ways: their institutional pedigree (an officer of Parliament); apolitical appointment (by the Governor-General on recommendation of the House of Representatives, conventionally with unanimous support of the House); security of tenure (dismissal threshold similar to judges); and personal characteristics (typically filled by former judges or former senior civil servants).[49]

The Ombudsman investigates matters of maladministration,[50] and also has specific supervisory powers in relation to official information requests,[51] and cruel and inhumane treatment in places of detention.[52] Their maladministration jurisdiction extends to almost all departments and organisations, as well many sub-national government organisations such as local authorities and schools.[53] However, political members of the executive, such as ministers and governing bodies of local authorities, are beyond their jurisdiction. Decisions made by police constables are also exempt from investigation, with complaints about police being subject to investigation by the Independent Police Complaints Authority.

Investigations are usually triggered by complaints but the Ombudsman may also choose to investigate a matter on their own motion. The mode of inquiry is inquisitorial and relatively informal. Most investigations involve exchanges of correspondence between the state sector agency and the Ombudsman, occasionally with informal meetings. Although the Ombudsman has various coercive powers, they are rarely invoked. These investigations are usually undertaken by case officers within the Office of the Ombudsman, in the name of the Ombudsman. Personal involvement of the Ombudsman in the investigation is generally reserved for the most serious cases. Some complaints are settled informally, in the early stages of triage, without any need for a formal investigation or report.

[49] Ombudsmen Act 1975, ss 3 and 6; A Satyanand, 'The Office of Ombudsman in New Zealand' (1995–1997) 6 *Canterbury Law Review* 470.

[50] Ombudsmen Act 1975, s 13.

[51] Official Information Act 1981; Local Government Official Information and Meetings Act 1987.

[52] Crimes of Torture Act 1989, ss 16 and 27.

[53] Ombudsmen Act 1975, s 13.

The Ombudsman's mandate on matters of maladministration is broad. The Ombudsman may rule that a decision or recommendation is 'contrary to law', 'unreasonable, unjust, oppressive, or improperly discriminatory', 'was based wholly or partly on a mistake of law or fact' or, notably, 'was wrong'.[54] They may also offer an opinion that the legislation on which a decision or recommendation was based is 'unreasonable, unjust, oppressive, or improperly discriminatory', although this power has been rarely invoked. In principle, this allows the Ombudsman to engage in the comprehensive assessment of a decision or recommendation, assessing its propriety and value in the round. In reality, however, the focus of investigations tends to echo the focus of the courts on matters of law and process, with the assessment of the merits and wrongness retained as a residual lens for unusual cases.[55]

Following investigation, the Ombudsman's powers are recommendatory only but, in practice, carry much force. The Ombudsman may recommend that a decision or practice be cancelled or varied, an omission varied, a matter reconsidered, reasons be provided or any other steps be taken. They may also recommend that legislation on which the decision, recommendation, act or omission was based should be reconsidered. This is a significant power but one that is rarely employed and has not reached its full potential. If their recommendations are not implemented, the matter is reported to the Prime Minister and then the House. In practice, decisions of the Ombudsman are usually accorded significant respect, particularly by the public service.

The style of grievance resolution deployed by the Ombudsman tends to emphasise the constitutional and learning dimensions of accountability. That is, a strong thread of the Ombudsman's work is about ensuring power is not abused by the administration and is exercised consistently with expected norms. The Ombudsman's brief also sometimes encourages a more wide-ranging assessment of the propriety of a decision than is undertaken by the courts. The Ombudsman is attentive to systemic and structural conditions of administrative action, and promotes best practice in decision-making. Thus, there is a significant learning dimension to their work, where the Ombudsman builds trusting relationships with administrative actors and provides feedback, in a non-punitive fashion, to improve the quality of the decisions.

[54] Ibid s 22(1).

[55] See eg B Wakem, 'Charge for supply of information about DOC Recommended Area for Protection' (January 2007).

E. Controller and Auditor-General

The Controller and Auditor-General is Parliament's financial watchdog and guardian, responsible for financial integrity within the public sector. An independent office, first filled in 1846, the Controller and Auditor-General is appointed as an officer of Parliament for a seven-year non-renewable term.[56] They have two main functions: the controller function ensures government spending is lawful and consistent with Parliament's appropriations; and the audit function ensures the activities of government departments and other organisations are prudently undertaken and accurately reported.

The first function, as Controller, involves ongoing supervision of governmental spending – both operating expenses and capital expenditure. As explained in Chapter 6, the spending of public money by the Crown (in this context, including government departments but not Crown entities, state-owned entities and a number of other organisations), and offices of Parliament must be expressly authorised by legislative appropriation.[57] The Auditor-General provides independent assurance that spending complies with the legislative appropriation.[58] The Treasury provides monthly statements of departments and offices to the Auditor-General, who examines whether the spending is lawful and consistent with the scope, amount and period of the appropriation. If spending is outside the appropriation, the Auditor-General can direct the responsible minister to report to the House of Representatives. The Auditor-General can also stop payments from a Crown or departmental bank account to prevent money from being used for an unlawful purpose.

The audit function has several dimensions. First, the Auditor-General is the auditor of every public entity (in this context, all government departments, offices of Parliament, and numerous sub-national organisations such as local authorities).[59] As auditor, the Auditor-General examines the annual financial statements of these departments and organisations to ensure that they are consistent with generally accepted accounting practice and accurately present the activities and spending of the department. A large portion of this auditing process is undertaken by private accounting firms commissioned by the Auditor-General.

[56] Public Audit Act 2001.
[57] Public Finance Act 1989, s 5; Constitution Act 1986, s 22.
[58] Public Finance Act 1989, ss 65U–65ZB.
[59] Public Audit Act 2001, s 14.

An audit opinion, reporting the accuracy or otherwise, is included in the annual report of the department or organisation. Matters arising from the audits may also be reported to the department or organisation. Secondly, the Auditor-General audits the draft and final long-term plans of local authorities.[60]

Thirdly, the Auditor-General may, at any time, conduct a performance audit of the activities of a public entity (in this context, ministers are also subject to annual audits, in addition to public entities).[61] Performance audits may examine effectiveness and efficiency, compliance with statutory obligations, wastage, lack of probity or financial prudence. However, performance audits may not question any applicable government or local authority policies. The Auditor-General's authority is limited to examining the extent to which activities are carried out effectively and efficiently in a manner consistent with the policies. Fourthly, and allied to the power to undertake performance audits, the Auditor-General may inquire into any matter relating to a public entity's use of resources (again, in this context, ministers, departments and other organisations).[62] The Auditor-General ultimately has an absolute discretion about what matters to inquire into, although they often receive complaints and suggestions from the government, other members of Parliament and the public. In recent years, the Auditor-General has been careful about when to undertake an inquiry, typically reserving the function for serious matters and avoiding duplicating other accountability processes already underway.

F. Inquiries

An inquiry can be established under the Inquiries Act 2013 to investigate and report on any matter of public importance or concern. New Zealand has a long tradition of constituting commissions of inquiry to determine the cause of major calamities and other things that have gone wrong, with the aim of changing the conditions and settings that contributed to the problem. Some examples include inquiries into the treatment of civil casualties in a defence force operation abroad, building failures caused by an earthquake, fatal explosions in a mine, contamination in

[60] Local Government Act 2002, s 94.
[61] Public Audit Act 2001, s 16.
[62] Ibid s 18.

milk production, and a controversial appointment of a deputy commissioner of police. In addition to inquiries looking at things that have gone wrong, inquiries are also used as an independent means to develop policies on matters of major importance. Examples include commissions on local governance in Auckland and genetic modification.

There are two main types of inquiries. Public inquiries are formally established by the Governor-General, on advice of ministers. Sometimes, usually when addressing a rarefied matter, a public inquiry may be designated as a Royal Commission and is then constituted under the prerogative but this difference is only in form, not substance. Governmental inquiries are established directly by ministers by notice in the *Gazette*.

Public inquiries are usually multi-person bodies, often chaired by current and former judges and including former senior civil servants and subject-matter experts. Governmental inquiries are often undertaken only by one person, usually a senior lawyer or civil servant. The conduct of inquiries largely depends on their terms of reference. The virtue of inquiries is that the mode and style of investigation can be tailored to particular matters being investigated. Public and governmental inquiries have the same – and extensive – powers to hear evidence, obtain information and summons witnesses.

Inquiries report their findings and recommendations: for public inquiries, the report is sent to the Governor-General and then tabled in Parliament; for governmental inquiries, the report is sent to the appointing minister. Importantly, findings and recommendations of inquiries do not have direct legal consequences – they are advisory only.

III. TRANSPARENCY

Transparency is a pre-requisite to accountability. Knowing about what the government has decided, the reasons for the decision and the relevant surrounding context is the first part of any accountability conversation. Without that, the decision cannot be interrogated, appraised or quashed.

Transparency may arise in a number of ways. The generic regime for providing transparency in government is the Official Information Act 1982 – New Zealand's freedom of information regime. This regime requires the disclosure of official information on request and, in some cases, the provision of reasons for decisions. More bespoke forms of transparency are provided in the course of other accountability relationships, as we have explained elsewhere.

A. Official Information

The Official Information Act 1982 promotes transparency by providing a freedom of information regime where official information must be disclosed on request. Similar legislation – the Local Government Official Information and Meetings Act 1987 – applies to local authorities and local organisations. Because the latter echoes the former, with only a few differences, our explanation focuses on the Official Information Act 1982.

The Act was passed following the recommendations of the Danks Committee on Official Information and inverted the then secrecy that applied to official information under the Official Secrets Act 1951.[63] At its core is a presumption that official information should be made available unless there is a good reason for it to be withheld. The regime is founded on the belief that increasing the availability of official information will 'promote public participation and government accountability'.[64] In essence, the Official Information Act sets up a request-based regime where disclosure is assessed on a case-by-case basis, in the light of the presumption of availability, mandated withholding grounds and the public interest.

Official information is defined in the Act very broadly, to include any information held by ministers, departments and other public organisations. The definition is not restricted to documents, thereby allowing requests for, for example, recollections of meetings and documents no longer in existence. Institutional coverage is almost comprehensive for executive government, including ministers, departments and other listed public organisations.[65] Parliament and the judiciary are not covered. The Attorney-General (in their law officer capacity) and a number of parliamentary-related agencies, such as the Parliamentary Counsel Office and the Parliamentary Service, are also excluded. Information known or possessed by ministers becomes official information when it is held by them in their 'official capacity'. This excludes information they know or possess in their party political or personal capacity. For example, coalition documents negotiated between the Labour, NZ First and

[63] Danks Committee on Official Information, 'Towards Open Government' (December 1980; July 1981).

[64] Official Information Act 1982, s 4. Local Government Official Information and Meetings Act 1987, s 4.

[65] Official Information Act 1982, s 2 'official information', 'department', 'organisation'.

Green parties were ruled not to be official information because they were generated before ministers assumed office and were not subsequently used by ministers in their ministerial capacity.[66]

Citizens, permanent residents and New Zealand bodies corporate may request official information, without any formality or specific reliance on the terms of the Act. Requests are usually made in writing but requests made orally or via social media are also valid requests. Ministers, departments and public organisations are obliged to make a decision on a request as soon as reasonably practicable and, in any event, within 20 working days. Once a decision on a request is made, information must be released without undue delay, although usually information is provided at the same time a decision on release is communicated. There is also provision for extensions and transfer to other ministers, departments or public organisations.

Requests must be granted unless there is a good reason for withholding the information requested. The regime sets out three different types of reasons. First, a set of conclusive (and other) reasons, including matters such as prejudice to security, defence, international relations or maintenance of law; likelihood of serious damage to the economy; and danger to personal safety.[67] Secondly, a set of other reasons for withholding information may be relied on but only when these are not outweighed by any public interest in disclosure.[68] These reasons include protecting personal privacy, trade secrets, or legal professional privilege; maintaining constitutional conventions and the effective conduct of public affairs (especially the free and frank expression of opinion of ministers and officials); and allowing ministers and departments to undertake commercial activities and negotiations. Finally, a set of administrative reasons to withhold the information may be relied on. These include reasons such as the information not existing; the information being publicly available or soon to be available; substantial collation and research being required; the request being frivolous or vexatious; and other legislation requiring the information not be disclosed.[69]

Information that is made available is normally released in documentary form, with redactions as necessary to protect parts that can be

[66] P Boshier, 'Ombudsman's finding on request for document related to coalition negotiations between Labour and New Zealand First' (December 2017).

[67] Official Information Act 1982, s 6.

[68] Ibid s 9.

[69] Ibid s 18.

withheld. However, other means can be used to meet the request, such as inspection, disclosure of an excerpt or written summary, or an oral briefing. Charging for making information available is permitted but any charges must be reasonable. Guidelines suggest charges should not be the norm for simple requests and the Act requires liaison with the person making the request before charges are imposed.[70]

If a request is refused in whole or part, the person who requested the information may complain to the Ombudsman. The Ombudsman then investigates and determines whether the information should be disclosed. Their recommendations are binding on the ministers, department or public organisations, unless an order-in-council is issued otherwise – a power so far never used. In addition, the Ombudsman may use their general maladministration jurisdiction to investigate a department's or public organisation's actions, policies and systems more generally and make recommendations about how transparency should be improved.[71]

The Privacy Act 2020 also provides a parallel regime for individuals to access and obtain personal information about themselves held by agencies, including public sector agencies.[72] The right of access is subject to a similar but not identical set of withholding grounds. Corporate bodies have a similar right of access to personal information under the Official Information Act 1982.[73] People can also request access to internal rules governing decisions made about them that affect them in a personal capacity.[74]

The Official Information Act has been successful in bringing much transparency to the business of government but it is not without some ongoing frustrations. In the most recent major review, the then Chief Ombudsman Beverley Wakem concluded the Act has 'caused greater openness and transparency about the plans, work and activities of the government', 'increased the ability of the public to participate', and 'led to greater accountability in the conduct of public affairs'.[75]

[70] Ombudsman, 'Charging: a guide to charging for official information under the OIA and LGOIMA' (August 2019), 4; Ministry of Justice, 'Charging Guidelines for Official Information Act 1982 Requests' (March 2002), [1.1].

[71] See eg P Boshier, 'Auckland Council's processing of a request for official information' (July 2018).

[72] Privacy Act 2020, s 22, principle 6.

[73] Official Information Act 1982, s 24.

[74] Ibid s 22.

[75] BA Wakem, *Not a game of hide and seek* (December 2015) 2–3.

The regime provides cherished access to information held by government without formality or technical impediments. Recent data shows that around 80,000 official information requests are made each year to departments and other central government organisations alone, with more also being made to ministers and local organisations.[76] Fewer than 2,000 lead to complaints to the Ombudsman and as few as 100 of those complaints are upheld (although many are resolved without or during an investigation).[77]

Increasingly, ministers, departments and public organisations are proactively making information available in accordance with the culture of transparency promoted by the Act. In 2018, Cabinet directed that all Cabinet and Cabinet committee papers and minutes (other than those of the Cabinet appointments and honours committee) must be published online within 30 working days of final decisions being taken by Cabinet, unless there is good reason not to release or to delay release.[78]

At the same time, frustrations remain.[79] Requestors often complain that the process is gamed by ministers and officials so as to avoid timely and meaningful disclosure. Common complaints include successive extensions of time for making decisions on requests; requests by particular requestors (especially media and opposition parties) being treated differently; ministerial influence over the departmental decisions on requests; and baseless refusals, especially in relation to requests for information about formative policy development information, personal information, security information and commercially sensitive information. There is a sense that the regime operates with a dual track: most non-contentious requests are processed in a full and often timely manner but a small group of politically sensitive requests are processed less benevolently.[80] Departments and organisations also note the increasing administrative burden associated with processing requests, especially due to the vast increase in information held by government and public eagerness for access. Calls for reform of the legislation have not been

[76] State Services Commission, 'Latest OIA statistics released' (4 March 2020) (ssc.govt.nz).

[77] Office of the Ombudsman, 'Complaints Data' (2019) (www.ombudsman.parliament.nz).

[78] Cabinet Office, 'Proactive Release of Cabinet Material' (23 October 2018) CO (18)4.

[79] Wakem (n 75), 134; N White, *Free and Frank* (Wellington, Institute of Policy Studies, 2007).

[80] S Price, 'The Official Information Act' [2006] *New Zealand Law Journal* 276.

taken up but significant steps have been taken recently to improve institutional capability, especially in relation to the timeliness of decisions, and to clarify some of the less certain withholding grounds.[81]

B. Public Records

Transparency and freedom of information rely on good recordkeeping. The Public Records Act 2005 aims to promote the accountability of government by ensuring that 'full and accurate records of the affairs of central and local government are created and maintained' and records of long-term value are preserved.[82]

The chief archivist is responsible for leadership in recordkeeping within public offices and management of public archives. Public officers in both central and local government are directed to 'create and maintain full and accurate records of [their] affairs, in line with normal prudent business practice'.[83] Public records must be kept until their disposal is authorised. After 25 years, public records must be transferred to a central archive, where they are classified as either 'open' or 'restricted access'. The central archive also accepts for deposit parliamentary records, ministers' papers and significant private records.

The maintenance of public records brings particular challenges, especially with the vast mass of electronic documents and communications that characterises modern government. Sometimes maintaining government files can be treated as a low priority compared to other departmental work.

C. Reason-giving

Another aspect of the process of accountability is reason-giving: the right of those affected to know the legal and factual basis for a decision. Those affected may find out reasons by requesting information relating to a decision under the Official Information Act or Privacy Act. However,

[81] State Services Commission, 'Capability Development Toolkit' (www.ssc.govt.nz). See Law Commission, 'The Public's Right to Know' (NZLC R125, 2012); A Kibblewhite and P Boshier, 'Free and Frank Advice and the Official Information Act' (2018) 14(2) *Policy Quarterly* 3.

[82] Public Records Act 2005, s 3(c).

[83] Ibid s 17.

there may also be more direct obligations imposed on the government to explain decisions.

First, it is commonplace for legislation containing decision-making powers to explicitly direct the decision-maker to provide reasons to affected persons, usually on an obligatory and contemporary basis. For example, the department providing social welfare must give a beneficiary notice of reasons if the beneficiary's benefit is to be suspended. The Legal Services Commissioner must give reasons to an aided person if legal aid is withdrawn. And local authorities must provide reasons when deciding applications for resource consents. The scope and form of reasons is bespoke to the particular regimes. On rare occasions, such as in relation to some immigration decisions, the legislation disavows any obligation to provide reasons.

Secondly, the Official Information Act allows citizens, permanent residents and New Zealand bodies corporate to request reasons for a decision that affects them in a personal capacity.[84] The minister, department or organisation must provide a written statement setting out the findings on material issues of fact, a reference to the information on which the findings were based, and the reasons for the decision. A request must be made within a reasonable time after the decision and a less extensive set of grounds for refusal apply than for requests for official information.

Thirdly, the courts are increasingly recognising a duty to give reasons in some circumstances, although they have not yet definitely adopted a general and universal obligation on the part of all decision-makers to give reasons.[85] Regardless, while not formally recognised as a free-standing ground of review, in practice the absence of reasons makes a decision vulnerable to judicial review or appeal because of the absence of contemporary justification. Decision-makers are almost always well advised to give (good) reasons for their decisions.

IV. CONCLUSION

Numerous mechanisms require the government explain its actions and justify the effect of its decisions on citizens and their rights and liberties. These accountability mechanisms test the propriety of governmental

[84] Official Information Act 1982, s 23.

[85] T Cochrane, 'A General Public Law Duty to Provide Reasons' (2013) 11 *New Zealand Journal of Public and International Law* 517.

decisions against different standards, through processes with varying degrees of formality, and result in different consequences if the decision fails to pass muster.

FURTHER READING

Chen, M, *Public Law Toolbox*, 2nd edn (Wellington, LexisNexis, 2014).

Taylor, GDS, and Roth, PA, *Access to Information* (Wellington, LexisNexis, 2017).

Smith, M, *Judicial Review Handbook*, 2nd edn (Wellington, Thomson Reuters, 2016).

Taylor, GDS, *Judicial Review: A New Zealand Perspective*, 4th edn (Wellington, LexisNexis, 2018).

9

Human Rights

Introduction – Bill of Rights Act – Fundamental Rights and the Common Law – Other Statutory Rights Protections – Conclusion

I. INTRODUCTION

IN THIS CHAPTER we look at rights, especially the way that accountability shifts gears when moving from public wrongs to human rights.[1] If government action affects protected human rights, the demands of law and justification are increased. Fundamental rights are preserved and protected by law in different ways.

In the international sphere, New Zealand has been an active participant in the long-running international human rights project. New Zealand has committed to important human rights instruments, such as the International Covenant on Civil and Political Rights, and joined the international community in championing specific rights, such as the rights of workers, minorities and indigenous peoples. '[I]nternational human rights law matters for how New Zealand operates as a country', Geddis observes, 'because New Zealanders accept that human rights themselves ought to matter, they think that other States ought to accept this too, and they are anxious to maintain a good name on rights matters.'[2]

In the domestic sphere, the New Zealand Bill of Rights Act 1990, or Bill of Rights Act as we call it, recognises and enshrines many fundamental rights in statute, though it is not supreme law. This shapes parliamentary law-making and governmental decision-making. We explain the

[1] See M Taggart, 'Proportionality, Deference, Wednesbury' (2008) 3 *New Zealand Law Review* 423.

[2] A Geddis, 'The Philosophical Underpinnings of Human Rights' in M Bedggood, K Gledhill and I McIntosh (eds), *International Human Rights Law in Aotearoa New Zealand* (Wellington, Thomson Reuters, 2017) 59.

various ways the Bill of Rights Act enhances protection for specified human rights and how it changes the ways judges scrutinise government action when these human rights are impugned. The common law also enhances protection of some fundamental rights. We look at examples of doctrine developed by the courts which seek to ensure that fundamental human rights are not unduly compromised by the legislature or executive. Other legislative regimes also provide tailored protections and deliberative mechanisms for specific rights. This suite of interwoven protections aims to give greater priority to fundamental rights in decisions taken by Parliament, the executive and others when governing in the public interest.

II. NEW ZEALAND BILL OF RIGHTS ACT 1990

The Bill of Rights Act recognises and affirms fundamental rights and provides some protection against unjustified breach by the different branches of government, subject to the ultimate power of Parliament to legislate contrary to those rights. While formally only an ordinary Act of Parliament without elevated status or security against amendment, the Bill of Rights Act is the centrepiece of rights-protection. It provides an important deliberative framework for conversations about fundamental rights and their relationship with government initiatives and activities. Since its enactment, the Bill of Rights Act has had a discernible, though patchy, effect on human rights culture and compliance. It is now usually described as a constitutional instrument.

The Bill of Rights Act was enacted in 1990 following a manifesto commitment from the Labour Party and an important White Paper setting out the case for a human rights instrument, promoted by Sir Geoffrey Palmer, the father of one of us.[3] Originally a supreme bill of rights was proposed – one that also proposed recognition and affirmation of te Tiriti o Waitangi / the Treaty of Waitangi. However, adverse public reaction saw the proposal watered down to a statutory or parliamentary bill of rights; that is, an ordinary statute that does not invalidate other inconsistent legislation. Te Tiriti o Waitangi protections did not

[3] G Palmer, 'A Bill of Rights for New Zealand: A White Paper' [1984–1985] I *Appendix to the Journals of the House of Representatives* A.6; KJ Keith, 'The New Zealand Bill of Rights Act 1990 – An Account of Its Preparation' (2013) 11 *New Zealand Journal of Public and International Law* 1.

proceed. The move away from a supreme, judicially enforced human rights instrument to a parliamentary bill of rights requires the legislature, executive and judiciary to share the responsibility for human rights protection. The creation of joint responsibility should foster genuine dialogue between the different branches of government.

A. Protected Rights

The Bill of Rights Act recognises and affirms a diverse range of civil and political rights for natural and other legal persons, including the security of the person; the right to vote; freedom of thought, conscience, religion, belief and expression; rights of assembly, association and movement; and freedom from discrimination on specified grounds. Protections against search, seizure, arrest and detention are also included, as well as a number of specific protections for the criminal justice process. The Bill of Rights Act also contains a generalised natural justice right and a right to seek judicial review. This catalogue of rights does not purport to be comprehensive. The Act confirms that other rights and freedoms are not abrogated or restricted due to their non-inclusion. Rights notably not featured in the Bill of Rights Act include the right to property, the right to privacy and any socio-economic rights.

The rights in the Bill of Rights Act are generally expressed in broad terms. For example, freedom of expression is protected in the following way: 'Everyone has the right to freedom of expression, including the freedom to seek, receive, and impart information and opinions of any kind in any form.'[4] Also, the rights are, by-and-large, expressed without specific derogation. Instead, the Act contains a generally applicable limitations provision; limitation of the specified rights is permissible if the limitation is demonstrably justified in a free and democratic society (section 5). Much of the reach and operation of the Bill of Rights Act depends on the assessment of whether limitations on rights are justified under this calculus. However, the definitions of some rights are subject to internal modifiers or qualifications, such as '*unreasonable* search and seizure' and '*disproportionately* severe treatment or punishment', which incorporate some natural limitation into the expression of the right itself.

[4] New Zealand Bill of Rights Act 1990, s 14.

B. Operational Scheme

The question of whether the Bill of Rights Act has been breached is governed both by definition of the right itself and the generic operative provisions – analysis of which is sometimes complex. As a statutory bill of rights without supremacy, the operative provisions provide a framework which allows the catalogue of rights to be applied in the surrounding legislative context. Legislative and administrative acts which limit or circumscribe protected rights do not necessarily amount, in themselves, to actionable breaches of the Bill of Rights Act.

First, the Bill of Rights Act applies to acts done by the 'legislative, executive, or judicial branches' of government and other bodies performing a 'public function, power, or duty' (section 3). Public bodies are not permitted to breach the rights, although the influence and burden of the Bill of Rights Act differs depending on which branch of government is implicated and the function they are engaged in.

Secondly, inconsistent legislation is protected against invalidation, implied repeal or disapplication (section 4). This recognises and preserves the principle of legislative supremacy and the power of the legislature to enact legislation which is inconsistent with the protected rights. This applies to legislation already on the books and legislation subsequently enacted.

Thirdly, the Bill of Rights Act contains a generally applicable limitations provision (section 5). Limitation of the specified rights is permitted, if the limitation is prescribed by law and demonstrably justified in a free and democratic society. This provision has the potential to circumscribe the ambit of protected rights and is a natural consequence of the individual rights generally being defined in unqualified form. The requirement for prescription by law captures the notion of prior legal authorisation, as the rule of law expects.[5] Whether a limitation is demonstrably justified under section 5 anticipates a complex, structured assessment of the proportionality of its objectives and effects. The questions to be addressed, as set out in the current leading case, *R v Hansen*, are as follows:[6]

(a) Does the limiting measure serve a sufficiently important purpose to justify curtailing the right or freedom?
(b) Is the limiting measure rationally connected with its purpose?

[5] *Borrowdale v Director-General of Health* [2020] NZHC 2090, [2020] 2 NZLR 864.
[6] *R v Hansen* [2007] NZSC 7, [2007] 3 NZLR 1, [104] (Tipping J), drawing on *R v Oakes* [1986] 1 SCR 103.

(c) Does the limiting measure impair the right or freedom no more than is reasonably necessary for sufficient achievement of its purpose?
(d) Is the limit in due proportion to the importance of the objective?

Fourthly, the Bill of Rights Act directs that, where an enactment can be given a meaning consistent with the protected rights and freedoms, 'that meaning shall be preferred' (section 6). This key interpretative direction promotes consistency between legislation and the protected rights, potentially requiring the adoption of harmonious meanings. Because legislation is also the key means by which most government action is empowered, this interpretative direction may also have the effect of narrowing the scope of lawful government activity to rights-consistent activity.

Looking at these operational provisions in the round, they inevitably sit in tension with each other. Much of the jurisprudence on the Bill of Rights Act has sought to grapple with the relationship between these provisions, especially the appropriate sequencing of each.[7] For example, the steps set out by Tipping J in *Hansen* are usually taken as charting a useful way through the operational provisions:[8]

> Step 1. Ascertain Parliament's intended meaning [of the enactment in issue].
> Step 2. Ascertain whether that meaning is apparently inconsistent with a relevant right or freedom.
> Step 3. If apparent inconsistency is found at step 2, ascertain whether that inconsistency is nevertheless a justified limit in terms of s 5.
> Step 4. If the inconsistency is a justified limit, the apparent inconsistency at step 2 is legitimised and Parliament's intended meaning prevails.
> Step 5. If Parliament's intended meaning represents an unjustified limit under s 5, the Court must examine the words in question again under s 6, to see if it is reasonably possible for a meaning consistent or less inconsistent with the relevant right or freedom to be found in them. If so, that meaning must be adopted.
> Step 6. If it is not reasonably possible to find a consistent or less inconsistent meaning, s 4 mandates that Parliament's intended meaning be adopted.

[7] See A Butler and P Butler, *The New Zealand Bill of Rights Act*, 2nd edn (Wellington, LexisNexis, 2015) chs 6 and 7; PA Joseph, *Joseph on Constitutional and Administrative Law* (Wellington, Thomson Reuters, 2021) [28.4.3].

[8] *Hansen* (n 6) [92] (Tipping J), [60] (Blanchard J) and [192] (McGrath J).

However, the Supreme Court also left the door open for other sequences, where those are more appropriate in other contexts.[9]

Finally, the Act itself does not contain any remedial provision and it has been left to the judiciary to fashion the consequences for breaching rights. These remedies now include declaratory relief, exclusion of evidence and public law damages. However, much of the force of the Bill of Rights Act comes from the courts' interpretative role, without any need for specific sanctions. The availability of some of these remedies, especially public law damages and declarations of legislative inconsistency, have been born out of constitutional dialogue between the different branches of government.

C. Impact on the Functions of Government

In relation to legislative functions, the Bill of Rights Act is designed to influence the content of legislation and promote human rights consistency by providing 'navigation lights' for the legislative process.[10] However, it is still open to Parliament to pass legislation that breaches rights, as section 4 recognises.[11] The key formal mechanism for encouraging rights-consistent primary legislation is the Attorney-General's obligation to vet and advise the House on the (in)consistency of bills with the protected rights (section 7). They have a duty to table a report – known as a section 7 report or 'vet' – at the first reading of any bill they consider unjustifiably breaches rights. For bills considered to be consistent, there is no obligation to table a report. But a practice has developed that the official advice, prepared either by the Ministry of Justice or the Crown Law Office, is generally made publicly available.[12]

Other aspects of the policy and legislative process also encourage compliance with the Bill of Rights Act. For example:

(a) when submitting a legislative bid or proposed legislative text for approval by Cabinet, ministers must draw attention to any aspect of the bill that has implications for the Bill of Rights Act;[13]

[9] Ibid [94].

[10] Palmer, 'White Paper' (n 3) 6.

[11] C Geiringer, 'The Dead Hand of the Bill of Rights?' (2007) 11 *Otago Law Review* 389. Compare Butler and Butler (n 7) 7.7.1–7.79.

[12] Ministry of Justice, 'Advice on consistency of Bills with the Bill of Rights Act' (www.justice.govt.nz).

[13] Cabinet Office, *Cabinet Manual 2017*, [7.65] and [7.66].

(b) the executive's internal committee of officials who monitor and advise on legislative quality, the Legislation Design and Advisory Committee, is alert to rights-implications of draft bills;[14] and
(c) when considering bills, subject select committees often address any issues arising under the Bill of Rights Act and any section 7 report on a bill is formally referred to the relevant subject committee in tandem with the bill.[15]

Since the Bill of Rights Act was passed, the Attorney-General has issued a section 7 report for over 100 bills, roughly split between government and non-government bills. Almost all of the government bills subject to a section 7 report were still enacted. However, most members and private bills receiving a section 7 report did not proceed. It is difficult for an outsider to discern whether these statistics suggest a cavalier attitude of the legislature towards human rights. We think it is not as troubling as it might seem.

First, the Attorney-General has been relatively vigilant in this reporting duty, perhaps more so than in some comparative jurisdictions, so reports arise more frequently. Secondly, the section 7 report represents one opinion on rights-consistency, albeit an authoritative one. It is open to the House to take a different view, either on the scope of the protected right or justifiability of any infringement. Committees in the House often touch on rights implications, although these deliberations do not tend to match the formal analytic voice of a section 7 report, and disagreement may be expressed more informally. Thirdly, the formal vetting function has a deeper – but largely hidden – prophylactic role in earlier stages of the policy and legislative drafting process. The Bill of Rights Act vetting function has ensured that many potential rights breaches are ironed out before the legislative text sees the light of day. This vetting function is a key aspect of the so-called Commonwealth model of bills of rights.[16]

Regulations and other secondary legislation must be rights-consistent, because their delegated character has a status more akin to an administrative decision. Although, strictly speaking, regulations fall within the meaning of an enactment that would be protected against invalidation by section 4, the courts have reasoned that the legislative scheme does not

[14] Legislation Design and Advisory Committee (www.ldac.org.nz). Cabinet has mandated expectations about compliance with the Committee's Legislation Guidelines: Cabinet Circular, 'Legislation guidelines' (CO (18)1, July 2018).

[15] Standing Orders of the House of Representatives 2020, SO 269.

[16] S Gardbaum, 'The New Commonwealth Model of Constitutionalism' (2001) 49 *American Journal of Comparative Law* 707, 710 and 747–48.

protect regulations that unjustifiably breach rights.[17] Any empowering provision must be given a rights-consistent interpretation by virtue of section 6 and the discretion to make regulations necessarily excludes regulations which unjustifiably breach rights. Any such regulations are ultra vires, or outside the law, in the ordinary administrative law sense.

In relation to administrative functions, discretionary decisions made under legislative or other authority must be compliant with the Bill of Rights Act. Empowering legislation must, if possible, be read consistently with protected rights unless otherwise justified under section 5 – effectively circumscribing the scope of delegated discretion. It follows that non-compliance with the Bill of Rights Act provides a basis on which a decision may be invalidated under standard principles of administrative law. Although rarely articulated, non-compliance with the Bill of Rights Act amounts to a type of unlawfulness or error of law.

In addition, the Bill of Rights Act has a procedural dimension because it fortifies the principle of natural justice, although the courts have tended to read this protection co-extensively with its common law sibling (section 27(1)).[18] The right to seek judicial review is also enshrined (section 27(2)). Any substantive dimension of the Bill of Rights Act is, perhaps surprisingly, more muted. In principle, the interaction between sections 4, 5 and 6 should bring a strong focus on whether an administrative decision amounts to a justified limitation on rights. Yet, the courts rarely test administrative decisions against the proportionality calculus of section 5.[19] This also means speculation that the Bill of Rights Act might usher in proportionality as the standard measure for testing the substantive merits of administrative decisions has not been realised. Geiringer observes that: 'New Zealand judges tend to associate proportionality with the most rigid and structured version of proportionality analysis that is available, that is the version that is most in tension with New Zealand's contextualist administrative law culture'.[20] That is perhaps ironic given administrative decisions were originally slated as one of the Bill of Rights Act's key targets.[21]

[17] *Drew v Attorney-General* [2002] 1 NZLR 58 (CA).

[18] *Combined Beneficiaries Union Inc v Auckland City COGS Committee* [2009] 2 NZLR 56 (CA).

[19] C Geiringer, 'Sources of Resistance to Proportionality Review of Administrative Power under the New Zealand Bill of Rights Act' (2013) 11 *New Zealand Journal of Public and International Law* 123, 137.

[20] Ibid 158.

[21] J McLean, P Rishworth, and M Taggart, 'The Impact of the Bill of Rights on Administrative Law' in *The New Zealand Bill of Rights Act 1990* (Auckland, Legal Research Foundation, 1992) 62, 63.

The judiciary is expressly subject to the Act. The courts naturally have an enforcement role, ensuring the government and other bodies subject to the Bill of Rights Act comply with their human rights obligations. The guardianship role also manifests itself in a number of different ways. First, the Bill of Rights Act interpretive direction in section 6 means the courts have significant power to read and apply legislation in a rights-consistent way – where such meaning is available and not otherwise excluded. No formal remedy is required, because the promotion of rights takes place in the course of the courts' traditional responsibility for determining legal meaning. Other legal consequences may follow, though. For example, a rights-consistent interpretation of an administrative power may, as discussed earlier, lead to a ruling that the executive has acted unlawfully as a matter of administrative law. Much of the influence of the Bill of Rights Act in practice is attributable to this interpretative approach.

Secondly, the Bill of Rights Act inevitably influences the common law, although how it does so is slightly uncertain. The Bill of Rights Act does not directly apply to disputes between private parties because its scope is restricted to governmental bodies or others performing a public function. But rights might be relevant if the dispute involves questions of legislative meaning and the rights-consistent directive is engaged. It follows that, in the absence of any public dimension, the Bill of Rights Act does not explicitly address the consistency of the common law with rights and freedoms. The courts, however, will still usually be mindful of the Bill of Rights Act when developing the common law. For example, judges have sometimes seized on the constitutional character of the Bill of Rights Act and its role in expressing our legal system's normative values in order to justify developing the common law in a rights-friendly manner.[22] The precise path by which the Bill of Rights Act informs this development of the common law is unclear, though. Some argue the principle of horizontal effect demands a rights-consistent common law.[23] The New Zealand courts have not explicitly adopted this principle. But they have still been content for the Bill of Rights Act to inform common law developments, indirectly at least.

Thirdly, the courts can award damages to anyone affected by a breach of the Bill of Rights Act. This remedy was recognised by the Court of Appeal in *Baigent's case*, based on the need to provide effective remedies

[22] *Hosking v Runting* [2005] 1 NZLR 1 (CA), [178].
[23] Butler and Butler (n 7) 5.8.23.

for breaches.[24] In a nice example of constitutional dialogue, the executive branch formally considered but decided against legislative change of that decision.[25] Damages for breaches of the Bill of Rights Act were treated as a public law action, rather a private law action in tort, in order to avoid the immunity provisions in the Crown Proceedings Act 1950. However, the trigger for awarding compensation for rights breaches is high. Damages are only awarded if non-monetary relief does not sufficiently vindicate or redress the breach.[26] Amounts awarded are usually relatively modest and most commonly arise in cases of unlawful detention.[27]

Finally, the courts have the power to formally declare legislation inconsistent with the Bill of Rights Act, even though they do not have the power to invalidate legislation. Although the possibility of such a remedy was often floated,[28] the power to grant declarations of legislative inconsistency was only definitively recognised by the Supreme Court in 2018 in *Attorney-General v Taylor*.[29] The Supreme Court declared that disenfranchising all prisoners unjustifiably breached the right to vote protection (a point conceded by the Attorney-General, consistently with the section 7 report issued on the relevant legislation). A majority of the Supreme Court ruled that the scheme of the Bill of Rights Act was consistent with the judicial development of such a remedy and such declarations were consistent with the usual functions of the court.[30] This ruling has generated constitutional dialogue. After the declaration was granted, the government eventually moved to address the inconsistency and Parliament passed a bill restoring the vote to prisoners serving terms of imprisonment of less than three years.[31] The government has also introduced a bill to recognise this declaratory remedy, by requiring the Attorney-General to report to Parliament on any declarations of inconsistency granted by the courts.[32]

[24] *Simpson v Attorney-General (Baigent's Case)* [1994] 3 NZLR 667 (CA).

[25] See Law Commission, 'Crown Liability and Judicial Immunity' (NZLC R37, 1997); Interpretation Act 1999, s 27.

[26] *Taunoa v Attorney-General* [2007] NZSC 70, [2008] 1 NZLR 429, [258] and [300].

[27] See eg *Dunlea v Attorney General* [2000] 3 NZLR 136 (CA); *Attorney-General v Udompun* [2005] 3 NZLR 204 (CA), [210].

[28] C Geiringer, 'On a Road to Nowhere' (2009) 40(3) *Victoria University of Wellington Law Review* 613.

[29] *Attorney-General v Taylor* [2018] NZSC 104, [2019] 1 NZLR 213.

[30] Ibid [53].

[31] Electoral (Registration of Sentenced Prisoners) Amendment Act 2020.

[32] New Zealand Bill of Rights (Declarations of Inconsistency) Amendment Bill 2020 (230-1), proposing to insert a new s 7A (Attorney-General to report to Parliament declaration of inconsistency) into the Bill of Rights Act.

The institutional activities of the different branches must also be rights-consistent. Parliament's non-legislative activities, such as its proceedings, hearings and regulation of the parliamentary precinct, are subject to the Bill of Rights Act (although parliamentary privilege blocks judicial supervision of some aspects of those activities). The courts also must, in their institutional role, ensure the conduct of court proceedings and other judicial activities are rights-consistent. This includes ensuring they give effect to the various protections that apply in the criminal justice process and the general obligation to act in accordance with the principles of natural justice.

D. Sites of Contest

While the Bill of Rights Act is relatively ubiquitous in its reach, a few sites of contest have been particularly vigorous in practice, especially regarding criminal process rights, expressive rights and, more recently, protections against discrimination and bodily security. A handful of cases are illustrative.

The Bill of Rights Act has been particularly active in the area of criminal procedure and punishment – fortifying the rights of individuals against the coercive muscle of the state. Many of the early landmark rights cases addressed the legality and fairness of search, arrest, detention and trial, including *Ministry of Transport v Noort* (right to a lawyer when detained for drink-driving tests), *Baigent's case* (compensation for unreasonable search), and *Martin v District Court at Tauranga* (right to be tried without delay).[33] The leading case on the methodology in Bill of Rights Act cases, *Hansen v R*, addressed the burden of proof in drug possession and supply cases.[34] Other notable cases, including *Poumako*, *Pora* and *Taunoa*, have grappled with severe penal regimes, guarding the protections against retrospective penalties, double jeopardy and other liberty protections – with mixed success for criminal defendants.[35]

Expressive rights have been tested in a number of different ways. In *Moonen*, the Court of Appeal looked at how freedom of expression should be factored into the interpretation of censorship legislation,

[33] *Ministry of Transport v Noort* [1992] 3 NZLR 260 (CA); *Simpson v Attorney-General (Baigent's Case)* [1994] 3 NZLR 667 (CA); *Martin v District Court at Tauranga* [1995] 2 NZLR 419 (CA).

[34] *Hansen v R* [2007] NZSC 7, [2007] 3 NZLR 1.

[35] *R v Poumako* [2000] 2 NZLR 695 (CA); *R v Pora* [2001] 2 NZLR 37 (CA); *Taunoa v Attorney-General* [2007] NZSC 70, [2008] 1 NZLR 429.

emphasising the interpretative force of the Bill of Rights Act.[36] The Court ruled the classification of publications as objectionable (and thus prohibited) needed to take into account freedom of expression. A series of protest-related cases have also seen public order offences read down to accommodate expressive rights. Convictions for disorderly and offensive behaviour were quashed by the Supreme Court in *Brooker* (intimidatory musical protest outside police officer's house) and *Morse* (disruptive flag burning protest at an Anzac Day memorial service).[37] And, in *Hopkinson*, a conviction against a specific flag burning offence was overturned, after the High Court ruled the 'dishonour' element in the offence should be given a rights-consistent meaning tantamount to 'vilify'.[38]

The protection against discrimination has generated some significant litigation, both directly in the courts and via the related work of the Human Rights Review Tribunal. However, the influence of this right has been patchy, as the courts have wrestled with the methodology for appraising government policies which inevitably target different class of people. In the early days of the Bill of Rights, in *Quilter*, a challenge to the exclusion of same-sex couples from marriage failed, with judges ruling the exclusion was non-discriminatory – analysis now out of step with subsequent jurisprudence elsewhere – or was more appropriately addressed through legislative reform.[39] More recent discrimination claims arising from differential policy treatment have had mixed success, including *Atkinson* (exclusion of family members from disability support caregiver payment discriminatory and unjustified), *Child Poverty Action Group* (tax credit for working families discriminated against beneficiaries with child but was justified), *Re AMM* (meaning of spouse in adoption legislation should and could be read to include opposite sex de facto couples in order to avoid marital status discrimination), and *Ngaronoa* (ban on prisoner voting did not indirectly discriminate against Māori, even though Māori are significantly over-represented in the prison population).[40]

[36] *Moonen v Film and Literature Board of Review* [2000] 2 NZLR 9 (CA).

[37] *Brooker v Police* [2007] NZSC 30, [2007] 3 NZLR 91; *Morse v Police* [2011] NZSC 45, [2012] 2 NZLR 1.

[38] *Hopkinson v Police* [2004] 3 NZLR 704 (HC), [81].

[39] *Quilter v Attorney-General* [1998] 1 NZLR 523 (CA), 526 and 578.

[40] *Ministry of Health v Atkinson* [2012] NZCA 185, [2012] 3 NZLR 456; *Child Poverty Action Group Inc v Attorney-General* [2013] NZCA 402, [2013] 3 NZLR 729; *Re AMM* [2010] NZFLR 629 (HC); *Ngaronoa v Attorney-General* [2017] NZCA 351, [2017] 3 NZLR 643.

Security of the person and mobility rights have also generated some prominent cases. In *New Health*, an argument that the right to refuse medical treatment prevented local authorities from adding fluoride to public water supply failed; a majority ruled the public health benefits of avoiding dental decay justified (or might in some cases justify) the lack of choice over ingesting fluoridated water.[41] In *Seales*, a terminally ill woman was unsuccessful in obtaining declarations that medically assisted death was not criminal or that legislation preventing such assistance breached her right to life or the protection against cruel treatment.[42] In *Borrowdale*, an attack on the coronavirus pandemic lockdown largely failed (but is under appeal at the time of writing).[43] The High Court held the stay-at-home order was reasonable, proportionate and justified, and the power to issue these health orders did not need to be read down because the emergency purpose of the legislative regime contemplated limitation of mobility rights. Finally, inconsistency between electoral rights and legislation disenfranchising prisoners notably led to the Supreme Court embracing the declaration of legislative inconsistency in *Taylor*.[44]

The Bill of Rights Act has generated some controversial moments in the parliamentary domain too. Legislative debates about matters such as same-sex marriage and civil unions, physical discipline of children, search and seizure controls, euthanasia, prisoner voting, anti-terrorism and penal policy have included some fiery rights discourse. These have often involved complaints about the undue limitation of rights but also endorsement of legislation based on protection of rights. The Attorney-General's vetting function has occasionally prompted argument. The absence of any section 7 report on legislation imposing heavy electoral finance and campaigning restrictions was the subject of criticism (and was subsequently but unsuccessfully litigated).[45] When legislation was passed vesting the foreshore and seabed in the Crown and codifying, in heavily diminished form, related Māori customary rights, the Attorney-General's opinion that doing so did not unjustifiably breach the rights of Māori was contentious.[46] At other times, Parliament has

[41] *New Health New Zealand Inc v South Taranaki District Council* [2018] NZSC 59, [2018] 1 NZLR 948.

[42] *Seales v Attorney-General* [2015] NZHC 1239, [2015] 3 NZLR 556.

[43] *Borrowdale v Director-General of Health* (n 5).

[44] *Attorney-General v Taylor* (n 29).

[45] *Boscawen v Attorney-General* [2009] NZCA 12, [2009] 2 NZLR 229.

[46] Attorney-General, *Report on the Foreshore and Seabed Bill* (2004).

passed legislation, despite the identification of unjustified limitations on rights, without much fuss or concern. It is difficult to see a strong pattern in the rights engaged but disregarded in the legislative process because the section 7 reports issued by Attorney-General tend to span the full gamut of rights.

E. Efficacy

The Bill of Rights Act has changed the way the legal and political system deals with rights. This is not the place for a full appraisal of its efficacy but it is fair to say the influence of the Bill of Rights Act has been patchy. As its original promoter, Sir Geoffrey Palmer, puts it, the Act 'has had positive achievements but it has not resulted in the transformational change that propelled the initial proposal for an entrenched, supreme law bill of rights' (although he still advocates for a supreme bill of rights and the dilution of Parliament's full power to make law).[47] Similarly, leading bill of rights scholar, Professor Claudia Geiringer, charts its effect on New Zealand law and practice as follows:[48]

> [A] picture starts to emerge of a legal instrument that has never quite grown into the skin that some of the academic literature tried, valiantly, to clothe it in. I'm not suggesting that it's made no difference to our legal system; clearly it has. Nor that it didn't make *more* difference than some initially expected. … But I *do* want to suggest that the Bill of Rights hasn't lived up to the promise shown in some of those early criminal procedure decisions. And that, in many areas of operation, it hasn't had the transformative effect that some have hoped or claimed for it.

Much like our constitutional development generally, we see the influence of the Bill of Rights Act as incremental and complex. Revolutionary moments are rare and are often teamed with instances of disappointment. But dialogical developments will continue and the jurisprudence will evolve, especially as the Bill of Rights Act continues to inject itself into the culture of all branches of government.

[47] G Palmer, 'What the New Zealand Bill of Rights Act Aimed To Do, Why It Did Not Succeed and How It Can Be Repaired' (2016) 14 *New Zealand Journal of Public and International Law* 169.

[48] C Geiringer, 'Mr Bulwark and the Protection of Human Rights' (2014) 45 *Victoria University of Wellington Law Review* 367.

III. FUNDAMENTAL RIGHTS AND THE COMMON LAW

The New Zealand courts have also recognised fundamental rights inherent in the common law and have worked to ensure they are adequately respected in governmental decision-making. One of the favoured mechanisms to do so is the common law principle of legality, which favours rights-consistent readings of legislation in a similar way to the Bill of Rights Act. But there are a range of judicial techniques which seek to give rights extra prominence and protection.

First, the principle of legality is now a common interpretative technique deployed by the courts, where legislation is read as compatibly as possible with fundamental human rights. As Lord Hoffmann explained in *Simms*: 'In the absence of express language or necessary implication to the contrary, the courts therefore presume that even the most general words were intended to be subject to the basic rights of the individual.'[49] The principle demands that Parliament express a deliberate and unambiguous intention in law to abridge rights. This raises the political stakes when passing such a law, with a view to squarely engaging the practical and extra-legal pressures against doing so. The interpretative technique deftly keeps legislative supremacy intact, by ultimately conceding that a law that unequivocally abridges rights must be applied by the courts on its terms.

This principle has been endorsed in New Zealand in a number of cases.[50] The potential force of the principle is seen in the *Poumako* case, where the Court of Appeal narrowed the impact of a retrospective penalty.[51] A majority suggested the retrospective effect did not need to apply fully and could be 'confined' to the 15-day period before the new penalty was passed into law when the concept of home invasion was first mentioned on the statute book. The normative force of the principle of legality has yet to be fully charted, especially the extent to which it might be limited by some sense of reasonable limitations analogous to the methodology under the Bill of Rights Act.[52] Also, as yet unanswered is whether the principle extends to rights afforded to iwi and hapū under te Tiriti o Waitangi. There seems no reason for it not to and

[49] *R (Simms) v Secretary of State for the Home Department* [2000] 2 AC 115, [1999] 3 WLR 328 (HL), 131.

[50] *Cropp v Judicial Committee* [2008] NZSC 46, [2008] 3 NZLR 774; *New Health* (n 41).

[51] *Poumako* (n 35).

[52] H Wilberg, 'Common Law Rights Have Justified Limits' in D Meagher, M Groves and R French (eds), *The Principle of Legality in Australia and New Zealand* (New South Wales, Federation Press, 2017) 139.

this potential has been nodded to by the courts although it has yet to crystallise definitively.[53]

Secondly, the courts have sometimes increased the depth of scrutiny when reviewing administrative decisions if fundamental human rights are implicated. The Court of Appeal in *Kim* explained this type of review as requiring an assessment of whether 'the decision has been reached on sufficient evidence and has been fully justified, while recognising that Parliament has entrusted the Minister (not the courts) to undertake adequate enquiries and to exercise her judgment on whether surrender should be ordered'.[54] This judicial method is often traced back to English developments in the unreasonableness ground of review, where a more intensive or demanding standard is expected or a 'hard look' is applied.[55] But, in principle, this more demanding supervisory eye could apply more generally.[56] The parameters of this approach remain oddly unsettled. A general impression that human rights are at stake, especially in the case of vulnerable people, seems to be the most common trigger. The direct engagement of human rights instruments is also common. The way in which this more demanding standard is expressed is also not yet universally settled. Some common instances include application of a simple standard of reasonableness (*Wolf*), 'anxious or heightened scrutiny' (*Kim*) or 'hard look' (*Gwynn* and *McGrath*).[57] One of us stated in a recent judgment that, in practice even if not in theory, a label such as heightened scrutiny 'serves as a signal to courts of the degree of priority of attention and care to be accorded to one case compared to another in their busy workloads' and 'that is good reason for the appropriate "intensity" of judicial review being explicitly signalled, depending on its context'.[58]

[53] See *Ngaronoa v Attorney-General* (n 40) [39]–[52].

[54] *Kim v Minister of Justice* [2019] NZCA 209, [2019] 3 NZLR 173, [45], adopting *Kim v Minister of Justice* [2016] NZHC 1490, [2016] 3 NZLR 425, [7]. On appeal, the Supreme Court did not express any views on heightened scrutiny: *Minister of Justice v Kim* [2021] NZSC 57.

[55] *Bugdaycay v Secretary of State for the Home Department* [1987] AC 514, [1987] 2 WLR 606 (HL); *R (Smith) v Ministry of Defence* [1996] QB 517, [1996] 2 WLR 305 (CA).

[56] DR Knight, *Vigilance and Restraint in the Common Law of Judicial Review* (Cambridge, Cambridge University Press, 2018) ch 4.

[57] *Wolf v Minister of Immigration* [2004] NZAR 414 (HC), [72]; *Kim v Minister of Justice of New Zealand* [2019] 3 NZLR 173 (CA); *Gwynn v Napier City Council* [2018] NZHC 1943, [2018] NZAR 1410; *McGrath v Minister of Justice* [2014] NZHC 3279, [2015] NZAR 122.

[58] *Hauraki Coromandel Climate Action Inc v Thames-Coromandel District Council* [2020] NZHC 3228, [49].

Thirdly, human rights are also often protected by instruments at international law. There are two distinct approaches to animation of domestic decision-making by international law norms. The relevancy principle demands that decision-makers take into account any relevant international law obligations the government has agreed to.[59] However, as with all mandatory relevant considerations, the weight to be given to human rights commitments remains with the decision-maker, subject to usual reasonableness expectations. In the Court of Appeal's decision in *Tavita*, Cooke J, in an obiter comment, condemned as 'unattractive' an argument that international obligations not mentioned in the governing statute could be ignored by a minister when making discretionary deportation decisions.[60] This crystallised, without further firm judicial determination, into a requirement that decision-makers turn their mind to, and take seriously, relevant international commitments.[61] A more powerful approach echoes the principle of legality, by inviting the courts to read legislation in a way that preserves and gives effect to human rights (and other) commitments at an international level, except in cases where the text of the legislation cannot be so read.[62] For example, in *Ye*, discretionary powers to make and cancel removal orders for overstayers were read subject to an implicit requirement that those powers should be exercised consistently with humanitarian considerations and that children's interests should be given special consideration in decisions affecting them.[63] This approach appears to have largely taken over from the softer relevancy approach in *Tavita*.[64]

Fourthly, the courts have suggested that the principle of implied repeal might be read narrowly, so that constitutional laws enshrining fundamental human rights can only be amended or repealed expressly. For example, in *Pora*, a minority of the Court of Appeal said 'Parliament must speak plainly if it wishes to derogate from [such] principles' and they would have not given the penalty any retrospective effect.[65] The majority thought Parliament had made a 'clear pronouncement' and felt obliged to give effect to the new law over the earlier one, but conveyed

[59] *Tavita v Minister of Immigration* [1994] 2 NZLR 257 (CA).

[60] Ibid 266.

[61] C Geiringer, '*Tavita* and All That' (2004) 21 *New Zealand Universities Law Review* 66.

[62] *Puli'uvea v Removal Review Authority* [1996] 3 NZLR 538 (CA); *Zaoui v Attorney-General* [2005] 1 NZLR 577 (CA); see generally C Geiringer, 'International Law through the Lens of *Zaoui*' (2006) 17 *Public Law Review* 300.

[63] *Ye v Minister of Immigration* [2009] NZSC 76, [2010] 1 NZLR 104.

[64] Geiringer (n 62).

[65] *Pora* (n 35), [40] and [56].

a similar sentiment that some 'leading' laws might not be able to be overridden by the implied repeal doctrine.[66] The notion that implied repeal might not apply in relation to fundamental provisions is consistent with developments elsewhere, including *Thoburn* in England.[67] This approach potentially gives a degree of quasi-constitutional status to human rights and unsettles the otherwise flat legislative hierarchy that traditionally operates in New Zealand.

Finally, as explained in Chapter 6, some judges have historically toyed with the idea that some common law rights might lie so deep that their abridgement lies beyond the competency of Parliament.

All these techniques are emblematic of how the common law, especially proceedings supervising government action, has the potential to shift gears when fundamental rights are implicated. But, of course, the protection of rights (broadly defined) has been an important thread of the common law in its everyday work too. Law students are still taught famous common law cases protecting individual rights such as the 1762 ruling that the King's messengers committed trespass when they entered John Entick's home and seized his papers without any legal mandate.[68] Other more contemporary New Zealand common law cases protecting important rights abound too.

IV. OTHER STATUTORY RIGHTS PROTECTIONS

Fundamental rights are also protected or reinforced in bespoke legal regimes, in addition to their general protection under the Bill of Rights Act or at common law.

The Privacy Act 2020 sets up an extensive regime for protection of personal information and data protection generally. A privacy commissioner oversees this domain and determines complaints from individuals about interference with their privacy. Complaints can be escalated to the Human Rights Review Tribunal.

The Human Rights Act 1993 provides a detailed anti-discrimination regime, in the public and private spheres, prohibiting direct and indirect discrimination on the grounds of sex, marital status, religious belief, colour, race, ethnic or national origins, disability, age, political opinion, employment status, family status and sexual orientation.

[66] Ibid [114].
[67] *Thoburn v Sunderland City Council* [2003] QB 151, [2002] EWHC 195 (Admin).
[68] *Entick v Carrington* (1765) 19 Howell's State Trials 1029, 95 ER 807.

There are a handful of specific and narrow exceptions, in areas such as employment, education and training, access to places and facilities and provision of goods and services. Discrimination by government or others performing a public function is unlawful if it amounts to an unjustified limit on the freedom from discrimination under section 19 of the Bill of Rights Act, read in conjunction with section 5. For discrimination by private or public bodies, the Human Rights Act provides a remedial regime based around investigations and conciliation by the Human Rights Commission and, if unresolved, adjudication by the Human Rights Review Tribunal. The Human Rights Review Tribunal has a wide range of remedies and may make declarations, order compliance, award damages and grant a declaration of legislative inconsistency with the Bill of Rights Act.

Other statutory regimes regulating search and surveillance, social security, housing and education also protect human rights in particular areas.

V. CONCLUSION

While there are many dimensions to human rights, the enactment of the Bill of Rights Act marked out a special place for fundamental rights – setting out a framework to mediate the interaction between those rights and government action. Disproportionate and unjustified limitations on rights are discouraged but Parliament retains its legislative supremacy and can still enact inconsistent laws. Policing the balance is a shared responsibility but one where the courts are especially busy and engage in relatively searching examination of the rights implications of the government action.

FURTHER READING

Butler, A, and Butler, P, *New Zealand Bill of Rights Act: A Commentary*, 2nd edn (Wellington, LexisNexis, 2015).

Rishworth, P, and others, *The New Zealand Bill of Rights Act* (Oxford, Oxford University Press, 2003).

Geiringer, C, 'Mr Bulwark and the Protection of Human Rights' (2014) 45 *Victoria University of Wellington Law Review* 367.

Palmer, G, 'The Bill of Rights after Twenty-One Years: The New Zealand Constitutional Caravan Moves On?' (2013) 11 *New Zealand Journal of Public and International Law* 257.

10

Te Tiriti o Waitangi

Introduction – A Brief History of the Status of te Tiriti – Te Tiriti in the Constitution Now – Conclusion

I. INTRODUCTION

THERE IS NO doubt that te Tiriti o Waitangi / the Treaty of Waitangi is a significant constitutional document today. It affects, in various ways and to varying extents, how public power is exercised in New Zealand. It provides some ways for Māori to vindicate their rights at law. But, as one of us observed over a decade ago, the interesting question is not whether te Tiriti is constitutional but exactly how te Tiriti affects and reflects the exercise of public power in New Zealand.[1] The answers to that question reflect a remarkable period in New Zealand's constitutional development, from the 1970s to the 1990s. In that period, the meaning and legal status of te Tiriti o Waitangi was fundamentally re-interpreted in the contemporary New Zealand law and constitution. The process is an excellent example of the sort of constitutional dialogue we have seen elsewhere in this book: iterative decisions by different institutions exercising public power, reacting to each other over time, rethinking the same constitutional issues.

II. A BRIEF HISTORY OF THE STATUS OF TE TIRITI

A. Creation

Earlier in this book, we explained the creation of te Tiriti amongst the collision between the legal systems of Māori tribes and British settlers

[1] MSR Palmer, *The Treaty of Waitangi in New Zealand's Law and Constitution* (Wellington, Victoria University Press, 2008).

respectively. The operative provisions of te Tiriti, in te Reo and English, are as follows:[2]

Ko te Tuatahi

Ko nga Rangatira o te Wakaminenga me nga Rangatira katoa hoki ki hai i uru ki taua wakaminenga ka tuku rawa atu ki te Kuini o Ingarani ake tonu atu-te Kawanatanga katoa o o ratou wenua.

Article the First

The Chiefs of the Confederation of the United Tribes of New Zealand and the separate and independent Chiefs who have not become members of the Confederation cede to Her Majesty the Queen of England absolutely and without reservation all the rights and powers of Sovereignty which the said Confederation or Individual Chiefs respectively exercise or possess, or may be supposed to exercise or to possess over their respective Territories as the sole Sovereigns thereof.

Ko te Tuarua

Ko te Kuini o Ingarani ka wakarite ka wakaae ki nga Rangatira ki nga hapu-ki nga tangata katoa o Nu Tirani te tino rangatiratanga o o ratou wenua o ratou kainga me o ratou taonga katoa. Otiia ko nga Rangatira o te Wakaminenga me nga Rangatira katoa atu ka tuku ki te Kuini te hokonga o era wahi wenua e pai ai te tangata nona te Wenua-ki te ritenga o te utu e wakaritea ai e ratou ko te kai hoko e meatia nei e te Kuini hei kai hoko mona.

Article the Second

Her Majesty the Queen of England confirms and guarantees to the Chiefs and Tribes of New Zealand and to the respective families and individuals thereof the full exclusive and undisturbed possession of their Lands and Estates Forests Fisheries and other properties which they may collectively or individually possess so long as it is their wish and desire to retain the same in their possession; but the Chiefs of the United Tribes and the individual Chiefs yield to Her Majesty the exclusive right of Preemption over such lands as the proprietors thereof may be disposed to alienate at such prices as may be agreed upon between the respective Proprietors and persons appointed by Her Majesty to treat with them in that behalf.

[2] Treaty of Waitangi Act 1975, Sch 1.

Ko te Tuatoru Hei wakaritenga mai hoki tenei mo te wakaaetanga ki te Kawanatanga o te Kuini-Ka tiakina e te Kuini o Ingarani nga tangata maori katoa o Nu Tirani ka tukua ki a ratou nga tikanga katoa rite tahi ki ana mea ki nga tangata o Ingarani.	*Article the Third* In consideration thereof Her Majesty the Queen of England extends to the Natives of New Zealand Her royal protection and imparts to them all the Rights and Privileges of British Subjects.

The meaning of the English version differs from the meaning of the Māori translation, as outlined in Chapter 2.[3] Key differences include the authority ceded by Māori in article one (kāwanatanga/governance versus sovereignty) and the authority guaranteed to Māori in article two (te tino rangatiratanga/unqualified exercise of chieftainship versus exclusive and undisturbed possession). These differences continue to be matters of acute contest.

B. Te Tiriti o Waitangi Ignored

Over the 130 years after its signing there was continuing political and legal contest over the meaning and legal status of te Tiriti.[4] We sketch some of the key shifts in thinking over that time, as te Tiriti has been interpreted and re-interpreted.

There was ongoing physical conflict between the Crown and particular iwi and hapū from 1843 until the 1890s. Settlers outnumbered Māori by around 1858 and settler demand for land was strong. During the 1840s there was armed conflict between the Crown and iwi and hapū in Northland and Wellington and war in the 1860s in Taranaki and Waikato. The Native Land Court was established by the colonial government to convert collective native title to individual titles that could be sold. It was effective in doing that. By the end of the nineteenth century,

[3] Professor Sir Hugh Kawharu's English translation of the te reo text is widely acknowledged and has been endorsed by the Waitangi Tribunal: M Belgrave, M Kawharu and D Williams (eds), *Waitangi Revisited* (Oxford, Oxford University Press, 1989) 390–93; Waitangi Tribunal, 'Translation of the te reo Māori text' (www.waitangitribunal.govt.nz).

[4] For example see H Robinson, 'Simple Nullity or Birth of Law and Order?' (2010) 24 *New Zealand Universities Law Review* 259; M Hickford, 'John Salmond and Native Title in New Zealand' (2007) 38 *Victoria University of Wellington Law Review* 853.

Māori were around 6 per cent of the population and held around 17 per cent of the land.[5]

Many Pākehā seemed determined to forget about te Tiriti. The 50th anniversary in 1890 was notable for debate about what date in 1840 was the founding moment of the colony, sidelining te Tiriti. But Māori continued to push for te Tiriti to be honoured, trying several different strategies. Ngāpuhi initiated a deputation to London in the 1880s to request a royal commission and an audience with Queen Victoria.[6] Kotahitanga hui, particularly in the 1890s, established a Māori equivalent to Parliament in the 1890s. Individual Māori played increasingly prominent roles in Pākehā politics from around the same time. Māori attempted to form a Māori contingent of the New Zealand Division in the First World War, and did form a Māori Battalion in the Second World War. The Māori population increased again. In the 1920s the Māori prophet, Tahupōtiki Ratana, formed the Ratana Church which called for ratification of te Tiriti, organised a petition to Parliament, formed itself into a political party and was elected in a Māori seat. Ratana allied itself with the New Zealand Labour Party in 1935, a bond which endures today.

There were also legal forays to the courts but they yielded little recognition of a domestic legal status of te Tiriti. For example:

- In 1847, the Supreme Court partially relied on the English version of te Tiriti, but ignored much legal argument based on it, in upholding the common law of aboriginal title, and the Crown's exclusive right to extinguish it (*Symonds*).[7]
- In 1856, in a judgment lost and found again only in 2010, the Acting Chief Justice of New Zealand observed that recognition in te Tiriti of the continued right of Māori over their lands was a reason why New Zealand had not been acquired by the British Crown by cession (*McLiver v Macky*).[8]
- In 1877, New Zealand's third Chief Justice, Prendergast CJ, characterised te Tiriti as a 'simple nullity' in so far as it purported to cede

[5] Matthew Wright, *The Reed Illustrated History of New Zealand* (Auckland, Reed, 2004) 201.

[6] Matthew Wright, *Waitangi: A Living Treaty* (Auckland, Bateman Books, 2019) 170.

[7] *R v Symonds* (1840–1932) NZPCC 387 (SC).

[8] *McLiver v Macky* (1856), discussed in DV Williams, 'The Pre-history of the English Laws Act 1858' (2010) 41 *Victoria University of Wellington Law Review* 361.

sovereignty, since Māori did not and could not have had sovereignty (*Parata*).[9]

- In 1903, the Judicial Committee of the Privy Council appeared simply to assume te Tiriti had legal status, in a decision condemned by the then (Pākehā) New Zealand legal profession (*Wallis*).[10]
- In 1913, the Court of Appeal agreed te Tiriti was unenforceable at domestic law unless made so by legislative authority and that had not been done (*Korokai*).[11]
- In 1941, the Judicial Committee of the Privy Council affirmed the proposition that te Tiriti was not part of New Zealand law unless Parliament specifically so provides (*Te Heuheu Tukino*).[12]

This ambivalence about te Tiriti's legal status was not settled until Parliament opened the legislative gate to judicial consideration of the Treaty in 1986.

C. Te Tiriti Revisited

In the late 1960s, there was a renaissance of strengthening Māori cultural and political assertiveness. Māori protest about land claims was galvanised by the passage of the Maori Affairs Amendment Act 1967 and formation of Ngā Tamatoa, a group of young Māori activists, in 1970. In September 1972, Ngā Tamatoa presented a petition of 30,000 signatures to have te reo Māori (the Māori language) taught in schools. In 1975, an alliance of Ngā Tamatoa and traditional elders organised the Māori Land March, in which some 5,000 people marched from one end of the North Island to the other to protest against the loss of Māori land.

The political system reacted in different ways at different times. The differences between two Cabinet papers, in May 1971 and February 1974, are a fascinating example of the importance of changes in the contexts of politics, culture and academic scholarship, in less than three years.[13]

[9] *Parata v Bishop of Wellington & the Attorney-General* (1877) 3 NZJur (NS) 72 (SC); see DV Williams, *A Simple Nullity?* (Auckland, Auckland University Press, 2011).

[10] *Wallis v Solicitor-General* [1903] AC 173, (1903) NZPCC 23.

[11] *Korokai v Solicitor-General* (1912) 32 NZLR 321 (CA).

[12] *Te Heuheu Tukino v Aotea District Māori Land Board* [1941] NZLR 590 (PC); A Frame, 'Hoani Te Heuheu's case in London 1940–1941' [2006] 22 *New Zealand Universities Law Review* 148.

[13] This part of the chapter is drawn from Palmer, *Treaty of Waitangi* (n 1) 132–34 and MSR Palmer, 'Indigenous Rights: New Zealand' in DS Law (ed), *Constitutionalism in Context* (Cambridge, Cambridge University Press, forthcoming 2022).

On 1 March 1971, the Cabinet of the National government requested a paper 'on the reasons why the Treaty of Waitangi has not been given force of law, with a recommendation whether any action should now be taken'.[14] The resulting Cabinet paper of 27 May 1971, from the Ministers of Justice and Māori Affairs (both Pākehā), relied only on the English version of te Tiriti in summarising its provisions. The paper left open the question of whether te Tiriti was binding at international law, but observed that the Crown was at least morally bound by it. The paper took the view that ratification was superfluous since, if te Tiriti was binding in international law, it was in force without ratification and the government was clearly bound by it.

The only consideration of the meaning of te Tiriti in the 1971 Cabinet paper was of Article II, when it said '[t]he most important objection to giving the Treaty the force of law by Act of Parliament is the uncertainty to which the incorporation of the very general language of Article II into New Zealand law would give rise'.[15] Appendix II of the paper, by the Secretary of Māori and Island Affairs, included 'an accurate translation of the Maori version of the Second article' that would be regarded today as wrong: 'The Queen of England confirms and guarantees to the Chiefs and Tribes and to all the people of New Zealand the full possession of their lands, their homes and all their possessions'. In a statement that would today be regarded as breathtakingly mistaken, it said: 'It must be assumed, however, that the English version was the authoritative version and that the Maori version was simply a translation, albeit an inexact one'.[16] The paper noted there had been complaints that some legislation had been inconsistent with Articles II and III of te Tiriti, but stated '[t]hey are criticisms of detail that can properly be the subject of detailed examination and, if necessary, remedy'.[17]

The Cabinet paper went on to observe that 'what [some Māori] really want is a Maori Bill of Rights following or based on the text of the Treaty, which would presumably have a status superior to that of an ordinary Act of Parliament' which would be 'alien to New Zealand traditions and practice'.[18] Following the ministers' recommendation, Cabinet 'declined to take any steps to ratify the Treaty of Waitangi or to incorporate it in

[14] Cabinet Paper, 'Treaty of Waitangi', 27 May 1971, CP (71) 517, [1].
[15] Ibid [17].
[16] Appendix II, [4].
[17] Ibid [16].
[18] Ibid [17] and [18].

legislation', but it invited the Minister of Māori Affairs to consult with the New Zealand Māori Council 'with the object of ascertaining what provisions of the existing law the Council considers to be inconsistent with the Treaty of Waitangi'.[19]

The following year, in November 1972, a Labour government was elected, including Māori MPs from the four Māori electorates. Matiu Rata became the Minister of Māori Affairs and Cabinet asked Rata to consider how to deliver on Labour's 1972 election manifesto commitment to 'examine a practical means of legally acknowledging the principles set out in the Treaty of Waitangi'. Rata did so by chairing the government's Caucus Committee on Māori Affairs, made up of four Māori MPs and two Pākehā MPs, over 1973 and 1974. The Committee issued two reports.[20]

Both reports contained an extensive analysis of the differences in the Māori and English versions of te Tiriti and some of the background of its signing. They referred to a seminal article on the differences between the Māori and English language versions of te Tiriti that had been published in 1972 by academic Ruth Ross.[21] Professor James Rutherford's English translation of the Māori version of te Tiriti which translated 'kāwanatanga' as 'governorship', and 'rangatiratanga' as 'full chieftainship' was also appended.[22] The Caucus Committee regarded both language versions as 'equally valid' and recommended both warranted recognition, one complementing the other.[23] It considered 'the total significance of the Treaty of Waitangi as a document expressing mutuality is more important than the segments concerned with which provisions need legislative action'.[24]

The first report recommended a permanent standing committee of the House of Representatives be established to consider alleged breaches of the Treaty. But Cabinet preferred a legislative solution and invited the Caucus committee to revise its proposal accordingly, which it did in its second report. After several deferrals, the Cabinet effectively adopted

[19] Cabinet Minute, 'Treaty of Waitangi', 16 August 1971, CM 71/32/27.

[20] Cabinet Paper, 'Report of the Government Caucus Committee on Maori Affairs on the Treaty of Waitangi', 5 February 1974; Cabinet Paper, 'Report of the Caucus Committee on Maori Affairs on the Treaty of Waitangi', 25 February 1974.

[21] Ibid [10]–[12], citing RM Ross, 'Te Tiriti o Waitangi' (1972) 6 *New Zealand Journal of History* 129.

[22] Robinson (n 4) 269; M Belgrave, *Historical Frictions* (Auckland, Auckland University Press, 2005) 49.

[23] Cabinet Paper, 25 February 1974 (n 20) [7], [8] and [13].

[24] Ibid [13].

the Caucus Committee's revised proposal by approving in principle a preliminary draft Treaty of Waitangi Bill. This approval was subject to amending the operative clause to refer to 'the principles' of the Treaty of Waitangi, reflecting the wording of Labour's manifesto commitment.[25] There were further discussions of its drafting and effect by Cabinet after the death of Prime Minister Norman Kirk in August 1974, until its passage in October 1975, just before the Māori land march reached Parliament. Interestingly, initial drafting gave te Tiriti binding effect in law but that was reversed by Cabinet. And proposals to give it retrospective effect were turned down.[26]

D. The Waitangi Tribunal

The Treaty of Waitangi Act 1975 created the Waitangi Tribunal as a permanent commission of inquiry to inquire into and make recommendations on allegations of breaches of te Tiriti o Waitangi from that point onwards. Its recommendations were to relate to the 'practical application of the principles of the Treaty and, for that purpose, to determine its meaning and effect and whether certain matters are inconsistent with those principles'.[27] The Act defined the Treaty of Waitangi as it was to be recognised in law. It delegated to the Waitangi Tribunal the role of interpreting te Tiriti. The Act effectively incorporated te Tiriti into New Zealand law, giving it legal status, but without giving it binding effect enforceable through the courts.

The early days of the Waitangi Tribunal were fraught. The National government elected in November 1975 did not establish the Tribunal until the end of 1976 and appears only to have acted then on the basis of legal risk and once a complaint to the Tribunal had been received.[28] The early decisions of the Tribunal were conservative and legalistic.[29] But from 1980, the Tribunal was chaired by Sir Edward Taihakurei Durie, the first Māori Chief Judge of the Māori Land Court, and the Tribunal was composed of both Māori and Pākehā. In an impressive display of 'soft power', it developed a new approach: an inquisitorial, non-legalistic,

[25] Cabinet Minute, 'Report of the Caucus Committee on Maori Affairs on the Treaty of Waitangi', 1 April 1974, CM 74/11/22.

[26] Palmer, *Treaty of Waitangi* (n 1) 186–87.

[27] Treaty of Waitangi Act 1975, preamble.

[28] Palmer, *Treaty of Waitangi* (n 1) 187–88.

[29] Ibid 106.

relational approach, responsive to both Māori and Pākehā concerns and aiming to find pragmatic solutions.[30]

From 1983 to 1986, the Tribunal issued four substantive cornerstone reports that interpreted the meaning of te Tiriti o Waitangi in a contemporary context.[31] In the abstract, the Tribunal characterised te Tiriti as representing a comforting relational compromise: 'the gift of the right to make laws in return for the promise to do so, so as to acknowledge and protect the interests of the indigenous inhabitants'.[32] In relation to specific issues, it sought to recommend practical actions to remedy breaches. These Tribunal reports were careful, though increasingly assertive, in formulating an approach to interpreting te Tiriti. They were wide-ranging in their recommendations, including recommendations for statutory changes and compensation for breaches, but were carefully calibrated.

E. Legislative References and Judicial Enforcement

In 1985, a new Labour government delivered on an election campaign promise to pass legislation retrospectively extending the Tribunal's power to examine alleged breaches of te Tiriti back to 1840. The same year the government issued a White Paper proposing that an entrenched supreme law Bill of Rights Act that also included te Tiriti should be enacted. The consequence was that, in 1986, the government could hardly ignore the relevance of te Tiriti when fundamentally restructuring the organisation of government in relation to land by transferring land and assets from the Crown to separate state-owned legal entities. The Waitangi Tribunal issued an urgent interim report suggesting the honour of the Crown was at stake and recommending the Crown should not dispose of lands that are the subject of claims to the Tribunal.[33] Ultimately, Parliament passed the Environment Act 1986 and the State-Owned Enterprises Act 1986 which both referred to the principles of the Treaty of Waitangi. Section 9 of the State-Owned Enterprises Act 1986 provided: 'Nothing in this Act shall permit the Crown to act in a manner that is inconsistent with the principles of the Treaty of Waitangi.'

[30] Ibid 106–13.

[31] Waitangi Tribunal, 'Motunui-Waitara Report' (Wai 6, 1983); Waitangi Tribunal, 'Kaituna River Report' (Wai 4, 1984); Waitangi Tribunal, 'Manukau Report' (Wai 8, 1985); Waitangi Tribunal, 'Te Reo Maori' (Wai 11, 1986).

[32] Waitangi Tribunal, 'Motunui-Waitara Report' (n 31) [11.3].

[33] Waitangi Tribunal, 'Interim Report to the Minister of Maori Affairs on State-Owned Enterprises Bill' (Wai 1177, 1986).

Section 9 became 'a prompt for litigation'.[34] It supplied the legislative authority for the courts to interpret te Tiriti. In 1987, when the Crown sought to transfer land and assets to state-owned enterprises (SOEs), the New Zealand Māori Council sought an urgent interim injunction preventing the transfer. The result was simply the most constitutionally significant court judgment in New Zealand's history: *New Zealand Maori Council v Attorney-General* (the *Lands case*).[35] The Court of Appeal declared, on the basis of s 9 of the State-Owned Enterprises Act, that transferring the assets to SOEs would be unlawful, without a system to consider whether transfer would be inconsistent with the principles of te Tiriti. They delivered a unanimous decision expressed in five judgments. The Court followed the Tribunal's lead on the meaning of te Tiriti. President Cooke, on behalf of the whole court, summarised as follows:[36]

> [T]hose principles [of the Treaty of Waitangi] require the Pakeha and Maori Treaty partners to act towards each other reasonably and with the utmost good faith.
>
> That duty is no light one. It is infinitely more than a formality. If a breach of the duty is demonstrated at any time, the duty of the court will be to insist that it be honoured.

The Court used the language of 'partnership', picking up on the lead given by the Waitangi Tribunal in 1985, to describe the relationship between the Crown and Māori. It required the Crown and the New Zealand Māori Council to negotiate a regime to protect Māori claims to the Waitangi Tribunal. They did so. The outcome of these negotiations was legislated for in the Treaty of Waitangi (State Enterprises) Act 1988. The Act enabled the transfer of land to the SOEs to proceed on the basis that the Waitangi Tribunal would have the power to require, compulsorily, that the land be resumed by the Crown from whoever then owned it, at market value, and returned to a Māori claimant. The fiscal incentives of that regime have directly contributed to a comprehensive programme of settlement of historical land grievances of Māori claimants since 1994.

From 1987 to 1990, Māori further challenged Crown proposals to transfer coal, forestry assets and broadcasting assets to SOEs, and create

[34] For more detailed context on the drafting of s 9 see Palmer, *Treaty of Waitangi* (n 1) 93–94; M Hickford, 'Quasi-constitutionality and the Treaty of Waitangi' in R Albert and J Colón-Ríos (eds), *Quasi-Constitutionality and Constitutional Statutes* (Abingdon, Routledge, 2019) 94.

[35] *New Zealand Maori Council v Attorney-General* [1987] 1 NZLR 641 (CA) (*Lands case*).

[36] Ibid 667.

new forms of property rights in fisheries and radio frequencies. In these cases, the Court of Appeal, relying on legislative clauses referring to te Tiriti (or, in the case of fisheries, 'Māori fishing rights'), continued to hold firmly to its interpretation of the meaning and force of te Tiriti in the *Lands case*.[37] The final judicial reinforcement of the approach of the Court of Appeal and the Waitangi Tribunal came in 1993 from the Judicial Committee of the Privy Council, then New Zealand's highest court, sitting in London. In relation to broadcasting assets, it explicitly acknowledged and effectively endorsed the Court of Appeal's approach to te Tiriti in the *Lands case* and subsequent cases.[38]

In 2013, in a virtual re-run of the *Lands case* in relation to the effects of partial privatisation of electricity SOEs on Māori claims to water, the Supreme Court reaffirmed the re-interpretation. However, in considering a remedy, the Court recognised the progress of the Crown and Māori in settling Tiriti claims to date and took seriously Crown assurances of its intentions for future settlements in relation to water claims.[39]

F. Reinterpretation through Dialogue

The reinterpretation of the meaning and legal status of te Tiriti o Waitangi, effected from the 1970s to the 1990s, remains current. This reinterpretation occurred through the iterative interaction of institutions exercising public power: constitutional dialogue. Political pressure led the executive to propose and Parliament to create the Waitangi Tribunal, which subsequently recommended direct legislative reference to te Tiriti. That prompted litigation which gave a contemporary relational meaning to te Tiriti and, through negotiation with Māori and more legislation, greater legal power to the Tribunal. It has resulted in a reconciliation of authoritative views of the meaning of te Tiriti in the context of contemporary New Zealand social, economic, political and cultural conditions. And court decisions have, in turn, guided further decision-making by the Waitangi Tribunal and the executive.

This reinterpretation of te Tiriti occurred in the context of an ultimately political, rather than judicialised, constitution. Māori, at

[37] *Tainui Maori Trust Board v Attorney-General* [1989] 2 NZLR 513 (CA); *Attorney-General v New Zealand Maori Council* [1991] 2 NZLR 129 (CA); *Te Runanga o Muriwhenua v Attorney-General* [1990] 2 NZLR 641 (CA).

[38] *New Zealand Maori Council v Attorney-General* [1994] 1 NZLR 513 (PC).

[39] *New Zealand Maori Council v Attorney-General* [2013] NZSC 6, [2013] 3 NZLR 31.

16 per cent of the population, have the numbers and inclination to attempt to achieve their aims through both politics and law. Since the mixed-member-proportional (MMP) electoral system was introduced in 1996, the electoral system has facilitated that participation. Māori votes in the House have been crucial to the formation of successive governments since then. After the 2020 election, 25 of the 120 MPs (21 per cent) are Māori.[40] New Zealand's protection of indigenous rights through te Tiriti has been a political enterprise, interacting with the judiciary and the Waitangi Tribunal at crucial points. But, however loudly Māori voices are heard in New Zealand politics, Parliament is ultimately ruled by the majority and Māori do not now constitute a majority in New Zealand.

III. TE TIRITI IN THE CONSTITUTION TODAY

Today, te Tiriti is interwoven into the operation of modern government. We summarise its contemporary meaning and current legal status, as well as the main ways it conditions the exercise of public power.

A. Contemporary Meaning

The contemporary meanings attributed to te Tiriti by the courts, Parliament, the executive and the Waitangi Tribunal all share the perspective of its fundamental relational aspect. Its essence represents the value of the ongoing relationships between the Crown, Māori and other New Zealanders. Tiriti partners are obliged to act reasonably and in good faith, consulting with each other and compromising where appropriate.

This general meaning of te Tiriti o Waitangi is now embedded in the reality of the culture of New Zealand government. But we believe that the lack of a common formulation of the meaning of te Tiriti, in brief, comprehensible terms, has impeded public understanding of it. One of us characterised the contemporary interpretation of its meaning in the following way:[41]

> The Treaty of Waitangi, and its principles,
> should be interpreted broadly, generously and practically,
> in new and changing circumstances as they arise;

[40] Some additional MPs have Māori heritage but do not appear to self-identify as Māori.
[41] Palmer, *Treaty of Waitangi* (n 1) 150.

> As an agreement upholding the Crown's legitimacy, in governing New Zealand for the benefit of all New Zealanders,
> in exchange for the Crown's active protection of the rangatiratanga, or authority of hapū, iwi and Māori generally to use and control their own interests,
> especially in relation to land, fisheries and te reo Māori and their other tangible and intangible taonga or valued possessions.
> The Crown must also ensure that Māori enjoy the rights and privileges of Pākehā New Zealanders.
> Since this agreement involves a continuing relationship
> akin to partnership between the Crown and Māori,
> the parties should act reasonably and in good faith towards each other,
> consulting with each other,
> compromising where appropriate,
> and reasonably redressing past breaches of the Treaty.

We consider this brief statement continues to capture the contemporary meaning of te Tiriti and is a useful, comprehensible way of expressing that meaning.

B. Legal Force and Effect

The reinterpretation of the meaning of te Tiriti has been settled through constitutional dialogue in New Zealand. It is now firmly entrenched in the reality of the operation of New Zealand's constitution. But te Tiriti is still only half in and half out of the law. The legal status of te Tiriti in New Zealand is incoherent and its legal force inconsistent.[42] The meaning and effect of te Tiriti are decided by different institutions in different areas of law. Their views have different levels of power when expressed for different purposes.

At international law, we consider te Tiriti may well be regarded as a valid international treaty. If so, that would place the Crown under a duty at international law to honour its terms in good faith. This would have political and moral bite, since New Zealand regards itself as required by the recognised rules of the law of treaties to give effect in its law and practice to obligations imposed on it by a treaty. But the orthodox legal view is that international treaties do not have direct domestic legal effect unless and until domestic legislation gives them legal effect,

[42] Ibid ch 4.

as we explain in Chapter 11. The Privy Council agreed with that in 1941.[43] But their conclusion was based only on the English version of te Tiriti and may now be open to revision, as the Waitangi Tribunal has suggested.[44]

Te Tiriti can be said to be incorporated into New Zealand law through those Acts which mention te Tiriti explicitly in their preambles and go on to provide detailed schemes of legislative provisions in relation to any subject particularly relevant to te Tiriti. So, te Tiriti is effectively incorporated into: the law relating to Māori land by Te Ture Whenua Maori Act 1993; the law relating to Māori language and television by Te Ture mō te Reo Māori 2016 / the Māori Language Act 2016 and the Māori Television Service (Te Aratuku Whakaata Irirangi Maori) Act 2003; and into the law relating to Māori fisheries by the Maori Fisheries Act 2004.

Since 1986, and by mid-2021, Parliament has also referred to the 'principles of the Treaty of Waitangi' in 30 Acts of the New Zealand Parliament other than those implementing Treaty settlements. Under those Acts, decision-makers are variously required to 'give effect to' the principles; 'not act in a manner inconsistent' with the principles; 'ensure full and balanced account is taken' of the principles; and 'give particular recognition', 'take into account', 'have regard to' and 'acknowledge' the principles of te Tiriti o Waitangi.[45] Since 2000, more Acts have tended to use variations on a formula of general wording that begins 'in order to recognise and respect the Crown's responsibility to take appropriate account of the Treaty of Waitangi …' before making specific provisions which elaborate Parliament's intended meaning of te Tiriti. All these Acts effectively incorporate te Tiriti into aspects of the law.

The law of equity recognises that some 'fiduciary' relationships carry special obligations when one person reposes trust and confidence in another person in the management of their affairs. Fiduciary obligations include duties of good faith, of loyalty, and not to profit from a fiduciary position. In Canada and the United States, the courts have applied this law to particular relationships between governments and indigenous peoples. In 2017, the New Zealand Supreme Court did something similar in *Wakatū v Attorney-General* in holding the Crown

[43] *Te Heuheu Tukino v Aotea District Maori Land Board* [1941] AC 308 (PC).
[44] Waitangi Tribunal, 'Ngai Tahu Report' (Wai 27, 1991), 4.3.1 and 4.3.7.
[45] Palmer, *Treaty of Waitangi* (n 1) 182–83.

owed fiduciary duties to reserve 15,100 acres of land for the benefit of the customary Māori owners near Nelson.[46]

The courts also give legal force to te Tiriti directly when an issue in a case requires interpretation of a statute with a Treaty clause in it. And the courts have said that te Tiriti can be an aid to statutory interpretation even without explicit legislative reference.[47] It is conceivable that a court could apply the principle of legality, explored in Chapter 9, to reinforce te Tiriti. Cooke P appears to have done so in the *Lands case*.[48]

Te Tiriti o Waitangi is directly invoked in judicial review challenges to government decision-making. One of us analysed 53 cases of judicial review since 1987 that rely on te Tiriti.[49] They challenge: (initially) decisions by the Crown to divest itself of land and assets that might prejudice Tiriti settlements (with success); Tiriti settlements themselves (with less success); resource management and conservation decisions (with some success); commercial regulatory decisions (with no success); and social services and other decisions (with little success).

So, the legal force of te Tiriti is a patchwork quilt of statutes passed by Parliament, darned together by the judiciary. Whether te Tiriti has legal force, and how much legal force it has in a particular context, depends on whether there is a Treaty clause in the relevant statute or whether the judiciary considers it is so salient it must be a relevant consideration to an official decision. We consider the legal force and effect of te Tiriti continues to reflect incoherence and inconsistency – though perhaps that is less obvious than it used to be. And as we note in Chapter 7, the role of tikanga or Māori customary law is currently assuming an increasing role in New Zealand's legal system. That is related to the established role of te Tiriti in New Zealand law but also independent of it.

C. Reconciliation and Settlement

The Waitangi Tribunal was, as mentioned above, set up initially to address contemporary breaches of te Tiriti, before its jurisdiction was later extended to also address historic claims.

[46] *Proprietors of Wakatu v Attorney-General* [2017] NZSC 17, [2017] 1 NZLR 423.

[47] *Huakina Development Trust v Waikato Valley Authority* [1987] 2 NZLR 188 (HC), 210; *Barton-Prescott v Director-General of Social Welfare* [1997] 3 NZLR 179 (HC), 184; *Trans-Tasman Resources Ltd v Taranaki-Whanganui Conservation Board* [2020] NZCA 86, [2020] NZRMA 248, [171].

[48] *Lands case* (n 35) 656.

[49] MSR Palmer, 'Indigenous Rights, Judges and Judicial Review in New Zealand' in JNE Varuhas and SW Stark (eds), *The Frontiers of Public Law* (Oxford, Hart, 2019) 123.

Historic claims, for breaches of te Tiriti that took place before 21 September 1992, have represented the large bulk of the Tribunal's work to date. The Tribunal investigates claims lodged by Māori alleging they have been prejudicially affected by Crown acts or omissions that were or are 'inconsistent with the principles of the Treaty'. Crown acts or omissions that can be subject to scrutiny extend to primary and secondary legislation, as well as any governmental policy or practice – whether done or proposed. A deadline of 1 September 2008 was set for the lodging of historic claims, with over 2,000 lodged.

The Tribunal is constituted as a standing commission of inquiry and consists of up to 20 members – about half are Māori – comprising people with a broad range of expertise, including law, tikanga, governance and history. The chair of the Tribunal must either be a High Court judge or chief judge of the Māori Land Court (currently the latter, Chief Judge Isaac). The Tribunal adopts an inquisitorial approach to its work.[50] Historical research is undertaken by Tribunal staff, the Crown and claimants. Hearings are then held, often on the marae of claimant groups. Reports are then issued, setting out the Tribunal's findings and associated historical accounts. The Tribunal's recommendations are non-binding, except for the return or resumption of SOE or Crown forest land.[51] The Tribunal is barred from making recommendations about private land.[52]

The settlement of historic grievances began in 1994 with Waikato-Tainui. One of us was a lead Crown negotiator for the Crown with Waikato-Tainui. Settlements have involved uncertainty, innovation and political courage on all sides. The process has now largely been systematised.[53] Waitangi Tribunal findings on historical events and grievances are often important in settlement negotiations but the Tribunal itself is not directly involved in negotiations. However, the Tribunal may be called on to address some matters which affect the process of negotiations, such as issues about claimant mandates and overlapping claims.

The Minister for Treaty of Waitangi Negotiations, advised by Te Arawhiti, the Office for Māori-Crown Relations (formerly the Office of

[50] Waitangi Tribunal, 'Guide to the Practice and Procedure of the Waitangi Tribunal' (May 2012), [2.1].

[51] Treaty of Waitangi Act 1975, ss 6(3), 8A, 8HB and 8HJ.

[52] Ibid s 6(4A).

[53] C Jones, *New Treaty, New Tradition* (Wellington, Victoria University Press, 2016) ch 4. For criticism of the settlement process, see M Mutu, 'Behind the smoke and mirrors of the Treaty of Waitangi claims settlement process in New Zealand' (2018) 14 *Journal of Global Ethics* 208.

Treaty Settlements), is responsible for negotiating directly with iwi and hapū to settle claims. In general terms, there are four different phases to negotiations: (a) preparation, involving historical research, and settling mandates to negotiate; (b) agreement on the terms of negotiations; (c) negotiation resulting in an agreement in principle and draft deed of settlement; and (d) ratification by the iwi and passage of legislation by Parliament.

Treaty settlements usually contain three types of redress. A historical account of the Crown-claimants relationship and Treaty breaches, often based on findings of the Tribunal, is agreed and reflected in legislation, along with a Crown apology. Cultural redress is offered, such as the vesting of culturally significant land, renaming sites precious to Māori, or acknowledgement of special association with specific sites (often concomitant governance roles or a right to be consulted). Commercial redress is agreed, usually in the form of a mix of direct financial payments and ability to purchase specific land from the government. As part of government policy for negotiations, claimants must establish a suitable post-settlement governance entity in order to receive and administer settlement assets. Legislation giving effect to settlements is, in formal terms, ordinary legislation passed via standard legislative processes, but has an important symbolic character. Iwi and hapū usually attend en masse at Parliament for the passing of their settlement legislation by the House. The Crown apology is an especially cherished act of reconciliation and its expression by ministers and receipt by iwi and hapū is cloaked in ceremony and emotion.

The inquiry into claims by Ngāi Tūhoe, an iwi based in Te Urewera, and its significant Treaty settlement with the Crown present an example of the nature and depth of reconciliation and settlement processes.[54] A Waitangi Tribunal report into claims from a number of iwi with interests in Te Urewera was produced – a report running to over 4,000 pages, generated through an inquiry process that took three decades. The report narrates numerous Treaty breaches, including military action causing death and destruction; aggressive purchase of tribal lands in order to undermine the iwi's mana motuhake (self-government); eventual consolidation of land into a national park; confiscation and other land alienation; and other Crown actions and neglect leading to

[54] Although Tūhoe were not signatories to te Tiriti, the Tribunal ruled the Crown's obligations under te Tiriti still extend to Tūhoe; Waitangi Tribunal, 'Te Urewera – Vol I' (Wai 894, 2017) 132.

severe socio-economic deprivation.[55] The Crown recognised Te Kotahi ā Tūhoe's mandate to represent Tūhoe and negotiated a comprehensive historical Treaty settlement. The settlement was implemented through the Tūhoe Claims Settlement Act 2014 and associated Te Urewera Act 2014. It includes a summary of historical account, acknowledgements of numerous breaches and Crown apology:[56]

> (1) To the iwi of Tūhoe, to the tipuna, the descendants, the hapū and the whānau, the Crown makes the following long-overdue apology.
>
> (2) The Crown unreservedly apologises for not having honoured its obligations to Tūhoe under te Tiriti o Waitangi (the Treaty of Waitangi) and profoundly regrets its failure to appropriately acknowledge and respect te mana motuhake o Tūhoe for many generations.

After detailed apologies for specific breaches, the apology concludes:

> (7) Through this apology and settlement the Crown hopes to honestly confront the past and seeks to atone for its wrongs. The Crown hopes to build afresh its relationship with Tūhoe and that this new relationship will endure for current and future generations.
>
> (8) Let these words guide our way to a greenstone door – tatau pounamu – which looks back on the past and closes it, which looks forward to the future and opens it.

Te Urewera land, formerly held as a national park, was vested by statute as its own legal entity with its own legal personality. A new board, comprising four Crown and five Tūhoe members, are charged with ongoing management of the land. The iwi's association with the land was acknowledged; a number of culturally significant sites were returned to the iwi; placenames were corrected; the iwi obtained a representative role on a river management board; and Tūhoe's ongoing relationships with the Crown and government agencies were recognised. Financial redress of $170 million was provided. Tūhoe obtained the opportunity to purchase a number of Crown properties (on the basis the properties would then be leased back to the Crown), as well as the exclusive right of first refusal over other Crown-owned land.

D. Constitutional Place

Finally, te Tiriti o Waitangi has also found its way into the reality of New Zealand's constitution, as well as its direct expression in law,

[55] Ibid Vols I-VI.
[56] Tūhoe Claims Settlement Act 2014, s 10 (apology).

politics and settlement. Throughout this book, we have addressed the way te Tiriti and the interests of Māori manifest throughout the constitution. We summarise this below, following the chapter structure of this book.[57]

(a) *Head of State:* Te Tiriti emphasises a relationship between the 'Crown' and Māori. In doing so it entrenches monarchical language as code for government and the state. There is a potent symbolic link between the Crown and Māori through te Tiriti that may complicate any future moves in a republican direction. Lord Cooke even questioned whether 'substantial Māori concurrence' might be required by the courts for such a move.[58]

(b) *Democratic government:* The Māori electoral seats in the House of Representatives are a crucial reflection and reinforcement of te Tiriti. Since the introduction of MMP, Māori MPs have played a crucial role in the formation of governments. They ensure Māori have a political presence. Te Tiriti, without question, is a major thread in modern-day civic discourse – in political exchanges and parliamentary debates across all levels of government. Government policies and actions are often scrutinised in terms of their implications for te Tiriti obligations and effect on Māori communities. It is fair to say, though, that attitudes and views continue to differ broadly about the proper place te Tiriti should have in government. Some argue for a more foundational role; some accept its current mixed role; some argue against its influence.

(c) *Executive:* The influence of te Tiriti has been formalised in executive policy-making and law-making processes. The executive branch of government has consistently affirmed its intentions to honour te Tiriti. It has published statements of its understanding of the principles of te Tiriti.[59] Ministerial portfolios and responsibilities have recognised te Tiriti and the particular importance of iwi and hapū as Treaty partners and distinct communities. A long-standing Cabinet portfolio has been the Minister of Māori Affairs (or Development). In 1991, a new portfolio of Minister in charge of Treaty of Waitangi Negotiations was created. As the programme of settlements winds down, a new ministerial portfolio was created in 2017, reflecting the ongoing relational nature of te Tiriti: the

[57] Palmer, *Treaty of Waitangi* (n 1) ch 5.

[58] R Cooke, 'The Suggested Revolution Against the Crown' in PA Joseph (ed), *Essays on the Constitution* (Wellington, Brookers, 1995) 28.

[59] 'Principles for Crown Action on the Treaty of Waitangi' (4 July 1989). And see Palmer, *Treaty of Waitangi* (n 1) 130–39.

Minister for Crown-Māori Relations.[60] Cabinet requires all Cabinet papers to identify whether legislative proposals are consistent with the principles of te Tiriti.[61] The Attorney-General and the Minister for Treaty of Waitangi Negotiations must be consulted about bills potentially affecting te Tiriti settlements.[62]

(d) *Parliament*: Parliament regularly passes legislation referring to te Tiriti o Waitangi and other legislation that implicates it. But that is not to say legislation passed by Parliament is always consistent with te Tiriti. Since 1995, it has also regularly passed legislation implementing settlements between the Crown and Māori claimants of claims of historical breaches of te Tiriti. But, effectively, the content of the legislation has been settled by the negotiations. The choice of the House of Representatives is to agree or disagree. It has always agreed.

(e) *Judiciary:* The judiciary is regularly confronted with cases calling for the interpretation or application of te Tiriti o Waitangi. Familiarity with basic te reo Māori and tikanga is regarded as essential for all judges. Significant issues relating to te Tiriti are explicitly stated by Parliament to be matters of general or public importance, in section 74(3) of the Senior Courts Act 2016, for the purpose of permission to appeal to the Supreme Court. Since 2019, there have been Māori judges at all levels of the courts, but there are still not yet enough Māori senior court judges for Māori perspectives to be consistently reflected in judgments.

(f) *Accountability and transparency:* Judicial review is frequently invoked by iwi and hapū in relation to te Tiriti disputes. Te Tiriti o Waitangi is also directly relevant to the complaints jurisdiction of the Human Rights Commission, including the Race Relations Commissioner. The Waitangi Tribunal increasingly deals with contemporary issues, such as policy development and the administration of government. The Tribunal may also inquire into a specific claim that current or proposed government action is inconsistent with the Crown's obligations under te Tiriti. An example is the Tribunal's inquiry into the operation of Oranga Tamariki (Ministry for Children) and the taking of tamariki Māori (Māori children) into state care.[63] And the Tribunal has worked to systematise some

[60] Such a portfolio was proposed in Palmer, *Treaty of Waitangi* (n 1) 326–27.

[61] Cabinet Office, *Cabinet Manual 2017*, [7.65].

[62] Ibid [5.14].

[63] Waitangi Tribunal, 'He Pāharakeke, he Rito Whakakīkinga Whāruarua' (Wai 2915, 2021).

of its inquiry work around nationally significant issues affecting Māori which may incorporate both historic and contemporary grievances.[64] For example, the Tribunal recently inquired into housing policy and services.[65]

(g) *Human rights:* Te Tiriti was not incorporated in the Bill of Rights Act, despite initial proposals to do so. However, the Act enshrines the right of people belonging to ethnic (and other) minority groups to enjoy the culture and language of that group in community with others (section 20), although little jurisprudence has developed around this right. The obligations of government to iwi and hapū under te Tiriti, broadly speaking, have a fundamental character that may invite particular focus by the common law, in a similar way to human rights.

(h) *Local and global governance:* Te Tiriti is a matter of significant practical moment for local government bodies in exercising their powers under the Resource Management Act 1991 and the Local Government Act 2002, both of which have Tiriti clauses. After voting against it in the United Nations in 2007, New Zealand eventually endorsed the UN Declaration on the Rights of Indigenous Peoples, along with other international agreements relevant to Māori. Te Tiriti is regularly a feature of international negotiations, in preserving government freedom to meet Tiriti obligations in international trade agreements.

IV. CONCLUSION

Overall, the Treaty of Waitangi is a significant feature of New Zealand's constitutional landscape.[66] But its constitutional place is uncertain and that uncertainty causes tension. The Treaty is a bit like Mt Ruapehu in New Zealand's physical landscape. It dominates the skyline of a significant area of the country, though it is often clouded over. There are ways around it but people constantly want to climb it. It can blow hot or cold.

[64] Waitangi Tribunal, 'Memorandum of the Chairperson Concerning the Kaupapa Inquiry Programme' (27 March 2019).

[65] Waitangi Tribunal, 'Housing Policy and Services Inquiry' (Wai 2750, report forthcoming).

[66] Palmer, *Treaty of Waitangi* (n 1) 278.

It can erupt unexpectedly. It taps some deep subterranean roots and conflicts with others. But it is here to stay.

FURTHER READING

Orange, C, *The Treaty of Waitangi* (Wellington, Bridget Williams Books Ltd, 1987).

Palmer, MSR, *The Treaty of Waitangi in New Zealand's Law and Constitution* (Wellington, Victoria University Press, 2008).

Waitangi Tribunal, 'He Whakaputanga me te Tiriti: The Declaration and the Treaty' (Wai 1040, 2014).

11

Local and Global Governance

Introduction – Local Government – Māori Governance – Non-state Bodies and the Private Sector – Global Institutions and International Relationships – Conclusion

I. INTRODUCTION

IN THIS CHAPTER we look at local and global governance, beyond central government. Public power is exercised by some sub-national governance bodies, such as local government. Other institutions, such as Māori authorities or international organisations, lie outside the state but increasingly exercise some public powers. Others, such as companies, are traditionally regarded as 'private' but, where their decisions can affect the exercise of public power, we regard them as part of New Zealand's constitutional arrangements. And New Zealand itself exists within a world of global governance and international law, which we explore briefly.

II. LOCAL GOVERNMENT

As a unitary state, power in New Zealand is formally vested in centralised national government. There is no sub-national provincial government. Early experimentation with federalism failed, with the abolition of provincial government in 1875. However, central government always chooses to devolve some functions to local and regional institutions. Localism, through sub-national government, creates a closeness between the governors and the governed. This closeness more readily allows communities to 'decide for themselves … what kind of services they want and what kind of environment they prefer'.[1] This form of

[1] 'Royal Commission on Local Government in England 1966–69' (1969) Cmnd 4040, 10.

democracy in the neighbourhood promotes participation in the business of government, encourages responsiveness to community needs, and brings pluralism to the national political system.[2] Local government is the main form of sub-national government, although there are numerous other localised institutions with specific mandates and some provision for democratic governance.

Local government has no formal constitutional status in New Zealand but its total abolition now would be unthinkable. In a formal legal sense, the continuing existence of local authorities and the generous framing of their operating mandates are dependent on the benevolence of central government. In reality, though, the importance, existence and traditional activities of local government are generally assumed. Calls for formal constitutional recognition of local democracy – along with the associated notion of subsidiarity – occasionally bubble up.[3] We consider that, regardless of formal legal status, local government's operating framework has important constitutional characteristics threaded through it.[4]

While the existence of local democracy has generally been enduring, the institutional and operational blueprint for local government has not been so stable. Its history is plagued with fragmentation, ad hoc arrangements and constant reorganisation and revision.[5] In modern times, both the 1970s and 1980s saw major reorganisation and merging of many of the multitude of authorities, as well as the imposition of strict financial management and other operating expectations as the wave of new public management swept the country. Early in the new millennium, the Labour-led government undertook a major reform of local government, in an effort to update and generalise its mission, shape and operation, as well as emphasising its institutional autonomy. The Local Government Act 2002, together with the Local Electoral Act 2001 and Local Government (Rating) Act 2002, continue to be the key legislation

[2] 'The Conduct of Local Authority Business', Report of the Committee of Inquiry (1986) HMSO, Cmnd 9797.

[3] See eg M Reid, 'Local Government's Quest for Constitutional Status' in J Drage and others (eds), *Along A Fault-Line* (Auckland, Dunmore Publishing, 2011); G Palmer and A Butler, *A Constitution for Aotearoa New Zealand* (Wellington, Victoria University Press, 2016) 188–91.

[4] MSR Palmer, 'What is New Zealand's Constitution and Who Interprets It?' (2006) 17 *Public Law Review* 133, 137; DR Knight, 'Constitutional Practice in Local Government' (Address to Society of Local Government Managers, January 2019).

[5] See K Palmer, *Local Authorities Law in New Zealand* (Wellington, Thomson Reuters, 2012) ch 23.

governing local authorities. Since that major sectoral reform, the most significant development was the establishment of Auckland Council as a 'supercity', when eight local authorities were merged into one large council, supported by numerous local boards operating under its ambit. While still formally a local government institution, its size means Auckland Council brings a more monolithic regional flavour to sub-national government. There are periodic proposals for other regions to follow suit.[6] There are also hints that some particular functions might more strongly regionalised or centrally coordinated. Moves to reform the provision of water infrastructure and resource management regulation along these lines are underway.

Local government is made up of numerous local authorities, with two distinct and overlapping tiers: 11 regional councils; and 67 territorial authorities. Fifty-three of those territorial authorities are designated as district councils and 12 as city councils (although the different names have no legal consequences).[7] The remaining two are established as councils under their own specific statutes.[8] Six of the territorial authorities also have the duties and functions of regional councils and are known as unitary authorities.[9] Local and community boards can be constituted to provide subordinate and more neighbourly electoral units. Council-controlled organisations can also be established, emulating central government's state-owned enterprises and bringing together both private and public sector accountability. These organisations are commonly used to place some commercial activities at arm's length, subject to general direction being set through statements of intent.

Each local authority has a governing body made up of members elected under the Local Electoral Act 2001, in electoral arrangements settled by the local authorities (either first-past-the-post or single transferable vote systems, organised in district wards or across the district as a whole). Local authorities may establish Māori electoral wards. Only two local authorities had Māori wards in place for the 2019 local elections but a law change in 2021 making them easier to establish has seen the number rise substantially. Mayors of territorial authorities are directly elected to the governing body by local electors; chairpersons of regional councils are decided by their governing bodies. As holders of

[6] Wellington Region Local Government Review Panel, 'Future Wellington' (October 2012).

[7] Local Government Act 2002, s 21.

[8] Local Government (Auckland Council) Act 2009; Chatham Islands Council Act 1995.

[9] Local Government Act 2002, Sch 2, pt 3, cl 3.

the senior civic office, the mayor and chairpersons are responsible for chairing and leading the governing body and local authority, although they only have a handful of minor executive powers.[10] Ultimately, the responsibility for governance is vested in the governing body as a plenary committee. The absence of any Cabinet or formal lead executive group, along with limited and usually weak party representation, means the fate of each and every proposal coming before the governing body turns on the whims of the aggregated views of individual elected members. As a result, informal allegiances can crystallise. Finally, in accordance with the standard division between governance and management, a chief executive leads an administration made up of local authority officers and staff, and implements policy agreed by elected members.

Local authorities have a broad mandate to promote 'community well-being' (after a short recent period with a more circumscribed, outputs-focused service delivery mandate).[11] In reality, much of the business of local government continues to focus on things like: infrastructure (roads, water, waste, etc); environmental and building regulation; environmental health; disaster management; and community amenities (such as libraries, parks, community centres, recreational facilities, etc). To differing degrees, local authorities also engage in more amorphous forms of community development, including place-shaping and low-key economic development. Miscellaneous regulatory activities are also increasingly delegated to local authorities by central government.

The Local Government Act 2002 sets out a detailed framework for the operation of local authorities. The legislation promotes prudential and accountable decision-making by imposing universal but flexible generic requirements across the full gamut of decisions.[12] These requirements include, among other things, a requirement to have processes that allow Māori to contribute to decision-making and fostering their capacity to do so. The relationship of Māori with ancestral lands, water, sites, wāhi tapu (burial grounds), valued flora and fauna, and other taonga (treasures) is also a mandatory relevant consideration in decision-making. The Local Government (Rating) Act 2002 sits alongside the Local Government Act and provides authority for local authorities to

[10] Local Government Act 2002, s 41. See also Local Government (Auckland Council) Act 2009, s 8.

[11] Local Government Act 2002, s 10; DR Knight, 'Rhetoric or Reality?' (2015) 26 *New Zealand Universities Law Review* 895.

[12] DR Knight, 'Local Democracy and the Consideration of Community Views' in C Charters and DR Knight (eds), *We, the People(s)* (Wellington, Victoria University Press, 2011) 284.

impose rates on property-owners in their districts. Local authorities also have some important legislative powers, including enacting bylaws and district/regional plans under environmental legislation.[13]

Legal and constitutional practice within local governance is quite patchy, with some local authorities embracing good governance and local democracy, and others falling short of the legislative and customary expectations.[14] Some breaches need to be, and occasionally are, validated by Parliament.[15]

In addition to local authorities, a range of other institutions also incorporate democratic representation and local democracy, usually in relation to the delivery of specific functions (district health boards, school boards of trustees, university councils, liquor licensing trusts and some utility providers). The mood seems to be shifting towards greater central coordination of some of these functions. For example, district health boards are set to be centralised.

III. MĀORI GOVERNANCE

A Māori legal system has operated throughout Aotearoa, pre- and post-colonisation, with distinctive constitutional traditions, law and governance, as we explained in Chapter 2. Its organisational units are based around iwi, hapū and whānau (tribe, sub-tribe and family).

There have also been periodic attempts to establish national Māori entities. The establishment of the Māori kingitanga was such an attempt by Māori in 1858 which has endured. The position of the Māori King or Queen, chosen by consensus at the death of the previous incumbent, has always been held by descendants of the first king, of Waikato-Tainui. The Māori King or Queen has occasionally performed an important role in coordinating iwi or mediating disputes. Parliament also created a pan-tribal self-government organisation, the New Zealand Māori Council, by enacting the Maori Community Development Act 1962. The Māori Council has had a pivotal role in litigating against the Crown on the

[13] D Knight, 'Power to Make Bylaws' [2005] *New Zealand Law Journal* 165; Knight (n 11).

[14] Knight (n 4).

[15] See eg Kaipara District Council (Validation of Rates and Other Matters) Act 2013. See also *Mangawhai Ratepayers' and Residents' Association v Kaipara District Council* [2014] NZHC 1147, [2014] 3 NZLR 85.

basis of te Tiriti o Waitangi. The Council also has responsibility for the office of volunteer Māori wardens which arose around 1860.

Māori political organisation has, however, always been inherently tribal. Statutory trust boards have often acted as governance organisations. But the process of settling historical te Tiriti claims has seen the creation of new Māori and iwi institutions, in part to facilitate the provision of redress and to provide vehicles by which Māori could express ongoing governance over different areas.[16] These organisations often deploy a tailored mix of company, trust and public board accountabilities, to match the complex commercial and social interests of the iwi that are intended to endure indefinitely. Treaty settlements usually require these organisations to maintain certain standards of governance. The total assets that post-settlement entities control now sits at around $9.2 billion, and the Māori economy as a whole was worth more than $50 billion in 2019.[17]

As major iwi have gained control over considerable resources, the significance of their governance systems and power within communities and across the nation have increased. Since 2005, they have also come together, in the Iwi Chairs Forum, to share knowledge and information across iwi. The forum regularly invites the Crown, MPs and community groups to make presentations and has become an effective channel of communication between the Crown and Māori.

The creation of newly resourced iwi organisations with modern Māori governance has also attracted some devolution of state activities to Māori, either absolutely or in partnership with government. An especially novel approach has been the conferring of legal personality on natural resources as part of te Tiriti settlements.[18] Te Urewera, formerly a national park, and the Whanganui River acquired their own legal rights and interests as parts of te Tiriti settlements by the Crown with Tūhoe in 2014 and Whanganui in 2017. Mt Taranaki is set to do the same. A mutually acceptable means of governance is usually negotiated between the Crown and iwi.

[16] C Jones, *New Treaty, New Tradition* (Vancouver, UBC Press, 2016) ch 5; Office of Treaty Settlements, *Ka tika ā muri, ka tika ā mua*, 2nd edn (Wellington, Ministry of Justice, 2002).

[17] P Barry, L Graham and M Barry, 'Iwi Investment Report 2019' (TBD Advisory, 28 February 2020), 5; 'Te Ao Māori' (Chapman Tripp, March 2018) 2.

[18] A Geddis and J Ruru, 'Places as Persons' in JNE Varuhas and S Wilson Stark (eds), *The Frontiers of Public Law* (Oxford, Hart Publishing, 2019) 269.

IV. NON-STATE BODIES AND THE PRIVATE SECTOR

Non-state bodies and the private sector are engaged in governance, some of which involves public power. Corporatisation and then privatisation in the 1980s and 1990s saw many activities formerly undertaken by government move to the private sector.[19] Obvious examples include the full or partial privatisation of financial services, utility networks, transport operations and primary industry operations. Some areas of regulation were also occasionally opened up to private providers, such as for example, building consent and inspection. Techniques normally associated with private law – whether corporatisation or self-regulation – were also relied on to achieve desired outcomes. While the pendulum has since swung back from the heyday of these policies, devolution, privatisation and reliance on private governance remain techniques sometimes relied on by government. This is also matched by traditional private law functions and activities that, by reason of their nature, impact or consequences, became of interest to the public law. Especially common is industry or professional self-regulation that obviates the need for, or is assumed by, direct governmental regulation; for example, the self-regulation of some professionals in the health, accounting, insolvency or legal sectors or media and advertising standards.

Modern frameworks and principles recognise the role of the private sector in public governance and sometimes demand commensurate public accountability for those activities. Administrative law and the Bill of Rights Act may impose expectations on private actors when their activities have public dimensions. For example, the courts have been called on to clarify the authority of an industry body to self-regulate advertising when complaints related to promotion of a public referendum;[20] assess the fairness of the discipline of surgeons by a professional body;[21] and require a private television broadcaster to add party leaders to a key electoral debate.[22] Such activities lie sufficiently far towards the public end of the public/private continuum that we consider there are good arguments for them being exposed to the supervisory jurisdiction of the courts over the exercise of power.

[19] M Taggart, 'Corporatisation, Privatisation and Public Law' (1991) 2 *Public Law Review* 77; D Gill, 'By Accident or Design' (2008) 4 *Policy Quarterly* 27.

[20] *Electoral Commission v Cameron* [1997] 2 NZLR 421 (CA).

[21] *Royal Australasian College of Surgeons v Phipps* [1999] 3 NZLR 1 (CA).

[22] *Dunne v Canwest TV Works Ltd* [2005] NZAR 577 (HC).

In the twenty-first century, social media giants such as Facebook, Google and Twitter exercise at least as much public power as activities traditionally regarded as subject to that jurisdiction. The courts in New Zealand are yet to grapple with the question of whether some of their activities should be subjected to public law standards and expectations.

V. GLOBAL INSTITUTIONS AND INTERNATIONAL RELATIONSHIPS

New Zealand's legal system sits within an international community of states and a global system of international law.[23] Viewed as a legal system, the international legal order is 'loose and decentralised'.[24] It lacks an elected legislature or centralised rule-making body, a responsible executive with across-the-board authority to enforce laws, and a judiciary with full and generalised adjudicative authority. States are the key agents in this system of governance. The system is largely based on horizontal relationships between nation states, rather than the vertical relationships between governors and the citizens found in domestic legal systems (although international law increasingly reaches out into these domestic relationships now).[25] Numerous independent intergovernmental organisations, such as the United Nations, World Health Organisation and International Labour Organisation, also play a variety of roles within the international order.[26]

Rules in international law largely come from international treaties and custom.[27] States are bound by obligations they agree to at international law in international treaties. Treaties may be bilateral or multilateral and come with many labels, such as agreements, exchange of notes, conventions, protocols and so forth.[28] Beyond treaties, international custom may create binding norms reflecting general practice

[23] Law Commission, 'A New Zealand Guide to International Law and its Sources' (NZLC R34, 1996).

[24] American Law Institute, *Restatement of the Foreign Relations Law of the United States*, 3rd edn (Minnesota, St Paul, 1987) 16.

[25] MN Shaw, *International Law*, 8th edn (Cambridge, Cambridge University Press, 2018) ch 1.

[26] GF Sinclair, *To Reform the World* (Oxford, Oxford University Press, 2017).

[27] Statute of the International Court of Justice, art 38; see generally, A Costi, S Davidson and L Yarwood, 'The Creation of International Law' in A Costi (ed), *Public International Law* (Wellington, LexisNexis, 2020) ch 4.

[28] Law Commission (n 23) 6–7.

amongst states. Similar to constitutional conventions at domestic law, the emergence of an obligatory custom at international law depends on the existence of constant practice, along with an understanding by states that they are bound to continue that practice (opinio juris). Examples include the doctrine of state immunity or exclusive economic zones.[29] Custom binds all states, except those that have clearly and consistently dissented during the emergence of the practice. Thus, the creation of norms at international law – both via treaties and custom – is generally founded in notions of acceptance or agreement by states.[30] Finally, some peremptory norms (jus cogens) exist within the international legal order too – fundamental principles that cannot be derogated from and which prevail over contrary rules in treaties or custom. Prohibitions on torture or commission of acts of genocide are examples.[31]

As a small democracy within the global system, New Zealand is particularly dependent on, and invests heavily in, the international community of states.[32] Within New Zealand's constitutional system, the allocation of institutional responsibilities relating to international law is consistent with a 'dualist' tradition.[33] That British inheritance means international and domestic law exist side by side.[34]

The conduct of international relations is primarily an executive function, historically as part of the royal prerogative. The acceptance of treaty obligations depends on negotiation and agreement by ministers, diplomats and the Ministry of Foreign Affairs and Trade, in conjunction with other departments. This usually involves the executive first signalling an intention to be bound by signing a treaty and then subsequently ratifying the treaty, formally signalling consent to be bound. By convention, parliamentary engagement usually takes place between initial signature and subsequent ratification, as we explain below.

[29] *Governor of Pitcairn Islands v Sutton* [1995] 1 NZLR 426 (CA); *Continental Shelf (Libyan Arab Jamahiriya v Malta)* [1985] ICJ Rep 13.

[30] American Law Institute (n 24) 19.

[31] D Tladi, 'Fourth report on peremptory norms of general international law' (International Law Commission, 31 January 2019) 26; International Law Commission, *Draft Articles on the Law of Treaties with Commentaries* (1966) 248.

[32] K Keith, 'The Impact of International Law on New Zealand Law' (1998) 6 *Waikato Law Review* 1.

[33] T Dunworth, 'International Law in New Zealand Law' in Costi (n 27).

[34] *Attorney General for Canada v Attorney General for Ontario* [1937] UKPC 6, [1937] AC 326, 347; *Ashby v Minister of Immigration* [1981] 1 NZLR 222 (CA); *R (Miller) v Secretary of State for Exiting the European Union* [2017] UKSC 5, [2017] 2 WLR 583, [54]–[58].

The government may reserve the right not to be bound by specific provisions of multilateral treaties. In some cases, a multilateral treaty will provide that certain numbers of countries must ratify the treaty before it comes into force. Once New Zealand is a party to a treaty that has come into force, the government is accountable at international law for the performance of obligations to which it has agreed. Enforcement of treaties at international law is a matter of some complexity but may include retaliatory action by other states, complaints to international bodies, tribunals and courts, or a loss of credibility within the international community of states.

In the domestic sphere, the power to amend domestic law to give effect to international law obligations agreed to by the executive remains with Parliament.[35] In other words, unless and until Parliament incorporates or transforms treaty obligations into domestic law, by enacting or amending legislation, those treaty obligations do not in themselves alter domestic law and are not directly enforceable in domestic law by the courts. International treaty obligations can be incorporated into domestic law in a variety of ways, including providing that a treaty has force of law,[36] verbatim reproduction of treaty provisions into legislation,[37] or re-expressing the obligations in statutory language (either on similar or modified terms).[38] Once transformed into domestic law, those obligations are enforceable by the domestic courts according to the terms of domestic legislation.

While the dualist tradition frames this formal allocation of responsibility, the practice of, and dialogue between, the different branches of government encourage a more 'monist' approach to domestic and international law. The monist tradition sees law in the round, does not seek to distinguish the domestic and international spheres, and frowns on disharmony between domestic law and international law. A number of conventions and practices have developed to promote consistency between international law obligations and domestic law.

First, under standing orders of the House of Representatives, before the executive unequivocally enters a major treaty, it is presented to the

[35] For the dual rationale for this, see C McLachlan, *Foreign Relations Law* (Cambridge, Cambridge University Press, 2014) [5.20].

[36] Sale of Goods (United Nations Convention) Act 1994.

[37] Immigration Act 2009, s 127(3), reproducing in Sch 1 the Convention Relating to the Status of Refugees.

[38] New Zealand Bill of Rights Act 1990, affirming New Zealand's commitment to the International Covenant on Civil and Political Rights by enshrining many of the human rights protected under the covenant in legislative language designed for New Zealand.

House for consideration, albeit not for approval or veto, along with a supporting national interest analysis.[39] The Foreign Affairs, Defence and Trade committee or other relevant select committee considers the treaty and reports to the House on whether there are any matters which ought to be drawn to its attention.[40] The House may debate the report and make known to the executive any views on the treaty – but ordinary parliamentary processes do not provide for any power to approve or reject the treaty.

Secondly, by constitutional convention, the executive does not unequivocally bind the nation to any international law obligations unless and until Parliament has changed domestic law to ensure consistency.[41] In other words, by convention, transformation by Parliament usually comes before binding ratification by the executive. It follows that Parliament has some ability to influence or delay the adoption of international treaties and obligations by the executive, if it delays transformation.

Thirdly, Cabinet processes require ministers to consider whether any bills have implications for, or may be affected by, international obligations.[42] In doing so, this explanatory vetting obligation encourages conformity between proposed domestic law and existing international law.

Finally, the courts sometimes use techniques to ensure consistency between domestic and international law, while acknowledging the dualist orthodoxy that treaty obligations are not directly enforceable at domestic law unless and until formally incorporated. Common techniques include drawing on international law to assist with the interpretation of ambiguous domestic legislation;[43] requiring ministers and officials making discretionary decisions to take into account relevant international obligations;[44] and, where possible, reading domestic legislation consistently with international obligations.[45] The latter presumption of consistency (as it is sometimes called) has become especially dominant

[39] Standing Orders of the House of Representatives 2020, SOs 405 and 406.

[40] Standing Orders of the House of Representatives 2020, SOs 407 and 408.

[41] Cabinet Office, *Cabinet Manual 2017*, [5.79].

[42] Ibid [5.12].

[43] *Helu v Immigration and Protection Tribunal* [2015] NZSC 2; [2016] 1 NZLR 298; *R (Brind) v Secretary of State for the Home Office* [1991] UKHL 4, [1991] 1 AC 696.

[44] *Tavita v Minister of Immigration* [1994] 2 NZLR 257 (CA).

[45] *Ye v Minister of Immigration* [2009] NZSC 76, [2010] 1 NZLR 104; *New Zealand Airline Pilots' Association v Attorney-General* [1997] 3 NZLR 269 (CA).

in New Zealand, led in part by a number of especially internationally minded judges, particularly in relation to human rights treaties.[46]

VI. CONCLUSION

The sources of public power treated in this chapter sit towards either ends of a spectrum of local and global. For centuries, the nation state has monopolised the effective exercise of power in western societies. In New Zealand, a globalised British empire centralised national government away from Māori hapū and iwi in the 1840s to 1860s. In the late twentieth and early twenty-first centuries, communications and transport technologies have lowered the costs of globalism in both public and private spheres. Recent reaction against that has simultaneously heightened interest in localism.

We consider both localised and globalised exercise of power is likely to be increasingly relevant to New Zealand in the future. We wonder if, over (quite some) time, the bulging curve of monopoly power exercised by the nation state will continue to flatten at both ends by simultaneous demands for localism and the pressures of globalism. If this occurs, the effective exercise of public power by national government will be supplemented by both local and global sources. Our constitutional arrangements will need to respond to that, in order to enable, supervise and check the local and global exercise of power consistently with the national exercise of power. What is 'public' – and the reach of our constitution – will have to be redefined accordingly.

FURTHER READING

Costi, A (ed), *Public International Law: A New Zealand Perspective* (Wellington, LexisNexis, 2020).

Jones, C, *New Treaty, New Tradition: Reconciling New Zealand and Māori Law* (Vancouver, UBC Press, 2016).

Palmer, K, *Local Authorities Law in New Zealand* (Wellington, Thomson Reuters, 2012).

Sinclair, GF, *To Reform the World International Organizations and the Making of Modern States* (Oxford, Oxford University Press, 2017).

McLachlan, C, *Foreign Relations Law* (Cambridge, Cambridge University Press, 2014).

[46] C Geiringer, '*Tavita* and All That' (2004) 21 *New Zealand Universities Law Review* 66; H Wilberg, 'Administrative Law' [2010] *New Zealand Law Review* 177.

12

Constitutional Futures

Introduction – A Written Constitution – A Māori-Centred Nation State – A New Zealand Head of State – Pragmatic Tinkering – Enhanced Protection of Rights – Localism versus Globalism – Conclusion

I. INTRODUCTION

WHAT LIES AHEAD in New Zealand's constitutional future? This book does not advocate for any constitutional changes in New Zealand. But we end by speculating about some possibilities and assess the likelihood of them occurring, given our constitutional culture. Reforms that cut against the grain of constitutional culture are more likely to fail. Reforms that that run with the constitutional grain – that are consistent with constitutional culture – are more likely to endure, at least until the next realignment of constitutional culture.

II. A WRITTEN CONSTITUTION?

Some have promoted full codification and adoption of a supreme and entrenched written constitution. But written constitutions and associated greater judicial power have never really captured the popular (or governmental) imagination in New Zealand and run against our pragmatic instincts. So, in the New Zealand context, any project for a written constitution is really about a number of different issues:

- completeness: what constitutional rules should be contained in a single document?
- entrenchment: what constitutional rules should not be able to be changed by a bare parliamentary majority or otherwise?
- supremacy: should judges be able to strike down legislation that is inconsistent with constitutional rules?

The most serious and comprehensive campaign for a written constitution in recent times comes from Sir Geoffrey Palmer and Dr Andrew Butler.[1] They propose the adoption of a complete, entrenched and largely supreme constitution – seeking public input on their proposal through the course of its development. Their proposal is largely based on current institutions, with some significant tweaks:

- The state would be constituted as the 'State of Aotearoa New Zealand', as successor to the Crown. The head of state role would be patriated (a Kaitiaki or Guardian appointed by a free vote and by a super majority in Parliament).
- Cabinet would be formally recognised, both as a formal institution and as constituting, with its ministers, 'the Government'. Executive authority would be directly vested in Cabinet.
- Parliament would continue to be elected by the mixed-member-proportional (MMP) electoral system but with a four-year term, compulsory voting and extended franchise.
- A bill of rights would be a prominent part of the constitution – expanded to include socio-economic, environmental, property and other rights.
- Te Tiriti o Waitangi would be given the full force of law. But a panel would be charged with determining its authoritative meaning in the modern context and proposing necessary consequential amendments to the constitution. The Waitangi Tribunal would continue to have an advisory role.
- The constitution itself would be entrenched – changeable only by supermajority parliamentary vote or majority at a referendum – and subject to periodic review.
- Judges would be able to make authoritative declarations of legislative inconsistency. However, Parliament could respond to condone the inconsistency by supermajority vote for renewable five-year periods.

The proposal takes seriously the virtue of accessibility for important constitutional rules and favours certainty through written expression. It also seeks to weed out the various fictions underlying current arrangements by proposing to give many of the conventional rules full force of

[1] G Palmer and A Butler, *A Constitution for Aotearoa New Zealand* (Wellington, Victoria University Press, 2016); G Palmer and A Butler, *Towards Democratic Renewal* (Wellington, Victoria University Press, 2018). For an alternative model for codification, see DR Knight and J Whaipooti, 'EmpowerNZ: Drafting a Constitution for the 21st Century' (2012) 10 *New Zealand Journal of Public and International Law* 287.

law. It is quite detailed in its institutional design and mandating of associated processes, looking to lock down many of the previously flexible aspects of New Zealand's constitutional system. The proposal seeks to solve many constitutional and civic dilemmas through law and the definitive expression of judicial opinion, albeit subject to political override through constitutional dialogue.

This proposal is the leading blueprint for codification of the New Zealand constitution, based, to a large degree, on familiar government institutions and arrangements. It is yet to attract widespread publicly stated favour with government and the public. That may change, particularly in light of the impact of recent increased immigration importing new cultural assumptions and consequent perceptions by both Māori and Pākehā of the need to spell out what has been formerly assumed in New Zealand's constitutional arrangements. However, if it succeeds, the current government's modest reform to recognise declarations of inconsistency, while still preserving legislative supremacy might head off more radical codification of the kind proposed by Palmer and Butler or others – at least for a while.

III. A MĀORI-CENTRED NATION STATE?

Iwi groups have also promoted constitutional change for Aotearoa New Zealand, although some recent proposals demonstrate an appetite for constitutional transformation rather than reformation. Some proposals seek a fundamentally different approach than modification of the current Westminster constitutional system.

The most prominent example of a call for constitutional transformation is *He Whakaaro Here Whakaumu mō Aotearoa*, the report of Matike Mai Aotearoa – an independent working group on constitutional transformation.[2] This working group, chaired by Margaret Mutu and convened by Moana Jackson, was established by the Iwi Chairs' Forum and consulted with Māori about models for 'an inclusive constitution for Aotearoa'.[3] The mandate was for a constitution based on tikanga and kawa, he Whakaputanga, te Tiriti, and other internationally recognised indigenous human rights instruments. Rather

[2] M Mutu and M Jackson, *He Whakaaro Here Whakaumu Mō Aotearoa* (Matike Mai Aotearoa, Independent Iwi Working Group on Constitutional Transformation, January 2016).

[3] Ibid 7.

than asking how te Tiriti might fit within the current Westminster constitutional system, the report set out six indicative and alternative constitutional models:[4]

1. A tricameral or three sphere model consisting of an Iwi/Hapū assembly (the rangatiratanga sphere), the Crown in Parliament (the kāwanatanga sphere) and a joint deliberative body (the relational sphere).
2. A different three sphere model consisting of an assembly made up of Iwi, Hapū and other representation including Urban Māori Authorities (the rangatiratanga sphere), the Crown in Parliament (the kāwanatanga sphere), and a joint deliberative body (the relational sphere).
3. A further three sphere model consisting of an Iwi/Hapū assembly (the rangatiratanga sphere), the Crown in Parliament (the kāwanatanga sphere), and regional assemblies made up of Iwi, Hapū and Crown representatives (the relational sphere).
4. A multi-sphere model consisting of an assembly of Iwi/Hapū and other Māori representation (the rangatiratanga sphere) and the Crown in Parliament (the kāwanatanga sphere). It also includes a relational sphere which would have two parts – a constitutionally mandated set of direct Iwi/Hapū-Crown relationships to enable direct Iwi/Hapu-Crown decision-making, plus a unitary perhaps annual assembly of broader Māori and Crown representation.
5. A unicameral or one sphere model consisting of Iwi/Hapū and the Crown making decisions together in a constitutionally mandated assembly. This model does not have rangatiratanga or kāwanatanga spheres. It only has the relational sphere.
6. A Bicameral Model made up of an Iwi/Hapū assembly and the Crown in Parliament. This model has distinct rangatiratanga and kāwanatanga spheres but has no provision for a relational sphere.

These models are presented as conceptual sketches and a further process of dialogue with the Crown, local government and communities about these proposals is recommended.

The Matike Mai report presents a rich account of constitutionality viewed through a Māori lens, based around tikanga and related values. The proposals promoted in the report present a different vision for governance in New Zealand. As the label suggests, it would be a dramatic transformation of the current constitutional arrangements. In the current environment, it is difficult to see a popular pathway forward with these proposals absent some revolutionary moment. These proposals, too, run against the grain of suspicion of grand plans. But that might not be the important point of the Matike Mai

[4] Ibid 10.

Aotearoa project, compared with shifting the constitutional conversation. While that conversation is had, we think the looming recognition of Māori tikanga as an element of New Zealand law is likely to effect a far-reaching but largely unnoticed constitutional development, as we touched on in Chapter 7.

IV. A NEW ZEALAND HEAD OF STATE?

Arguments that New Zealand should become a republic and patriate its Head of State have simmered for decades, although serious momentum for change has failed to crystallise during the long reign of Queen Elizabeth II. Originally cast as a component of broader constitutional reformation, recent efforts – involving one of us (not the judge) – have focused attention on patriation of the role of Head of State, while retaining other constitutional settings.[5]

This model of simple republican transformation is premised on the fact that, in reality, the Governor-General discharges the functions and duties of Head of State, such that it could be argued that New Zealand is already a de facto republic.[6] Reform would be based around the elevation of the office of Governor-General to senior civic office and the continuing appointment of similarly qualified people to occupy that office. Otherwise, the ceremonial, community and constitutional duties of the office would be kept as is. This assumes the continuing operation of relevant conventions, without any need for further codification. Choices would need to be made about the mode of appointment – direct election or appointment by parliamentary supermajority. Parliamentary ratification of a candidate is more consistent with the idea of minimal reform. Changes to the office of Head of State would be combined with development of a juristic entity to succeed the Crown and Realm of New Zealand – perhaps the trickier dimension of republican reform. An independent state of Aotearoa New Zealand is proposed to succeed the Crown and Realm of New Zealand, similar to the proposal of Palmer and Butler, and the new state would assume the duties and responsibilities previously held by the Crown. This would include transfer of the

[5] DR Knight, 'Patriating our Head of State' in C Morris, J Boston and P Butler (eds), *Reconstituting the Constitution* (London, Springer, 2011) 107; DR Knight, 'A Republic for New Zealand' (Comparative Constitutional Law Roundtable, University of New South Wales, December 2020).

[6] FM Brookfield, 'Republican New Zealand' (1995) 3 *New Zealand Law Review* 310.

Crown's responsibilities under te Tiriti, unchanged, to the new entity. Such changes would inevitably be subject to referendum, thereby providing a technical revolution to mandate the reformation.

This model of republican reform has a degree of sympathy with New Zealand's incremental and pragmatic constitutional history. However, there is a question as to whether it is feasible without codifying the constitutional conventions associated with the head of state, reconceptualising the Crown as a juristic entity, or obtaining separate consent from the general and Māori electorates as a mandate for any reconfiguration of the Tiriti partnership.[7] Although recent polls suggest over 80 per cent Māori support for a republic, Māori reactions are likely to be complex and nuanced.[8] Otherwise, overall public opinion is relatively mixed: support for a New Zealand Head of State at the end of Queen Elizabeth II's reign ebbs and flows at around 45–55 per cent, partly depending on how the question is framed.[9] Despite many political leaders acknowledging the inevitability of republicanism in New Zealand at some point, there seems little prospect of reform taking place before the end of Queen Elizabeth II's reign or until countries like Australia or Canada make a similar move.[10]

V. PRAGMATIC TINKERING?

As will be clear from our speculation above, we suspect the most likely type of constitutional change in New Zealand will be ongoing pragmatic tinkering within aspects of the broad framework of current arrangements. Incremental reform has been a key aspect of New Zealand's constitutional tradition, as we have pointed out throughout this book. Dramatic revolutionary pressures have generally been avoided, even if we have experienced a couple of more fundamental constitutional moments. Given New Zealand's constitutional culture, we anticipate

[7] Palmer and Butler (n 1); A Quentin-Baxter and J McLean, *This Realm of New Zealand* (Auckland, Auckland University Press, 2017) ch 15 (Afterword); R Cooke, 'The Suggested Revolution Against the Crown' in PA Joseph (ed), *Essays on the Constitution* (Wellington, Brookers, 1995) 28.

[8] New Zealand Republic, 'Opinion Poll – Majority of New Zealanders Want a New Zealand Head of State' (17 May 2019) (www.republic.org.nz).

[9] Ibid; V Molyneux, 'Research reveals Kiwis over 60 support monarchy, while under-60s want a republic' (Newshub, 9 June 2021).

[10] D Williams, 'Genealogies of the Modern Crown' in C Shore and D Williams (eds), *The Shapeshifting Crown* (Cambridge, Cambridge University Press, 2019) 31.

ongoing incremental reform is most likely to be relatively modest, albeit occasionally important, with changes being mainly the continuation of institutional modernisation in directions already signalled.

We expect the fundamentals of democratic government will continue. The continuing public endorsement of MMP, alongside the positive appraisal widely held by experts and parliamentarians, means we see no prospect of proportional representation being repudiated. However, we expect increasing pressures to tweak some of the sharp edges of the electoral system. The Electoral Commission has repeatedly raised matters which should be addressed, including the 5 per cent party threshold and related electorate seat coat-tail rule. Population growth and territorial drift (north to Auckland) might also put pressure on the current settings for defining electorate numbers and boundaries, which consequentially affect the number of members elected via the party lists. These pressures may make it more difficult to maintain the essential proportionality of membership in the House. After the 2020 general election, the Labour-led government signalled a willingness to advance the Commission's recommendations, as well as to extend the parliamentary term to four years.[11]

Innovation in multi-party government is also bound to continue. Much will depend on electoral prospects in future elections, especially the relative size of parties within Parliament and the number of different ways any government commanding confidence might be jigsawed together. We suspect there will be an ongoing appetite within multi-party government for stronger party distinctiveness and voice, capable of being publicly expressed, in the interests of minor party survival. In other words, the unanimity aspect of Cabinet collective responsibility will face increasing pressure.

We mentioned recent reforms to the public sector in Chapter 5. In particular, there are moves to emphasise a more whole-of-government mission and to encourage a public service that is simultaneously more responsive and more prepared to offer ministers free and frank advice, along with moves to embed te Tiriti o Waitangi in the institutional culture of the public sector. And the budget process has been reorientated to channel financial and budgetary decisions through a well-being lens. We suspect that these will continue to be works-in-progress, dependent on the growth of human resource capacity and cultural change, and it will take some time for these ambitions to be fully realised.

[11] New Zealand Labour Party and Green Party of Aotearoa New Zealand, 'Cooperation Agreement' (1 November 2020) [17].

Parliament, as an institution, continually reviews its customs and practices each term with an inquiry into standing orders. Its current Speaker, Trevor Mallard, is well-known for encouraging modernisation of how things are done in the House and committees. We might see the continuation of efforts to open up the business of Parliament to the people, in order to enhance its status as the 'people's Parliament'. The recent coronavirus pandemic has forced Parliament to adjust its way of operating, by building in virtual committee meetings by Zoom, modifying its proxy voting rules and adopting more electronic administration. These changes may become established on an enduring basis.

Legislative reform in 2016 significantly modernised the framework for the judiciary, as explained in Chapter 7. Processes for the appointment of judges – informal and inconspicuous in nature – continue to come under scrutiny, especially in the light of modern expectations about the competencies needed for judging. As more adjudication draws judges into realms of human rights and complex political and public policy issues, the public rightly expect judges to better reflect the more diverse faces of New Zealand society and different views on these issues. Codification of the process for judicial appointment remains a possibility, especially if any controversy were to develop about particular appointments. The adoption of an independent panel to provide the Prime Minister with advice on candidates for appointment as Chief Justice in 2018 might indicate a possible route for that. Another area where pressures for reform might arise is in relation to institutional support for judges, as we discussed in the context of judicial independence. Some work on harmonising tribunal powers and processes has already been implemented and we might see further efforts to provide them with more coherent institutional structures and functions.

Legislative expression of norms and associated accountability processes will inevitably continue to evolve. Legislating aspirational goals, and reporting regimes, for climate change and child poverty have been notable recent innovations, following those for fiscal responsibility adopted in the 1990s. These reforms reflect successive governments' wishes to encourage longer term and enduring concern for these objectives.[12] But they butt up against the traditional constitutional theory of parliamentary sovereignty (ie legislative supremacy) and the reality of political change. Pressure to enrich human rights protections will no doubt continue. Cementing in judicial declarations of inconsistency and

[12] J Boston and others (eds), *Future Proofing the State* (Canberra, ANU Press, 2014).

parliamentary sequels to declarations will take some time to realise and will occupy attention in this field for some time. It would not surprise us to see campaigns to enlarge the suite of protected rights, such as for the recognition of more socio-economic, property or environmental rights. Indeed, the Constitutional Advisory Panel recommended some of these possibilities should be explored in 2013.[13] Practice in comparable jurisdictions and within the international community may add some pressures for reform so that more rights are formally recognised. But, as we noted earlier in this chapter, we think the attitude of New Zealanders to legally enforceable rights remains ambivalent and this might inhibit any rapid developments in this space.

Constitutional dialogue between the branches of government has essentially settled the contemporary legal meaning of the obligations in te Tiriti o Waitangi. But te Tiriti is still half in and half out of the law. Sometimes it has legal force and sometimes it does not, depending on whether the relevant legislation has a Treaty clause and whether the subject matter is closely connected with Māori interests. We consider te Tiriti is likely to gradually exhibit increasing legal salience on the same trajectory it has so far. But New Zealand's diversity is increasing and Auckland's ethnic mix is now distinctly different from that in other New Zealand cities. These cultural pressures could lead to either more or less emphasis on te Tiriti – as recent immigrants either question the relevance of older cultural relationships or embrace the invitation of te Tiriti to honour diverse cultures. A changing cultural landscape may even see more Pākehā join Māori in referring to te Tiriti as a constitutional touchstone. Ironically, that would reflect a return of Tiriti discourse to its original function of mediating the exercise of power between newer and more established groups of New Zealanders.

More generally, demands for constitutional transparency and enhanced civic literacy might see some changes about how the constitutional rules are presented, showcased and studied. Palmer and Butler's point about the importance of accessibility of fundamental constitutional rules and comprehension of the shape of government is well made. One possible reform might be a project to fill out the current partial sketch of our constitutional system in the Constitution Act 1986, without seeking to engage in normative revision. In other words, modest codification by either gathering up some of the existing constitutional rules found in other statutes or including cross-references to them in the Constitution

[13] Constitutional Advisory Panel, 'A Report on a Conversation / He Kōtuinga Kōrero mō Te Kaupapa Ture o Aotearoa' (November 2013).

Act. In addition, a chorus of calls for deeper and more extensive civics education must surely be heeded, in order to increase civic and constitutional consciousness amongst young people and the community.[14] But the content of civics or citizenship education is often controversial. Calls for pupils to be taught how government works sit awkwardly with a curriculum designed around skill development and self-directed discovery, rather than catalogues of mandated knowledge.[15] Already underway are efforts to ensure school students have a deeper appreciation of New Zealand's histories, especially colonisation and te Tiriti.

VI. ENHANCED PROTECTION OF RIGHTS?

By its very nature, the common law is always in an active evolutionary state. Constant change, driven by the demands of justice in individual cases, is one of the essential features of judicial adjudication, especially in public law where precedents can be easier to distinguish. The absence of barriers to progressive development does not necessarily mean that judges will take up the invitation for reform. Institutional comity and a deep appreciation of the conventional role of judges in a small democratic society weigh heavily on the judicial conscience. But generational change can work its effect on judges too. Against this backdrop, there are two areas where we wonder if the judicial voice might become more amplified – both building on seeds already seen in the common law: the heightened protection of rights and declaratory judgments. The current direction of travel suggests the judicial voice in these areas could become stronger and more frequent.

In Chapter 9, we looked at the common law's heightened protection of certain rights, through the principle of legality or imposition of heavier justificatory burdens. This style of judicial statecraft – colouring law in the values of human rights and implicitly re-ordering an otherwise flat legal hierarchy – has much potential. It has grown into a mainstream judicial technique in New Zealand's legal tradition. Its legitimacy stems in part from the way it ostensibly navigates democratic sensitivities, on the one hand, but still allows the possibility that the legislature might speak definitely to remove any wriggle room for rights values to infiltrate legislative text, on the other. It would not surprise us to see the range of

[14] New Zealand Political Studies Association, *Our Civic Future* (2018).

[15] B Wood and A Milligan, 'Citizenship Education in New Zealand' (2016) 12 *New Zealand Policy Quarterly* 65.

human rights used to trigger this enhanced protection of rights to grow beyond the familiar examples of security and liberty, political freedoms and natural justice. Judges may also become more comfortable with international law protections shading into the domestic sphere, through the similar legal presumption of consistency. Similarly, the principle of legality might enhance protection for rights through te Tiriti o Waitangi. But we do not expect human rights to sweep entirely through the common law. Matters of institutional competence and comity still give rise to reluctance on the part of judges to express legal views on issues of social, economic and political sensitivity that are better discussed in the language of policy and politics than the language of law.

We also identified, in Chapters 7 and 9, an increasing willingness in the judiciary to express judicial views on a declaratory basis, even if their determination has little direct legal consequence. Declarations of inconsistency under the Bill of Rights Act are an example. However, this technique has been used in other types of challenges too.[16] Here, a judicial voice does not immediately vindicate and protect rights but instead can induce inter-institutional dialogue and action. This delicate tango could prove an attractive tool for judges to participate constructively in constitutional dialogue when confronted with socially and politically sensitive questions, particularly if political processes are stuck. The judicial voice of reason can be expressed in constitutional dialogue, but leave to others the choices about what should be done. However, we doubt judges will necessarily embrace a fully advisory opinion function. New Zealand judges rightly remain cautious about forming views in the abstract without a full appreciation of the context of a particular dispute which is the natural home of the common law approach. It seems likely declaratory relief would be reserved for cases where someone can come to court to explain the specific context of how their grievance has arisen, how their rights have been unjustifiably impinged and how resolution is beyond politics at the time.

VII. LOCALISM VERSUS GLOBALISM?

We identified the ubiquity of international law and globalisation in Chapter 11, especially in the context of New Zealand as a small and open democracy. In an increasingly interconnected world, and despite

[16] *Ngāti Whātua Ōrākei Trust v Attorney-General* [2018] NZSC 84, [2019] 1 NZLR 116.

recent 'Trumpian' experiments elsewhere, it is difficult to see any serious retreat from the internationalism project. As a matter of reality, the domestic and international are probably too deeply interwoven in New Zealand for global dimensions to be ignored or side-lined. However, against that backdrop, we detect some parallel ambition for more distinctive nationalism, along with desire for returns to autonomous localism for some types of decision-making. A tension is obvious: between practical globalisation and idealistic localism.

It is difficult to predict how the ebb and flow between these competing values might play out. Some nation states have shown antagonism to aspects of the internationalisation project in recent years. Brexit by the United Kingdom is one example, along with former President Trump's withdrawal of the United States from intergovernmental institutions and processes (now largely restored under President Biden). But other states continue to seek solutions and outcomes through multinational partnership. New Zealand continues to hold itself out as a good international citizen. However, recent divisions within New Zealand communities about the trans-Pacific partnership trade agreement – especially its implications for domestic sovereignty – revealed increasing dissension about the implications of globalisation. The position of Māori also complicates the strength of New Zealand's commitment to internationalism. Iwi and hapū are increasingly mobilising through networks of indigenous peoples, and international instruments such as the United Nations Declaration of the Rights of Indigenous Peoples, to achieve outcomes for Māori within the domestic sphere. But a globalised world built on universal values may sit uncomfortably with the idea of Aotearoa New Zealand as a special and sacred place for Māori and their distinctive culture.

We doubt there is a natural way for these tensions to be resolved. Much like other aspects of New Zealand's constitutional story, ad hoc, pragmatic and perhaps even haphazard shifts and turns seem more likely. We write this during the coronavirus pandemic that has seen the unprecedented closure of national borders and New Zealand being confined in its own bubble for many months. So much in our world is currently cloaked in uncertainty. We rely on our constitutional character and culture to help us navigate through our constitutional future.

VIII. CONCLUSION

As Professor Quentin-Baxter once said:[17]

> A constitution is a human habitation. Like a city, it may preserve its life and its beauty through centuries of change. It may, on the other hand, become either a glorious ruin from which life has departed, or a dilapidated slum that no longer knows the great tradition of its builders.

As well as explaining how the 'city' is constructed and mapping its infrastructure, we have sought to explain how the inhabitants live their lives within that city. Constitutional realism demands seeing how power is actually wielded, by whom and how others keep that power in check in reality. Constitutional realism also requires listening to the chorus of chatter – the constitutional dialogue – among the polity. The story of the constitution is a human one – one where the character and values of the people within it provide essential colour. Throughout this book, we have offered our account of the character and culture of New Zealand's constitution. In this final chapter, we have speculated on what might change over time. We hope the health, life and beauty of our 'city' – the nation of Aotearoa New Zealand – remain but, as always, that is in the hands of the people who live within it.

FURTHER READING

Constitutional Advisory Panel, *New Zealand's Constitution: A Report on a Conversation* (November 2013).

Morris, C, Boston, J, and Butler, P (eds), *Reconstituting the Constitution* (London, Springer, 2011).

Mutu, M, and Jackson, M, *He Whakaaro Here Whakaumu Mō Aotearoa* (Matike Mai Aotearoa, Independent Iwi Working Group on Constitutional Transformation, January 2016).

Palmer, G, and Butler, A, *Towards Democratic Renewal: Ideas for Constitutional Change in New Zealand* (Wellington, Victoria University Press, 2018).

[17] RQ Quentin-Baxter, 'The Governor-General's Constitutional Discretions' (1980) 10 *Victoria University of Wellington Law Review* 289, 290.

Index

Introductory Note

References such as '178–79' indicate (not necessarily continuous) discussion of a topic across a range of pages. Wherever possible in the case of topics with many references, these have either been divided into sub-topics or only the most significant discussions of the topic are listed. Because the entire work is about the 'New Zealand Constitution', the use of this term (and certain others which occur constantly throughout the book) as entry points has been restricted. Information will be found under the corresponding detailed topics.

accountability 103–4, 121, 123, 156–57, 161, 163, 166–81
  judiciary 137, 160–62
  legal 173, 175
  mechanisms/arrangements 100–101, 122, 160, 173
  political 87, 121
adjudication 13, 138, 168, 175, 207, 249
administration 70, 72, 74, 77–78, 81–82, 87, 160
administrative decisions 153, 165, 174, 195–96, 204
administrative justice 173, 177
administrative law 89, 165–66, 175, 196–97, 236
administrative tribunals 151, 165, 174–76
adversarial mechanisms 108, 121
advice 38, 43–45, 73, 83–84, 94–97, 99, 153–54
  free and frank 8, 13, 24, 87, 93–94, 97–99, 248
  ministerial 6, 48
  of ministers 6, 43, 181
  to ministers 97, 99
  policy 87, 98, 159
advisors, responsible 38, 69
agents, Crown 100–101
agreements 67, 81–82, 115, 154, 220, 224, 237–38
  coalition 59, 67–68, 72, 81
  confidence-and-supply
    cooperation 59, 68
    inter-party 59
    support 59, 65–66, 71, 81
amendments 17, 61, 66, 109, 116–18, 128, 131
annual reports 123, 180
anonymity 94, 97, 99–100
Aotearoa New Zealand 15, 26–35, 189, 234, 244, 246, 253–54
appeal judges 148, 152
appeal(s) 145–50, 153–54, 161, 173–75, 197, 199, 203–5, 217–18
appellate courts 137, 174
appointments 38–40, 43–44, 84–85, 94, 152–55, 246, 249
  judicial 153–54, 249
Appointments and Honours Committee 77, 185
appropriation bills 103, 119–20
appropriations 95, 103, 112, 117, 119, 179
arbitrariness 139, 161
Ardern, Jacinda 16, 18, 58, 84, 97
armed conflict 3, 210
assent, royal 38, 44–45, 115, 118, 128
assertion of sovereignty 3, 26, 33–35, 50, 127
Assistant Speakers 110
Associate Judges 148, 152
Attorneys-General 43, 45, 118, 153–54, 161–62, 195, 198
Auditor-General 14, 111, 179–80

Australia 4, 21, 37, 40, 158, 247
authority 16–18, 35, 38–39, 127–30, 210, 231, 233
  executive 39, 43, 47, 73, 243
  faith in 16–18
  law-making 128–29, 131, 133
  legislative 30, 127, 129, 133, 212, 217
automatic votes of confidence 64, 103
autonomous Crown entities 101

balance 20, 53, 67–68, 82, 105, 172, 207
ballot box 17, 36, 170
barristers 151–52
behaviour 11–13, 90, 98, 104, 137–38, 140, 145
  offensive 200
bill of rights 11, 127, 130, 200, 202, 243
Bill of Rights Act 131, 135, 170, 172, 190–203, 206–7, 228
  efficacy 202
  impact on functions of government 194–99
  operational scheme 192–94
  protected rights 191
  sites of contest 199–202
boundaries 54, 60, 82, 136, 248
  organisational 93
branches of government 12–14, 22, 76, 110–11, 157–58, 163–64, 190–92
  executive 76–77, 87–88, 105, 141, 158, 160, 198
  judicial 137, 156, 192
  legislative 156
  political 23, 163
British settlers 2–3, 26, 31, 208
  see also **Pākehā**
budget 59, 64, 71, 103–5, 160
  process 104, 119, 123, 248
  statements 119–20
Business Committee 109, 111–13, 121
business of government 65–66, 73–74, 109, 124–25, 184, 231

Cabinet 7–8, 62–63, 67, 76–85, 89–91, 153–54, 213–15
  agendas 83
  collective responsibility 79–84
  committees 77–79, 83, 116
  confidentiality 83–84
  decisions 78–80, 82, 89, 93
  government 7, 76–85
  minutes 77, 79, 83
  papers 83–84, 142, 212–13, 227
  room 77–78
  unanimity and exceptions 79–83
Cabinet Manual 14, 17, 63, 69, 73, 78–80, 82
Cabinet Office 69, 77–79
Canada 21, 37, 152, 157, 221, 247
candidates 39–40, 52–57, 154–55, 246, 249
  electoral 54–55, 70
  potential 39, 154
candour 9–10
capacity
  collective 30
  personal 182, 184, 187
caretaker convention 65, 69–74, 79
casting vote 110
caucus 57–58, 85
Caucus Committee 214–15
central government 8, 47, 230–33
chairpersons 112, 232–33
Chief District Court Judge 150, 153
chief executives 89, 91, 93–95, 97, 99–100, 102–3, 123
  departmental 91, 166, 174
Chief High Court Judge 153–54
Chief Justices 41, 146, 149, 153–56, 158–60, 162, 211
chiefs *see* **rangatira**
chieftainship 32, 210, 214
children 101, 201, 205, 227
  poverty 105, 249
citizens 18, 23, 51, 53, 165–66, 183, 187
civics education 251
civil servants 74, 130, 177, 181
Clark, Helen 18, 83, 91, 97
Clerk of the Executive Council 38, 65, 79
Clerk of the House of Representatives 55, 110–11
coalition agreements 59, 67–68, 72, 81
coalitions 7, 59, 64–68, 71, 77, 79–82, 84
  Labour-Alliance 67, 81
  Labour-Progressive 67
  partners 72, 77, 83

codification 201, 242, 244, 246–47, 249–50
coercive powers 8, 23, 177
coherence 155, 175, 249
collective capacity 30
collective entity 7, 79–80, 90
collective interests 92–93
collective responsibility 7, 64, 67, 79–84, 87, 89–90, 248
confidence element 79–80, 82–83
and confidentiality 83–84
unanimity and exceptions 79–83
colonial legislature 6, 108, 128, 133
Colonial Office 3, 31, 33–34
Colonial Secretary 31, 34, 50
comity 111, 251–52
Commander-in-Chief 41
Commerce Commission 101, 174
commercial activities 102, 183, 232
commercial functions 101–2
Commissioner of Inland Revenue 89, 95
Commissioner of Police 89, 95
commissions of inquiry 151, 176, 180, 215, 223
committee reports on bills 117–18, 142
committees 59–60, 95, 111–14, 116–18, 123, 125–26, 195 *see also* ***individual committee titles***
scrutiny of bills 117–18
common law 12–14, 23, 130–31, 145–46, 168–69, 197, 251–52
and fundamental rights 203–6
and judiciary 144–45
rights 134, 206
companies 92, 155, 170, 230, 235
Crown entity 101
compensation 172, 174, 198–99, 216
competition 24, 96, 124
complaints 162, 176–77, 180, 185, 206, 213, 215
jurisdiction 101, 227
compliance 14, 99, 180, 190, 194, 207
conduct 29, 93–94, 96, 121, 123, 161–62, 180–81
confidence 6–7, 17, 43–44, 63–74, 79, 90, 135
commanding 44, 64, 69, 71
element of collective responsibility 79–80, 82–83
lost 69, 71
matters of 65–67, 82
mid-term loss 64–65, 73
votes 64, 66, 71–72, 119
confidence-and-supply arrangements 66, 68
confidentiality 7, 79, 83–84
conflicts 2–3, 41, 145, 149, 158, 162, 229
armed 3, 210
conscience 13, 125, 191
judicial 251
consensus 17, 77, 138, 234
consent 119, 124, 128, 130, 138, 236, 238
consistency 155, 193–94, 197, 239–40, 252
constitutional change 17, 20–21, 247
constitutional conventions 12–13, 43–44, 61, 63, 77–78, 80, 82–83
constitutional culture 1, 12, 14–19, 135, 242, 247
constitutional dialogue 1–3, 21–24, 141–42, 198, 218, 220, 252
constitutional functions 41–42, 80, 95, 152, 173
constitutional futures 242–54
constitutional norms 15–17, 19, 21, 163, 166
constitutional powers 40–41, 48
constitutional realism 1, 9, 11–12, 14, 142, 166, 254
consultation 67, 94, 101, 117–18, 126153, 155
control 11, 31–32, 96, 116, 128, 166, 220
parliamentary 115, 127
of public finances 119–20
Controller and Auditor-General 14, 179–80
conventions
constitutional 5–8, 11–13, 38–40, 43–44, 61, 63, 73–74, 77–78, 80, 82–83, 89–90, 237–40
of ministerial responsibility 7, 87, 89–90, 94
convictions 51, 161, 200
Cooke, Lord 26, 133–35, 205, 217, 222, 226
cooperation agreements 59, 68
coronavirus pandemic 100, 105, 201, 249, 253
corporatisation 236

courts 128–38, 140–50, 158–62, 169–76, 193–200, 203–5, 217–19
appellate 137, 174
Court of Appeal 145–49, 152–54, 197, 199, 203–5, 212, 217–18
District Courts 148–50, 152, 154, 157, 159, 161, 174
High Court 144, 147–50, 152, 154–55, 169, 173–76, 200–201
highest 5, 148–49, 218
judicial direction and executive operation of system 158–60
Māori Land Court 130, 150, 215, 223
senior 140, 147–49
structure and processes 147–51
Supreme Court 144, 146–49, 153–54, 173–74, 194, 198, 200–201
criminal justice process 191, 199
crisis, economic 4, 73
Crown 2–3, 33–36, 47–48, 86–88, 100–103, 216–27, 245–47
agents 100–101
entities 88, 92, 100–101, 104, 123, 179
autonomous 101
companies 101
independent 54, 101, 157
in law 46–47
culpability 8, 87, 89–90
cultures 11–12, 15, 151–52, 212, 219, 250, 253–54
constitutional 1, 12, 14–19, 135, 242, 247
New Zealand 2, 16–21
customary rights 3, 22, 145, 201
customs 13, 26, 57, 116, 144, 249

damages 22, 183, 194, 197–98, 207
debates, parliamentary 88, 122, 142–43, 226
debating chamber 108–9, 111–12
decision-making 79, 97–98, 167–68, 175, 178, 218, 233
powers 27, 187
decisions 77–80, 85, 89–91, 95–97, 156, 165–78, 186–88
administrative 153, 165, 174, 195–96, 204
discretionary 205, 240
invalid 172
judicial 156, 158, 163
Declaration of Independence of New Zealand, *see* **he Whakaputanga o te Rangatiratanga o Nu Tireni**
declarations 30, 70, 169, 172, 198, 201, 207
judicial 135, 249
of legislative inconsistency 22, 194, 198, 243–44, 252
declaratory relief 194, 198, 252
democracy 5, 17, 117, 124, 138, 231, 238
representative 1, 5–6, 8, 17, 21, 49–50, 121
democratic government 6–7, 49–75, 105, 166, 226, 248
democratic legitimacy 6, 38, 49, 66, 74
democratic society 191–92, 251
Department of the Prime Minister and Cabinet (DPMC) 79, 97, 99
departmental chief executives 91, 166, 174
departmental officials 117–18, 158, 160
departments 85–88, 91–94, 96–98, 102–4, 123, 179–80, 182–85
Deputy Speaker 110
detention 177, 191, 199
unlawful 198
devolution 235–36
dialogue 14, 22, 39, 135, 163, 167, 191
constitutional 1–3, 21–24, 141–42, 198, 218, 220, 252
Dicey, Albert Venn 10, 18, 129–31
disclosure 96, 98–99, 162, 181–85
discretion 82, 90, 100, 146, 171, 180, 196
discretionary decisions 196, 205, 240
discrimination 176, 178, 191, 199–200, 206–7
disputes 8, 140, 144, 149–50, 163, 175, 197
dissent 7, 81–82
expressions of 67, 81–82
District Courts 148–50, 152, 154, 157, 159, 161, 174
distrust 18, 20
diversity 40, 52, 58–59, 94, 152
domestic law 212, 220, 238–40

DPMC (Department of the Prime Minister and Cabinet) 79, 97, 99
duties 91, 93–94, 96–97, 99, 217, 220–21, 246
of loyalty 8, 94–95, 102

early elections 71–72
economic crisis 4, 73
education 157, 207
civics 251
institutions, tertiary 92, 101
egalitarianism 1, 16–17
elected House *see* **House of Representatives**
election day 54–55, 65, 70
elections 44–45, 50–52, 54–55, 58–60, 63–66, 68–70, 72–74
early 71–72
first-past-the-post (FPP) 4, 6, 49, 51–53, 58–60, 70, 125–26
general 24, 53–56, 58, 248
mixed-member-proportional (MMP) *see* mixed-member-proportional elections
electoral candidates 54–55, 70
Electoral Commission 54–56, 60, 101, 248
electoral process 54–55, 60, 69
electoral system 4–6, 58, 60, 75–76, 219, 243, 248 *see also* **mixed-member-proportional elections**
entrenched provisions 60–62
evolution 50–53
first-past-the-post (FPP) 4, 6, 49, 51–53, 58–60, 70, 125–26
electorates 53–56, 59–62, 95, 122, 160
Māori 51–52, 54, 214, 247
electors 51–54
Elizabeth II, Queen 36–38, 246–47
employees 89, 92–93, 100, 102, 130
employers 93, 101
employment status 96, 206
enforcement 3, 5, 13, 34, 81–83, 98
English language 30, 33, 214
entrenchment 52, 60–61, 131–33, 242
manner and form 62
single 61
equity 144, 221
errors 90, 148, 172, 174, 196
of law 172, 196
exceptional circumstances 43, 45
executive authority 39, 43, 47, 73, 243
executive branch 76–105, 141, 158, 160, 198, 226
Cabinet *see* Cabinet
individual ministerial responsibility 7, 83, 87–91, 94, 99
Executive Council 36, 38, 45–46, 65, 77, 79–80, 85
Clerk 38, 65, 79
Governor-General in 80
executive functions 137, 238
executive government 6–7, 43, 45–47, 49–50, 62–63, 74–77, 114–15 *see also* **executive branch**
formal acts of 46, 77
executive power 5, 18, 36, 76, 125, 233
exercise of public power 11–12, 14–17, 22, 27–29, 142, 208, 219
expectations 13, 16, 138, 140, 165–66, 234, 236–37
expenditure 103, 119–20
capital 179
expenses 19, 92
operating 179
expertise 172, 176, 223
special 117, 176
subject matter 97, 181
experts 114, 248
expressive rights 199–200

fairness 16, 18–19, 199, 236
faith in authority 16–18
financial management 76, 104–5, 231
financial reforms 105
first-past-the-post (FPP) 4, 6, 49, 51–53, 58–60, 70, 125–26
fiscal restraint 103–4
fiscal strategy 104
fisheries 32, 209, 218, 220–21
fixed terms 91, 93
force of law 46, 213, 239, 243
foreshore 22, 130, 145, 201
forestry assets 217
form(s) 67–69, 73–74, 82–83, 103, 132, 137, 143–45
of law 139, 141, 143
legal 9, 24, 47
formal legality 138

formality 19, 46, 48, 183, 185, 188, 217
FPP *see* **first-past-the-post**
franchise 5, 31, 50–51
free and frank advice 8, 13, 24, 87, 93–94, 97–99, 248
freedom 19, 22, 110, 113, 191–93, 197, 199
freedom of information 83, 98, 186
freedom of speech 110, 113
functions 86–87, 93, 95–96, 111–15, 122–24, 136–38, 159
  constitutional 41–42, 80, 95, 152, 173
  core 41, 76
  executive 137, 238
  Head of State 38–39
  judicial 137, 151
  legislative 113, 194
  parliamentary 114–24
  primary 115, 126, 140
  public 192, 197, 207
fundamental human rights 23, 134, 143, 172, 190, 203–5
fundamental rights 22, 139, 190
  and common law 203–6

general elections 24, 53–56, 58, 248
global governance 8, 228, 230–40
global institutions 230, 237–41
globalisation 252–53
globalism 241, 252–53
good faith 23, 32, 93, 217, 219–21
governance 3, 27–28, 34, 57, 63, 223, 233–37
  British 3, 28
  good 173, 234
  local and global 8, 181, 228, 230–41
  Māori 28, 230, 234–35
  non-state bodies and private sector 236–37
governing parties 4, 68, 71, 80, 82, 96, 125–26
government
  Cabinet 7, 77–85
  caretaker convention 65, 69–74, 79
  central 8, 47, 230–33
  coalition *see* coalitions
  democratic *see* democratic government
  departments *see* departments
  executive branch *see* executive branch
  expiration of mandate
    following election 69–70
    mid-term following loss of confidence 70–72
  formation 63–66
  incumbent 64, 70, 73–74
  provider of 118–19
  representative 17, 36, 49–61, 115, 124, 127
  responsible 3, 6, 17, 21, 49, 62–74, 120
  sub-national 230–32
  transition between governments 72–74
Government Statistician 89, 95
Governors 29, 33, 35, 39–40, 45, 50, 127–28
Governors-General 6–7, 36, 38, 40–46, 63–66, 69–74, 153–55
  constitutional, ceremonial and community functions 41–42
  as de facto heads of state 39–41
  functions and powers 36, 41–45
  parliamentary powers 45
  prerogative and statutory powers 42–43
  reserve powers 43–45
Greens 56, 59, 65, 67–68, 73, 183
grievances 2, 165, 168, 175, 177–78, 223, 228
groups of parties 64, 73–74
guardianship 28–29, 197
guidance 78, 80, 99, 152

hapū 2–3, 16–17, 27–30, 32–34, 224–28, 234–35, 245
Head of State 6, 36–48, 226, 247
  functions 38–39
  Governors-General as de facto 39–41
  New Zealand 246–47
  Sovereign as 37–38
heads of bench 153–54, 156, 158, 162
health 20, 100–101, 150, 163, 236, 254
hearings 35, 199, 223
he Whakaputanga o te Rangatiratanga o Nu Tireni 26, 29–30, 35
High Court 144, 147–50, 152, 154–55, 169, 173–76, 200–201
historic claims 222–23

history 27–28, 76, 163, 208–17, 223, 231
legislative 142–43
Hobson, Captain 31–34
Holyoake, Sir Keith 40
House of Representatives 4–7, 36, 43–45, 48–63, 107–11, 116, 160–61 *see also* **Parliament**
Clerk 55, 110–11
committees 112–14
debates 122
as forum for party-political contest 124
ministerial questions 121–22
proceedings 110, 125–26
select committees 59–60, 95, 107, 112–14, 117, 123–25, 195
Speaker 14, 109–13, 121–22
as symbol of representative government 115, 124
human rights 9, 134–35, 143, 189–207, 228, 249, 251–52
common law and fundamental rights 203–6
fundamental 23, 134, 143, 172, 190, 203–5
instruments 189–90, 204, 241, 244
protections 131, 191, 249
Human Rights Commission 20, 101, 207, 227
Human Rights Review Tribunal 151, 176, 200, 206–7

Immigration & Protection Tribunal 176
immunities 22–23, 47, 84, 113, 198, 238
impartiality 19, 65, 110, 162, 177
implied repeal 129, 192, 205–6
imprest supply bills 117, 120
imprisonment 51, 113, 156, 198
impropriety, personal 90
incentives 11, 65, 81, 96, 102, 159, 161
political 107, 160
inconsistency 131, 193–94, 198, 201, 243–44, 249, 252
independence 1, 4, 19, 26, 29–30, 33, 163
judicial 8, 19, 137, 156–61, 249
statutory 89
independent judgement 44, 71
Independent Police Complaints Authority 177
Independent Police Conduct Authority 20
individual ministerial responsibility 7, 83, 87–91, 94, 99
individuals, rights of 23–24, 192, 199
information 78, 83–84, 98, 119, 121–22, 157, 181–87 *see also* **transparency**
personal 184–85, 206
infrastructure 4, 14, 18, 56, 232–33, 254
innovation 7, 20, 59, 119, 223, 248–49
inquiries 123, 151, 176–77, 180–81, 215, 223–24, 249
inquisitorial approach 176–77, 215, 223
inspection 94, 145, 184, 236
institutions 11, 22–24, 48–49, 124, 126, 139–40, 147–56
formal 62, 243
global 230, 237–41
parliamentary 50, 57–58, 107–14
intentions 34, 60–61, 65, 132, 156, 218, 226
interests 1–2, 16, 18, 88, 139, 154, 235–36
collective 92–93
of justice 148, 169
public interest 84, 98, 121, 175, 182–83, 190
international community 189, 237–39, 250
international law 205, 213, 220, 230, 237–40, 252
obligations 205, 239–40
international relationships 230, 237–41
international treaties 34–35, 123–24, 220, 237, 239–40
inter-party agreement 59
interpretation 5, 8, 12, 14, 23, 140–44, 222
purposive 141, 143
rights-consistent 196–97, 203
techniques 143, 203
invalidation 128, 130–32, 134, 170, 172–73, 190, 192
investigations 91, 94, 168, 177–78, 181, 185, 207
iwi (tribes) 2–3, 27–30, 32–34, 209–10, 224–28, 234–35, 244–45
Iwi Chairs' Forum 235, 244

judges 137, 152, 155–63, 167–68, 171–73, 249, 251–52
appeal 148, 152
Associate 148, 152
daily practice 155–56
District Court 149–50, 161
as face of judiciary 151–53
former 155, 162, 177, 181
and judiciary 151–55
Māori 215, 227
selection and appointment 153–55
senior court 152–53, 157, 161
judicial appointments 153–54, 249
judicial branch 137, 156, 192 *see also* **judiciary**
Judicial Committee 5, 145, 148, 212, 218
Judicial Conduct Panel 157, 162
judicial independence 8, 19, 157–61, 249
protection 156–58
judicial review 144, 148, 162, 165, 167–74, 176, 222
judicial supervision 174, 199
judicial voice 251–52
judiciary 5–6, 8, 19–23, 40, 137–64, 222, 227 *see also* **judges**
accountability 160–62
and common law 144–45
court structure and processes 147–51
daily practice 155–56
direction and executive operation of court system 158–60
independence *see* judicial independence
as institution 147–56
and interpretation of legislation 140–43
and judges 151–55
removal and accountability 160–62
and tikanga 145–46
juristic entities 46–47, 100, 246–47
justice 19, 26, 29, 148, 154, 158–60, 164
administrative 173, 177
interests of 148, 169
natural 171, 176, 191, 196, 199, 252
Justice and Electoral Committee 154
Justice and Law Reform Committee 142

kāwanatanga (governorship/government) 30, 32, 34–35, 214, 245
Keith, Sir Kenneth 5, 17, 36, 38
Key, John 18, 83
ki te Kuini o Ingarani ake tonu Confederation 209
Kirk, Norman 18, 215

Labour 56–57, 59, 67–68, 73, 81, 211, 214
governments 52, 73, 149, 214–16
Labour-Alliance coalition 67, 81
Labour-Progressive coalition 67
Land Valuation Tribunal 151
language 10, 22–23, 88, 141, 151–52, 159–60, 163
English 30, 33, 214
of management 92, 160
Māori 30, 32–34, 212, 214, 220–21, 227
of policy 23, 86, 92, 252
of politics 23, 86, 252
versions 32–33, 214
Law Commission 22, 101, 141–42, 154
law-making 6, 50, 85–86, 115–18, 126, 135
authority 128–29, 131, 133
power 115, 127–28, 130–31, 134–36
process 123, 125–26, 131, 226
lawyers 14, 19, 139, 151, 155–56, 160–62, 199
leadership 97, 186
political 27, 135
styles 102
legal entities 8, 47, 93, 101, 216, 225
legal force 3, 22, 34, 220, 222, 250
legal personality 100, 225, 235
legal powers 6, 44, 48, 77, 86, 102, 218
legal status 2, 35, 208, 210–12, 215, 218–20, 231
legal system 2, 138, 197, 202, 208, 234, 237
legal traditions 2, 251
legality 169, 199, 203, 205, 222, 251–52
formal 138
principle 203, 205, 222, 251–52
legislation 44–45, 87–89, 129–31, 140, 192–94, 201, 227
interpreting *see* interpretation
secondary 85–86, 113, 195, 223
striking down 6, 21, 130, 242
legislative authority 30, 127, 129, 133, 212, 217

legislative branch 156
Legislative Council 4, 45, 50, 52, 108, 127
legislative history 142–43
legislative inconsistency
see inconsistency
declarations 22, 194, 198, 243–44, 252
legislative process 115, 117, 129, 194, 202, 224
legislative reform 47, 92, 144, 200, 249
legislative supremacy 1, 4, 6, 18, 126–36, 163, 165
nature 129–32
origins 127–29
procedural restrictions 132–33
substantive restrictions 133–35
legitimacy 72, 160, 163
democratic 6, 38, 49, 66, 74
judicial 153
Liberal Party 4, 56
liberties 156, 187, 199, 252
Liquor Licensing Tribunal 151
local and global governance 8, 181, 228, 230–41
local authorities 115, 175, 177, 179–80, 182, 187, 231–34
local democracy 231, 234
local government 186, 230–34
localism 230, 241, 252–53
loyalty 8, 87, 94–95, 99–100, 102, 221
duty of 8, 94–95, 102

majority
support 71–72, 74–75
votes 58, 109–10
maladministration 177–78, 184
mana (status) 27, 30, 32, 68, 146
manaakitanga (nurturing others) 27, 32
management 92, 98, 102, 159–60, 221, 225, 233
financial 76, 104–5, 231
resource 145, 155, 222
managerialism 76, 93, 102–3
manner and form 62, 109–10, 132–33
entrenchment 62
Māori 2–3, 26–29, 31–33, 145–46, 210–13, 215–20, 232–35
Appellate Court 146, 150
authorities 230
urban 245
claims 22, 217–18
communities 26, 226
electorates 51–52, 54, 214, 247
governance 28, 230, 234–35
judges 215, 227
land 145, 150, 212, 221
Land Court 130, 150, 215, 223
Land March 212, 215
language (te reo) 30, 32–34, 212, 214, 220–21, 227
MPs 58, 214, 226
tikanga *see* tikanga
Māori-Centred nation state 244–46
matters of confidence 65–67, 82
mayors 40, 232–33
meaning
and effect 215, 220
intended 193, 221
and legal status 2, 208, 210, 218
of legislation 140, 142
media 82, 100, 122, 185, 236
social 183, 237
statements 130
merits 94, 96, 168, 171, 178, 196
methodology 199–200, 203
Minister for Treaty of Waitangi Negotiations 223, 226–27
ministerial advice 6, 48
ministerial direction 89, 91, 102
ministerial portfolios 80, 87–88, 90, 120–22, 226
ministerial questions 121–22
ministerial responsibility 3, 87, 89–90, 100, 122
convention 7, 87, 89–90, 94
to explain and remedy 88–89
ministers 4–8, 62–63, 76–91, 93–104, 114–22, 165–67, 180–87
advice of 6, 43, 181
advice to 97, 99
culpability 89–91
individual ministerial responsibility 7, 83, 87–91, 94, 99
prime *see* prime ministers
responsible 43, 48, 100–101, 111, 123, 179
Ministry of Justice 154, 158–59, 194
minorities 58, 59, 64, 79, 117, 152–53, 189, 205, 228

minutes, Cabinet 77, 79, 83
missionaries 28–31, 33
mixed-member-proportional elections (MMP) 40, 49–50, 52, 63–68, 72–73, 75–76, 107–8
effect 58–60
introduction 17–18, 226
in operation 53–56
parliamentary dynamics under 124–26
monarchs 24, 42, 127, 166, 168
monarchy 6, 8, 24, 37, 43
money 87, 102–3, 119–20, 179
public 103, 119, 179
MPs 52–53, 55–60, 68, 70, 108–12, 120–22, 125
opposition 97, 113, 122
total number 55
Muldoon, Robert 4, 18, 73, 86, 129–30
multi-party politics 39, 59, 75

nation states 26, 237, 241, 253
national parks 224–25, 235
National Party 52, 56–57, 74, 85
natural justice 171, 176, 191, 196, 199, 252
natural persons 86, 88
negotiations 31, 59, 65–67, 73–74, 126, 217–18, 223–24
Treaty of Waitangi 223, 226–27
neutrality 65, 87, 94, 99
political 8, 91, 95–97, 99–100
New South Wales 28–29, 31, 33
New Zealand culture 2, 16–21
New Zealand First 56, 64, 67–68, 72–73, 81, 182
New Zealanders 2, 5, 16–21, 40, 42, 219–20, 250
Ngāi Tahu 29
Ngāti Toa 29
normative values 19, 197
norms 1, 11–13, 15, 24, 59, 63, 114
constitutional 15–17, 19, 21, 163, 166
social 12, 138
North Island 33, 54, 212
NZ First *see* **New Zealand First**

obligations 95, 100, 220, 225, 228, 237, 239–40
international law 205, 239–40
treaty 238–40
offensive behaviour 200
official information 83–84, 98–101, 165
requests 99, 177, 185, 187
transparency 182–86
officials 8, 88, 98–99, 117–18, 138, 158, 160165–66, 183, 185
Ombudsmen 19, 98–99, 101, 111, 173, 177–78, 184–85
opposition 59, 66–67, 89, 96, 117, 122, 126
MPs 97, 113, 122
parties 52, 80, 96, 125, 185
oral questions 57, 113, 121–22, 125
overstayers 85, 205

Pākehā (Europeans) 18, 26–28, 31, 34, 211–13, 215–16, 220
Palmer, Sir Geoffrey 190, 202, 243–44, 246, 250
panels 137, 148, 155, 162, 243
parks, national 224–25, 235
Parliament 5–8, 49–55, 61–63, 84–90, 107–37, 179–82, 201–7 *see also* **House of Representatives**
British 127–28
control of public finances 119–20
holding executive to account 120–24
legislative supremacy 126–35
as provider of government 118–19
term 51, 61, 69, 248
parliamentary business 55, 112–13
parliamentary control 115, 127
Parliamentary Counsel Office 116, 182
parliamentary debates 88, 142–43, 226
parliamentary functions 114–24
parliamentary institutions 50, 57–58, 107–14
parliamentary ministry 49, 62–74
parliamentary privilege 22–23, 110, 199
parliamentary scrutiny 120, 123
Parliamentary Service Commission 111
parliamentary sovereignty 6, 18, 61, 126, 130, 249 *see also* **legislative supremacy**
parliamentary votes 7, 82, 243
partial privatisation 218, 236

parties 47, 52–58, 60–74, 80–82, 110–11, 124–26, 140 *see also* ***individual party names***
governing 4, 68, 71, 80, 82, 96, 125–26
groups of 64, 73–74
leaders 57, 63, 65, 236
major 52, 104
minor 52, 55
opposition 52, 80, 96, 125, 185
smaller 67, 81
party lists 54–55, 59, 248
party votes 53, 55–57, 60, 110, 124–25
patriation 129, 246
penalties 82, 171, 203, 205
retrospective 199, 203
performance 91, 93–94, 97, 112, 121–24, 239
audits 180
permanent residents 51, 53, 183, 187
personal information 184–85, 206
Peters, Winston 72, 81
petitions 29, 113–14, 123, 211–12
police 23, 89, 95, 134, 177, 181, 200
policy advice 87, 98, 159
political accountability 87, 121
political attacks 96–97
political branch 23, 163
political leadership 27, 135
political neutrality 8, 91, 95–97, 99–100
political parties *see* **parties**
political processes 65, 96, 252
political rights 4, 189, 191
political settlement 44, 71, 119
politicians 16, 18, 20, 86, 152–53, 161, 163
politics 4, 8, 20, 23, 50, 212, 252
portfolios, ministerial 7, 62, 80–82, 84–85, 87–88, 90, 91, 120–21, 226
possession, undisturbed 32, 210
powers 7–8, 10–13, 22–24, 38–45, 85–90, 113–14, 239–41
coercive 8, 23, 177
constitutional 40–41, 48
decision-making 27, 187
executive 5, 18, 36, 76, 125, 233
judicial 134, 242
law-making 115, 127–28, 130–31, 134–36
legal 6, 44, 48, 77, 86, 102, 218
prerogative 42–43
public *see* public power
regulation-making 114
reserve 43–44
soft 29, 46, 215
statutory 42–43, 46, 89, 170
pragmatism 16, 20–21, 23
prerogative power 42–43
President of the Court of Appeal 153–54
presumptions 64, 83–84, 182, 240
primary functions 115, 126, 140
prime ministers 38–40, 62–64, 66, 69–72, 76–78, 82–85, 87–91 *see also* ***individual names***
prisoner voting 51, 198, 200–201
privacy 176, 183, 191, 206
privatisation 101, 236
partial 218, 236
privileges 32, 47, 113, 115, 167, 210, 220
parliamentary 22–23, 110, 199
Privileges Committee 112–13
Privy Council 5, 145, 148–49, 212, 218, 221
proclamation of sovereignty 33–34
proportional representation 7, 52–53, 78, 248 *see also* **mixed-member proportional elections**
proportionality 55, 58, 75, 171, 189, 192, 196
protected rights 191–94, 196, 250
provider of government 118–19
public bodies 138, 165–66, 169–70, 173, 192, 207
public consultation 117–18, 126
public entities 179–80
public finance 4–5, 14, 76, 91, 102–5, 114
control 119–20
public functions 192, 197, 207
public inquiries *see* **inquiries**
public interest 84, 98, 121, 175, 182–83, 190
public money 103, 119, 179
public opinion 14–15, 20, 163, 247
public policy 105, 115
public power 9, 11–14, 24, 208, 230, 236–37, 241
exercise of 11–12, 14–17, 22, 27–29, 142, 208, 219

public records 186
public servants 8, 78–79, 91–97, 99–100, 102–3, 152, 158
public service 4–5, 8, 23, 76, 85–86, 91–100, 102–3
  anonymity 99–100
  conventional duties 94–100
  departments 93–94
  duty of loyalty 94–95
  free and frank advice 97–99
  neutral 4, 24
  political neutrality 95–97
  principles 94, 97, 99
  state services 92, 94, 96–97, 99
Public Service Commission 94–97
Public Service Commissioner 93–94
purposive interpretation 141, 143

question time 121–22
questions
  oral 57, 113, 121–22, 125
  supplementary 121
  written 85, 88, 121–22

rangatira (chiefs) 17–18, 26–35, 93–94, 99–100, 209–10, 213–14, 245
rangatiratanga, tino (independence) 29–34, 209, 214, 220
ratification 119, 211, 213, 224, 238–40, 246
realism, constitutional 1, 9, 11–12, 14, 142, 166, 254
reasonableness 171, 203–5
reason-giving 161, 186–87
reconciliation 218, 222, 224
referenda 52–53, 56, 60–61, 132, 236, 243, 247
reforms 50–51, 91–93, 101–2, 104, 242, 246–47, 249–51
  financial 105
  incremental 247–48
  legislative 47, 92, 144, 200, 249
  republican 246–47
  state sector 96, 100, 166
regulation-making powers 114
regulations 46, 85–87, 113–14, 126, 134, 195–96, 199
Regulations Review Committee 86, 113
relief, declaratory 194, 198, 252
remedies 87–89, 194, 197–98, 207, 213, 216, 218
repeal 61, 129, 132
  implied 129, 192, 205–6
reports 112–14, 117–18, 123–24, 179–81, 194–95, 214, 223–24
  annual 123, 180
representation 51, 124, 128, 245
representative democracy 1, 5–6, 8, 17, 21, 49–50, 121
representative government 17, 36, 49–62, 115, 127
  parliament as symbol of 115, 124
republican reform 246–47
reserve powers 43–45
reserved provisions 60–61, 132
residents, permanent 51, 53, 183, 187
resources 28, 102, 180, 187, 235
resource management 145, 155, 222
responsibility 7, 87, 89, 156, 160, 233, 235
  collective *see* collective responsibility
  to explain and remedy 88–89
  ministerial *see* ministerial responsibility
  vicarious 100
responsible advisors 38, 69
responsible government 3, 6, 17, 21, 49, 62–74, 120
responsible ministers 43, 48, 100–101, 111, 123, 179
responsiveness 97–98, 100, 231
review
  appellate 173–74
  judicial 144, 148, 162, 165, 167–74, 176, 222
revision 116, 221, 231, 250
rhetoric 16, 91, 102
rights 134, 189–92, 194–98, 200–203, 206–9, 250, 252
  common law 134, 206
  customary 3, 22, 145, 201
  enhanced protection 251–52
  expressive 199–200
  of individuals 23–24, 192, 199
  political 4, 189, 191
  protected 191–94, 196, 250
royal assent 44, 116, 118, 128
Royal Commissions 52, 58, 181, 211
Royal Navy 31, 34

rule of law 8, 19, 138–41, 143, 145, 156, 171–72

sanctions 82, 90, 113, 115, 194
school boards 101, 234
scrutiny 47, 116, 118–20, 122, 128, 171, 204
of bills 112, 123
close 112, 117
parliamentary 120, 123
seabed 22, 130, 145, 201
seats 50–52, 55–56, 63–64, 70, 125
secondary legislation 85–86, 113, 195, 223
secret ballot 52, 54, 85
security 20, 40, 152, 177, 183, 190–91, 201
select committees 59–60, 95, 107, 112–14, 117, 123–25, 195
self-regulation 236
senior civic office 233, 246
senior court judges 152–53, 157, 161
senior courts 140, 147–49
settler society 17–18
early 16
settlers 2–3, 26, 29, 31, 127, 208, 210
Shipley, Jenny 72, 81
sitting days 108–9, 121
social media 183, 237
social norms 12, 138
society, democratic 191–92, 251
SOEs (State-Owned Enterprises) 4, 91–92, 101–2, 123, 216–17, 223, 232
soft power 29, 46, 215
South Island 33, 54
Sovereign 5–6, 11, 36, 38–43, 45–50, 107–8, 110
as Head of State 37–38
sovereignty 2–3, 18, 27, 32–35, 139, 209–10, 212
assertion of 3, 26, 33–35, 50, 127
parliamentary 6, 18, 61, 126, 130, 249
proclamation of 33–34
Speaker 14, 109–13, 121–22
specialists 10, 150
speeches 13, 42, 45, 66, 109–10, 113, 119
parliamentary 143
standards 94, 96, 166, 171, 188, 235
standing orders 13–14, 103, 108–9, 111–14, 116, 125, 239
state 6, 17–18, 23–24, 36–48, 237–39, 242–43, 246–47
unitary 1, 3, 24, 230
state sector 92, 100–102
reforms 96, 100, 166
state sector reforms 96, 100, 166
state services 92, 94, 96–97, 99
State Services Commission 94
State Services Commissioner 97, 99
State-Owned Enterprises *see* **SOEs**
statistics 121–22, 153, 195
status 27, 55, 80, 98, 131, 195, 208–17 *see also* **mana**
employment 96, 206
legal 2, 35, 208, 210–12, 215, 218–20, 231
special 42, 83
statute book 4, 203
statutes 89, 140–41, 143, 145–46, 148, 168–70, 222
ordinary 4, 190
statutory appeals 174–75
statutory independence 89
statutory interpretation *see* **interpretation**
statutory powers 42–43, 46, 89, 170
stewardship 93, 122, 135, 167
strategy 57, 91, 121, 211
fiscal 104
Strategy Committee 77
subject matter 129, 131, 175–76, 250
expertise 97, 181
sub-national government 230–32
sub-tribes *see* **hapū**
successors 61, 131–32, 243
supervision 45, 170, 179
judicial 174, 199
supervisory jurisdiction 169, 236
supplementary questions 121
supply bills 59, 71
imprest 117, 120
support agreements 59, 65–66, 71, 81
supremacy 192, 242
legislative 4, 6, 18, 126–27, 129–33, 135–36, 163 *see also* parliamentary sovereignity
Supreme Court 144, 146–49, 153–54, 173–74, 194, 198, 200–201

taonga (treasures) 32, 146, 220, 233
taxes 102, 119–20, 155, 157, 166
te reo Māori *see* **Māori, language**
te Tiriti o Waitangi 2, 26–27, 31–35, 208–29, 235, 243–45, 250–52 *see also* **Waitangi Tribunal**
  brief history of status 208–19
  in constitution today 219–28
  contemporary meaning 219–20
  legal force and effect 220–22
  negotiations 223, 226–27
  reconciliation and settlement 222–28
  reinterpretation through dialogue 218–19
Te Urewera 224–25, 235
tensions 2, 12, 40, 97–98, 193, 196, 253
tenure 40, 177
territorial authorities 232
tikanga 2–3, 5, 26–27, 30, 32, 146, 222–23
  enforcement 5
  and judiciary 145–46
  role 146, 222
torts 144, 172, 198
torture 134, 238
traditions 11, 63, 133, 254
  legal 2, 251
transformative effect 105, 202
transitions 7, 62, 72
transparency 9, 57, 65, 100, 104, 181–87, 227
  official information 182–86
  public records 186
  reason-giving 161, 186–87
Treasury 104, 159, 179
treaties 31, 47, 220, 237–40
treaty obligations 238–40
Treaty of Waitangi *see* **te Tiriti o Waitangi**
tribes *see* **iwi**
tribunals 150–51, 173, 175–76, 215–18, 223–24, 227–28, 239 *see also* ***individual tribunal titles***
  administrative 151, 165, 174–76
trustees 101, 234
Tūhoe 34, 224–25, 235

unanimity 79–83, 113, 248
undisturbed possession 32, 210
unfairness 100, 171 *see also* **fairness**
unitary state 1, 3, 24, 230
United Nations 152, 228, 237, 253
United States 18, 87, 158, 221, 253
unjustified limitations 193, 202, 207
unlawfulness 173, 179, 196
unreasonableness 171, 204 *see also* **reasonableness**
unwritten constitution 11, 21, 134
urgency 109, 116–17

validity 31, 169
vetting functions 195, 201
vicarious responsibility 100
Victoria, Queen 32, 34, 47, 211
voters 53–54, 60
votes 50–59, 64, 109–10, 112–13, 118–19, 125, 141
  casting 110
  majority 58, 109–10
  parliamentary 7, 82, 243
  party 53, 55–57, 60, 110, 124–25
voting 17, 52, 54, 61–62, 109, 112, 141
  age 51, 61
  prisoners 51, 198, 200–201

Waikato-Tainui 223, 234
Waitangi Tribunal 2, 5, 20, 22, 30, 215–19, 221–22
  legislative references and judicial enforcement 216–18
wars 18, 28, 32, 34–35, 210
welfare state 4, 18
whānau 16, 27, 225, 234
witnesses 169, 181
women 4–5, 10, 17, 32, 50–51, 58, 152–54
workloads 123, 204
written constitution 9, 11, 18, 21, 242–44
written questions 85, 88, 121–22

www.ingramcontent.com/pod-product-compliance
Ingram Content Group UK Ltd.
Pitfield, Milton Keynes, MK11 3LW, UK
UKHW020123290926
15471UKWH00003B/235